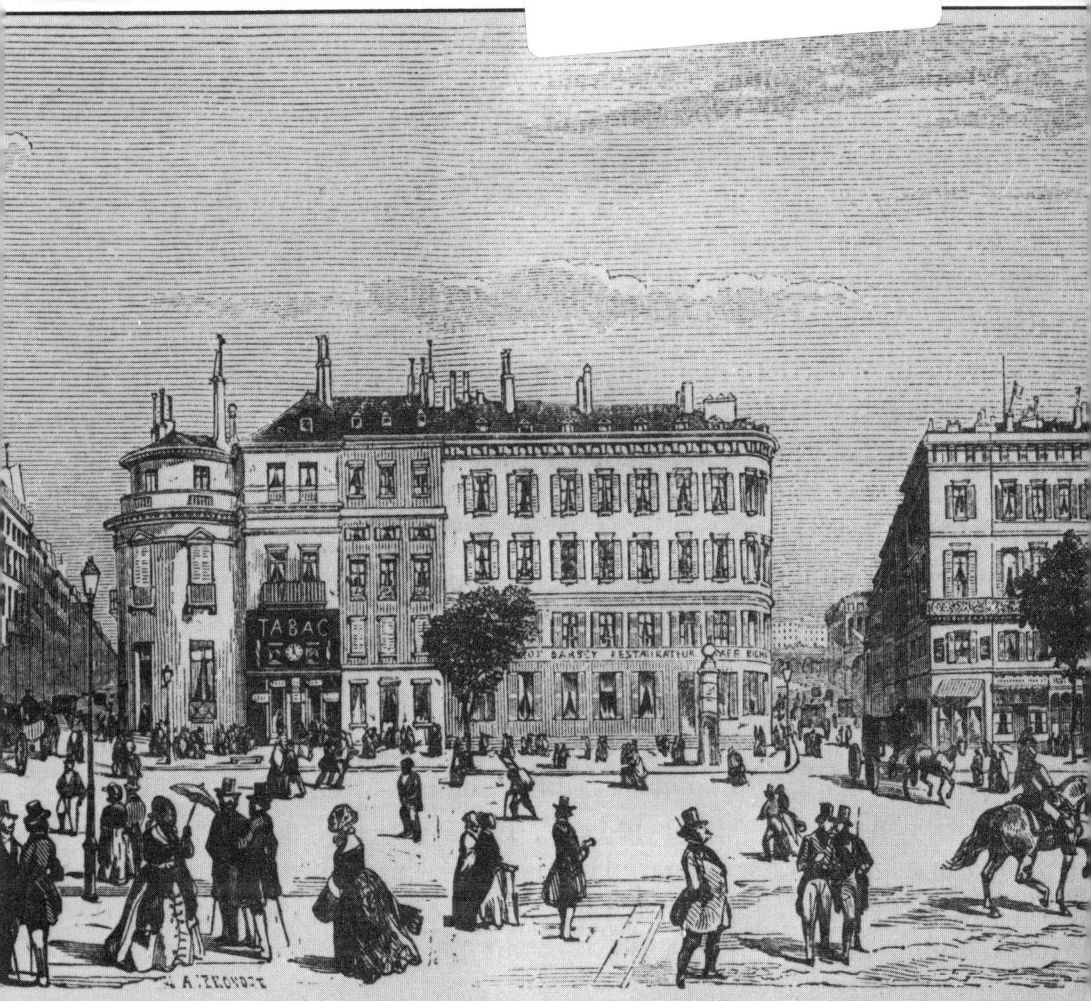

Rue Laffitte. Café Riche. Rue Lepelletier.

THE GREATEST COLLECTOR

Lord Hertford and the Founding of the Wallace Collection

THE GREATEST COLLECTOR

Lord Hertford and the Founding of the Wallace Collection

Donald Mallett

M

ISBN 0 333 24467 2

First published 1979 by
MACMILLAN LONDON LIMITED
4 Little Essex Street London WC2R 3LF
and Basingstoke
Associated Companies in Delhi, Dublin,
Hong Kong, Johannesburg, Lagos, Melbourne,
New York, Singapore and Tokyo

Printed in Great Britain by
BUTLER AND TANNER LTD
Frome and London

For Anda

Acknowledgements

I WISH TO ACKNOWLEDGE the gracious permission of Her Majesty the Queen to make use of material from the Royal Archives at Windsor Castle, which is among the papers I consulted at the Wallace Collection.

I also wish to thank the Harrowby MSS. Trust for permission to publish material concerning the Hon. Frederick Dudley Ryder, and Sir Richard Dashwood, Bt, for permission to publish extracts from the diary of the 5th Marchioness of Hertford.

Special thanks are due to the Trustees of the Wallace Collection who allowed me to consult the archives at Hertford House where I was given every assistance by the Director and staff. In particular I should mention Mr R. A. Cecil for his help and encouragement. He placed his great knowledge at my disposal and patiently answered my many queries.

Mr R. A. F. Wallis has very kindly allowed me to use new information about Agnes, the mother of Sir Richard Wallace, which he discovered in the course of his research into the families of Sir Thomas Wallace and Samuel Bickley.

Miss Elizabeth M. Aslin at the Bethnal Green Museum and Mr Anthony Burton at the library of the Victoria and Albert Museum both helped me to discover much valuable material, and the staff at the Department of Manuscripts at the British Library were also of great assistance.

In France I wish to record my gratitude to Monsieur Pierre Montagne, Directeur du Parc, who assisted me on my many visits to Bagatelle, and Monsieur Jacques Wilhelm, who was Conservateur en Chef at the Musée Carnavalet at the time I was doing research for this book.

I also wish to thank the president of the Jockey Club for permission to examine the records in the library of the club, and to acknowledge the help I received from Mademoiselle Françoise Marchand, the librarian.

Maître Robineau, *notaire*, who went to a great deal of trouble searching for a French will which may have been made by Lord Hertford, also deserves my thanks. Another who helped me in my research was the Rev. John Livingstone, Chaplain of St George's Church, Paris.

I am grateful to Mrs Mary Ann Harris at the Metropolitan Museum of Art, New York, for supplying information about Meissonier's painting *Friedland – 1807*.

Finally, I owe much to my friend Monsieur Olivier Perrin, who first encouraged me to write about Richard Wallace.

Contents

List of Illustrations

All illustrations are reproduced by permission of The Wallace Collection unless otherwise stated.

Foreword

ON 16 FEBRUARY 1897 a seventy-eight-year-old Frenchwoman died in London in a large house in Manchester Square just north of Oxford Street. She was a widow who had lived in almost complete seclusion since the death of her husband. Although she had been hostess to the Prince of Wales she had never been a well-known figure in society. She always dressed in black and refused to speak English so that she was scarcely an asset at a dinner party. But in her will, made only three years before she died, this Frenchwoman left the contents of her house to the British nation and, more surprising still, the gift consisted mainly of superb French works of art.

The Frenchwoman was Lady Wallace, widow of Sir Richard Wallace, and the contents of her house were what is known today as the Wallace Collection, which is still in the house in which she died and which, by the number and unrivalled quality of its treasures, is without doubt the greatest gift ever made by a private person to a state.

Lady Wallace was only nineteen when she had met her husband in Paris. At that time she was working in a shop on the boulevards selling scent. When she died the treasures which crowded the rooms of the house in Manchester Square were only part of the immense fortune she had inherited from her husband. There was a second equally important collection in France, mainly at a large apartment in the rue Laffitte in Paris, but also at Bagatelle, a little château in the Bois de Boulogne where Sir Richard had died. He also left her Sudbourn Hall in Suffolk, where twenty-three gamekeepers looked after the partridges which the Prince of Wales had been invited to shoot, and large estates in Ulster. All this Lady Wallace bequeathed to John Murray Scott, later Sir John, a man who had been her husband's secretary for the last twenty years of his life. To her grandchildren in France she left nothing.

Today only the Collection in London remains intact, drawing more than 120,000 visitors every year to Manchester Square. The collections in France have been dispersed. Some of the treasures can be seen in museums in Europe and America, but many have disappeared completely. A new building stands where the apartment in the rue Laffitte used to be, and Bagatelle now belongs to the City of Paris; the gardens are famous but the little château is empty.

Chapter One

THE WALLACE COLLECTION, the finest single collection of eighteenth-century French painting, furniture, porcelain and *objets d'art*, was built up over the years by successive Seymour-Conways, Marquesses of Hertford. The 4th marquess, the chief collector, bequeathed it to Richard Wallace, and this caused great bitterness and disappointment in the family. Two long and costly lawsuits were the result. In addition to this, the French have always thought that the Collection should have been left to France, instead of remaining in London where, by a curious irony, its home was the French Embassy during the reign of King Louis-Philippe.

The Seymours were always wealthy and held high positions at home or as ambassadors to foreign courts. Therefore they could indulge their passion for collecting unhindered by financial restrictions. They were clever and artistic and, however wild and dissipated they became in their later years, they always collected with intelligence and good taste. The family descends from Edward Seymour, Duke of Somerset and Earl of Hertford, the brother of Jane Seymour, Henry VIII's third queen. He rose to be Lord Protector of England during the reign of the young Edward VI, but he died on the scaffold, condemned for felony after a charge of treason broke down.

His titles and estates had been entailed by Act of Parliament in 1540 upon his issue by his second wife. This line became extinct in 1750, on the death of Algernon Seymour, 7th Duke of Somerset. The Earldom of Hertford was revived for Francis Seymour-Conway, Lord Conway (1719–94), who was a descendant of the Lord Protector's first marriage. Later he was created Earl of Yarmouth and 1st Marquess of Hertford. A nephew of Sir Robert Walpole, he became ambassador to France, Lord Lieutenant of Ireland and finally Lord Chamberlain from 1766 to 1782. (The Conway title and estates, which represented a considerable fortune, had also come to the family by marriage.) His wife, a daughter of the 2nd Duke of Grafton, bore him seven sons and six daughters. Portraits of two of these daughters, Elizabeth and Frances, were painted at Lord Hertford's request by Sir Joshua Reynolds, and this was the beginning of his collection. He probably was also the owner of the portrait of George III by Allan Ramsay. In the 1750s he is known to have bought some Dutch paintings at auction. They cannot be identified but they may still be in the Collection today.

Francis's eldest son, Francis Ingram Seymour-Conway (1743–1822), took the title Earl of Yarmouth when his father was made a marquess. He became, after his father's death, one of the most talked-of figures of the Regency. The Prince Regent became infatuated with his second wife, Isabella, when she was already forty-seven, fat, and a grandmother. For fourteen years she had considerable influence over him and at the same time firmly retained her virtue. He visited her at the Hertfords' house in Manchester Square at least once every day and often stayed for dinner with her and her husband. The arrival of his open yellow chariot brought heads to every window in the square.

After a political career in the House of Commons the 2nd Marquess had served as ambassador in Berlin. Then in 1804 he was appointed Master of the Horse and in 1812 Lord Chamberlain. He seems to have been the first Hertford to buy some of the fine French furniture which was put up for sale after the Revolution. In pictures his taste was not French. He preferred portraits by contemporary English painters and many are still in Manchester Square today. He bought Romney's *Mrs Robinson* and Reynolds's *Nelly O'Brien* for £21 and £64 respectively, and he must have commissioned the portraits by Downman of Isabella in her younger days and those of her family.

Even more notorious was his only surviving child, Francis Charles Seymour-Conway (1777–1842), the future 3rd Marquess. His extravagant life in pleasure-loving Georgian society was legendary and his name became a byword for debauchery; yet he was a collector of taste all his life.

At the age of twenty-one, when he was heavily in debt from gambling, Lord Yarmouth, as he then was, chose a day when his father was away in Ireland dealing with troubles on his estates in Antrim to run away to Southampton and get married. The fury of his parents knew no bounds when they discovered that their daughter-in-law was twenty-seven-year-old Maria Fagnani, daughter of the Marchesa Fagnani, a former Italian dancer. George Selwyn, the celebrated wit, and the Duke of Queensberry both claimed to have been her father; but although Selwyn renounced his bachelor ways to bring up Maria, the truth was that 'Old Q.' as Lord March, before he succeeded to the dukedom, was her father. The frivolous mother, finding the child an embarrassment, had made no objections when Lord March took her away and dumped her on Selwyn. To everybody's surprise Selwyn doted on the little girl whom he called Mie-Mie, a name by which she was to be known for the rest of her life. Later, when her mother demanded her back he was heartbroken and resisted all attempts to separate her from him. Mie-Mie was nearly twenty when he died in 1791 and he left her his considerable fortune.

At twenty-seven Mie-Mie was no fresh young beauty; nor, although she had money of her own, did she have any position in society. Her father, now a wealthy duke, knew that the young Lord Yarmouth was living far beyond his allowance. He hinted that if he married Mie-Mie he would prove a generous father-in-law and that a large part of the Queensberry fortune would come Lord Yarmouth's way on his death. So the deal was made and Mie-Mie could look forward to being Marchioness of Hertford one day. In the opinion of the Hertford family her doubtful origins and lack of social distinction made her an undesirable wife for the future head of the family. Although they had to recognise the marriage, they firmly ignored her.

Mie-Mie and her husband went to live in a large house in Piccadilly belonging to the Duke of Queensberry, who thereby showed that he, at least, was pleased with the marriage. Two children were born, first a girl, Frances Maria, and then a boy, Richard, in 1800. His birth was recorded at St George's, Hanover Square, the parish church for 105 Piccadilly, but there is no record there of his sister's birth. It has been suggested, since the exact date of her birth is not recorded, that she may have been born before the marriage and this, if true, would partly account for the Hertford family's annoyance.

Although now married and a father, Lord Yarmouth did not give up his wild ways. Indeed, he gambled more than ever and earned the reputation of one of the most daring, lucky and cunning card-players in London. He also extended his activities to the Stock Exchange, where he was again so fortunate that he was able to be financially independent of his father and mother. He did, however, follow the family tradition in taking his seat in Parliament. This was not difficult because the Hertfords controlled eight seats in the House of Commons. Only one other Tory peer, Lord Lonsdale, with nine seats in his gift, controlled more. So it came about that Lord Yarmouth represented in turn the family boroughs of Orford, Lisburn and Camelford until the death of his father.

Although she had brought him money and given him a son and heir, Mie-Mie was neglected by her husband and became lonely and unhappy. She determined to escape from this country where the society ladies turned their backs on her and where her husband gambled all night in the clubs to which women were not admitted. After all, she had Latin blood and had been to Paris and Milan as a girl when her mother had once claimed her back from Selwyn. Since Selwyn's death she had made many friends among the French *émigrés* who had come to live in London at the time of the Revolution. Like all refugees, they talked endlessly of the splendours of Paris and of the elegance and gaiety of life in their native city. Listening to them, Mie-Mie conceived the plan of moving to Paris when the war with Napoleon was over. The Treaty of Amiens, signed in the spring of 1802, made it possible to travel to the Continent once again and it became fashionable to go to Paris to see the wonders of Bonaparte. Mie-Mie had to work on Lord Yarmouth for six months before he agreed to take her to Paris, but in the autumn of that year they went, taking their two little children with them. What Lord Yarmouth did not realise was that his wife was determined never to return to London and his family.

They found Paris full of English sightseers and went to stay at a hotel in the place de la Concorde. The newly appointed British ambassador, Lord Whitworth, arranged a few formal calls; they were received by Cambacérès, the Second Consul, and if they did not meet the First Consul they did meet Joséphine. They were a striking couple, he good-looking and with red hair, she dark and possessing more ample Latin charms than the tall women from across the Channel. Also, he had money which he seemed pleased to spend and soon all the Paris hostesses were sending invitations to the English milord and his half-Italian wife.

Lord Yarmouth soon tired of the formal social rounds and, apart from accompanying his wife to the soirées given by Talleyrand, with whom he had struck up a friendship, he was seldom seen with her in the fashionable salons of the Consulate. He sought gayer company and it was not long before Madame Visconti, a famous Italian beauty, had become his mistress. She had started by making friends with Lady Yarmouth, their Italian blood being a bond between them, but, as is so often the case, she ended by going off with the husband. Nevertheless, he did not spend all his money on frivolous amusements. At the age of twenty-five he was already showing the Seymour passion for collecting and had started to buy pictures. One of the early purchases, *A Street Scene in Cologne* by Jan van der Heyden, is in the Wallace Collection today, and shows that he was already developing a taste for Dutch painters. Later he bought for his friend the Prince Regent many paintings of the Dutch School which are today in the royal collections at Windsor and Buckingham Palace.

Lord Yarmouth's extravagant living aroused the suspicions of the French police. He was followed and his daily life was watched. In March 1803 he is mentioned by name in a police report on the English in Paris. It was said that he allowed the most slanderous things to be said about the First Consul in his house which was always full of English people.

From time to time when he became bored with the pleasures of Paris Lord Yarmouth went back to London to see his old friends and to look in at the House of Commons. Mie-Mie never went with him. In Paris life was gay, she went everywhere, the women did not sneer at her and the men flirted with her. Her French friends included two famous beauties, Madame Récamier and Madame Tallien. Gabriel Julien Ouvrard, the rich army contractor, invited her to Raincy where she met most of the famous people under the Consulate. She quickly learned not to care what her husband did or whether he was there or not.

By April 1803 the precarious Treaty of Amiens was on the point of collapse and the honeymoon for the English in Paris was over. In London Lord Yarmouth saw the danger and urged his wife to return, but Mie-Mie refused. Exasperated, he decided to go to fetch her, but he left it too late. When he landed in France he was seized as an enemy and held for three days before being taken protesting to Paris where he was permitted to join his wife. There he was under constant surveillance, but it did not stop him from looking for pictures to buy. This comparative freedom did not last long, for Bonaparte very soon ordered that all Englishmen be interned at Verdun out of harm's way. Mie-Mie must have had some anxious moments, but by using her charms on General Junot, the military Governor of Paris, she obtained permission to stay in Paris with her two children. Perhaps being half-Italian had something to do with it, but the real reason was probably that Junot became her lover.

In Verdun Lord Yarmouth found a number of his old drinking and gambling friends. The French may have hoped that life in this dreary little town 150 miles east of Paris would break the spirits of the proud English. But the English have always been exasperating prisoners. Not for them moody reflection on the injustice of their lot or the drafting of defiant manifestos. They tend to make the best of things and see what can be done to amuse themselves. Since games and sport are their chief amusements they can soon get together and organise their favourite pastimes for themselves, since nobody else will. Lord Yarmouth conceived the idea of organising race-meetings. Despite the war he was able to receive large sums of money regularly through M. Perregaux, the Paris banker. Mie-Mie was also supplied with all she needed. General Wirion, the commander of Verdun, was easy to handle. Money could arrange everything so that horses were found and, to the astonishment of the population of Verdun, the first race-meeting was held under Newmarket rules on 5 May 1804.

But despite the card-playing and the horse-racing Lord Yarmouth did not settle down happily at Verdun. He missed his Paris life, and he tried to continue buying pictures and had them sent to him in case he should want to buy them. At this time he wrote regularly to Mie-Mie about the pictures that were sent to him, but it is also clear from these letters dating from the beginning of his internment that he regretted that he and Mie-Mie had grown so far apart and, like any normal father, he was anxious for news of his children. 'I am sorry Dick', he wrote, 'is tired of his playthings tho' I believe it is because they are spoilt and that he has grown older and wiser ... as to coming back I have little hopes of it ... God bless you. I wish I could write a more amusing letter.' He was clearly homesick.

In another letter, after dealing at some length with a scratch on a picture that had been sent to him he said it was not his doing and describes how he opened the case in which it had been sent, saw at a glance that he did not want it and nailed it down again, and he drew a picture of the tacks he used. Then suddenly he confesses his longing to return to Paris and his readiness to make it up with Mie-Mie.

I shall be very glad to return to Paris and to see you. I never wished to get rid of you or to be disagreeable. I only wished not to be reckoned a fool by you thats all for I certainly like you better than the rest of the world put together not but that we are very likely to quarrel but if we ever do it never shall be in such a manner as to prevent our meeting again when we think better of it....

Unfortunately, the letter has been cut and the manuscript ends there.

When he learns that two 'gentlemen' are going to Paris and he does not know how they obtained permission, he writes in despair: 'I should like to get out of this dungeon very much tho' I don't see much prospect of it; peace in three months or eternal war is what I expect, if the latter I had rather be dead than live the whole war in prison....'

None of Mie-Mie's letters to him in Verdun have survived, but from the sweetness of his letters to her it is clear that he was trying to persuade her to take him back. One such letter starts: 'I received two very amiable and agreeable letters from you this morning nobody can be more so than you when you like it....' He tells her to do what she likes with the poor grey horse which is 'eating off his head' and adds that a 'speedy decision is best for my purse if not for his comfort'. He suggests sending him to the veterinary hospital to be shot or cured.

Mie-Mie must have told him in one of her letters about a sale of pictures due to take place in Paris because in the same letter he tells her to go to the sale and 'commit any folly for any picture which particularly pleases your eye'. He warns her of the difficulty of getting trustworthy evaluations and adds that he is prepared to 'embark a thousand pounds or perhaps a little more if the speculation is good'.

There must have been a moment also when he tried to persuade her to join him at Verdun. In one letter he writes saying he is inquiring about lodgings 'in case you should come here', explaining that his present lodgings would not be suitable for them and the two children. 'You know I am always glad to see you,' he insists and then ends the letter with detailed instructions on how to play the latest gambling game and sets out the odds.

But Mie-Mie did not allow herself to be persuaded. Things had gone too far and she never went to Verdun. Past experience told her not to trust her husband's professions of love, nor, it must be admitted, was she pining for him. As the favourite of General Junot she was not treated as an enemy and she saw no reason for leaving Paris where she was enjoying herself. In all probability, Lord Yarmouth's letters were not her only source of information from Verdun and she may have known that he had found a good-looking widow who had become his mistress. So the year 1804 began with Lord Yarmouth still interned at Verdun and Mie-Mie and their children in Paris.

Later, in the spring, he was suddenly woken up in the middle of the night and, despite his protests, hurriedly bundled into a coach by two sturdy police agents from Paris. Not a word of explanation was forthcoming during the long drive to the capital. On arrival in the city Lord Yarmouth was greatly surprised when the coach headed straight for his own house and he was unceremoniously put out at his front door. Mie-Mie must have been responsible for his release, he thought. His joy knew no bounds. At last had come the reunion that he had wanted so much. Mie-Mie was waiting for him in the salon in the company of a man whom she introduced as Count Casimir de Montrond. The count was charming and the two men got on well together from the start. That night the three of them celebrated Lord Yarmouth's unexplained good fortune.

Lord Yarmouth's joy at being reunited with Mie-Mie would have been less intense if he had realised that Mie-Mie's feelings were more those of relief than love. The fact was that she was pregnant by none other than the amusing count who had replaced Junot in her affections. Alarmed at her news, Montrond had gone to see his friend Talleyrand, for whom he acted as a sort of private agent. He in turn had sent him to Fouquet, the resourceful chief of police. Fouquet knew what to do. He sent two trusted men to Verdun with orders to bring Lord Yarmouth back to Paris as quickly as possible and deliver him to his wife. Three days later he was home.

Such is the story which reveals much about the 'amiable and agreeable' Mie-Mie. She had no intention of starting life again with her husband and she was deceiving him if she let him think she would. Moreover, she saw to it that her husband was allowed to stay in Paris only long enough to make sure that it would be assumed that he was the father of her child. During that time he innocently allowed himself to be charmed by the unscrupulous adventurer Montrond, and they became firm friends. Then, again with no explanation, his permission to stay in Paris was suddenly cancelled and he was sent back to Verdun.

The baby, a boy, was born on 18 January 1805. He was always known as Lord Henry Seymour although, until his father succeeded to the title, he should have been called the Hon. Henry Seymour-Conway. In London, where the news of Mie-Mie's affair with Junot had already caused a scandal, it was generally believed that Junot was the boy's father. But in Paris it was well known that 'le beau Montrond' had replaced Junot and that he was the real father.

Not until August 1805 did Lord Yarmouth leave Verdun again. This time he was released on parole, but he was refused permission to live in the city of Paris and chose to go to Versailles. Whether or not this was Mie-Mie's doing we do not know. There is evidence that Talleyrand, who was thinking of using Lord Yarmouth to sound out opinion in England, was responsible for his release and during this period he invited him to stay with him in the country. But relations with England under Pitt went from bad to worse and by October Lord Yarmouth was back again in Verdun.

The death of Pitt early the next year, followed by the arrival of Fox at the Foreign Office, revived hopes for peace, and an exchange of prisoners was arranged as a result. Lord Yarmouth was among the first to be freed. This time he left Verdun for good. After spending a few days in Paris he left for London on 2 May, bearing a message from Talleyrand which assured the British government of Bonaparte's desire for peace. He was received by Lord Grenville, the new Prime Minister, and Fox, who decided to send him back to Paris to enter into preliminary peace negotiations with the French. He carried a personal letter from Fox to Talleyrand stating that Lord Yarmouth had his full confidence.

Lady Yarmouth by this time had moved again and was living at No. 1 rue Cerutti, which in 1814 became the rue d'Artois and finally, after 1830, the rue Laffitte. The disturbing habit of changing the names of streets in Paris every few years was evidently the practice then as it is today. Mie-Mie had broken with Montrond and, at the moment when her husband returned to live with her after so long an absence, she was the love of General Duroc. Lord Yarmouth was not a bit embarrassed by this irregular domestic situation. He installed his mistress from Verdun in a street not far away and settled down with Mie-Mie and the children. Mie-Mie was now thirty-five and rather plump, Frances Maria was seven, Richard six and Henry still a baby. Despite her endless flirtations Mie-Mie certainly never neglected her children. She was an excellent mother and retained their devotion all her life.

In his new role as an emissary of the British government Lord Yarmouth found his old friend Talleyrand not as simple to handle as he had hoped. The wily Foreign Minister was dealing with the Russians behind his back and negotiations made little progress. Then Fox fell ill and Lord Grenville took over the Foreign Office himself. Dissatisfied with the way Lord Yarmouth was handling things, he sent Lord Lauderdale, a shrewd Whig politician with a knowledge of French affairs, to join him. From the moment he arrived in Paris Lord Lauderdale, while appearing to be friendly, worked to get Lord Yarmouth withdrawn. In personal letters to Lord Grenville he reported all the damaging gossip about Lord Yarmouth's private life and later made the serious charge that he was using his position to make money for himself and others by profitable speculation in French and British securities. He also maintained that he was completely in the hands of Talleyrand

and passed on to him all the most secret instructions which were sent to him from London. In the end Lord Grenville had no option but to recall Lord Yarmouth, although when he was left to himself Lord Lauderdale did no better than Yarmouth had done. There was no peace.

Chapter Two

THE FAILURE OF HIS MISSION and the criticism of his conduct in Paris seems to have had little effect on Lord Yarmouth's spirits and still less on his fortunes. It is true that he moved out of his Piccadilly house and sent his paintings to be sold at Christie's in July 1807. The Van der Heyden of Cologne was Lot 52 in the sale, but it was bought in with five other pictures of the Dutch School which were unsold, all of which are in the Collection today. He moved to a new house in Seamore Place and was soon buying pictures for it.

He could not have chosen a better moment to return to London, for his mother, Lady Hertford, was just succeeding Mrs Fitzherbert in the affections of the Prince of Wales, the future George IV, and was about to become the dominant figure in the prince's life during the Regency. The star of the Hertfords was therefore very much in the ascendant. Delighted that Lord Yarmouth had left his wife behind, Lord and Lady Hertford received him back into the family with open arms, like the prodigal son.

Isabella, Marchioness of Hertford, despite her good looks, was a rather forbidding, stately woman. She was always beautifully dressed and very formal in her manners. A daughter of the last Viscount Irvine, she was rich in her own right and, like the marquess, held the most extreme Tory views.

The prince's passion for her was brought about by a little girl called Minny Seymour, a niece of her husband. Minny was the youngest child of Lord Hugh Seymour, a son of the 1st Marquess of Hertford, and when she was a baby her mother was ordered by her doctors to leave England and seek a warmer climate. She went to Madeira, but Minny was considered too small to travel so far, and she was left behind in the care of Mrs Fitzherbert. The Seymours' friendship with Mrs Fitzherbert dated from the time when Lord Hugh had been Master of the Robes and Keeper of the Privy Purse in the prince's household. Knowing of Mrs Fitzherbert's secret and illegal marriage to the prince in 1785, he had refused to remain in his household after his marriage to Princess Caroline, but both he and his wife had remained close friends of Mrs Fitzherbert. Then tragically in 1801, when Minny was only three, both her mother and father died within a few weeks of each other. She was not mentioned in her father's will because she had been born after it had been made, but Lord Hugh's executors took the view that she came within its terms and that she should be placed under the guardianship of her aunt, Lady Waldegrave. Mrs Fitzherbert, when asked to give up the child to whom she was so attached, became distraught and was determined to keep her. The prince, who was also very fond of the little girl, offered to settle £10,000 on her, provided that she was allowed to remain with Mrs Fitzherbert. But Mrs Fitzherbert was a Catholic and the executors argued that she had no right to the care and upbringing of a Protestant child. After two long and bitter court hearings, Mrs Fitzherbert appealed to the House of Lords. She and the prince persuaded the Marquess of Hertford, as Minny's uncle, to say that this was an intimate family matter and to avoid further distressing public discussion would their lordships agree to giving unconditional guardianship of his niece to himself and his wife? Surprisingly, their lordships did agree by a large majority – the prince had been very busy lobbying among them – whereupon Lady Hertford, despite her strong anti-Catholic views, gave Minny back to Mrs Fitzherbert, who was overcome with joy. But unhappily for her it was during these long, anxious months that the prince came under the curious, motherly spell of the haughty marchioness. As was to be said later, Mrs Fitzherbert had won a daughter but lost a husband.

So it was that the prince became a more and more frequent visitor to Manchester Square and went to stay at Ragley Hall, the Hertfords' country house in Warwickshire. In a short time there was no possibility of concealing the fact that the prince had developed a passion for Lady Hertford. He visited her every day when she was in London and wrote to her every day when she was not. Not only was she highly gratified, but she was also ambitious enough to see her opportunities for political influence.

Nevertheless, she had no intention of becoming his mistress. London society was at a loss to explain the prince's obsession. Lady Hertford was not a popular woman, and Lady Stafford put it down to a taste on the part of the prince for 'elderly dames'. But no one could doubt that it was serious. The more Lady Hertford resisted him the more emotional the prince became. He sat up all night to write to her, he lost his appetite, he became ill, he went about looking wretched. Only the Hertfords could console him. He addressed her always as 'my ever dearest Lady B(eauchamp)' and in one of his letters, in which he tells her he is persevering with his medicine, he calls her 'my dearest nurse'. After her mother, Lady Irvine, had died he wrote: 'Do, my best and ever dearest friend, let the voice of the purest and most acute feeling in everything in which you are concerned claim your attention for a short moment....'

The Hertfords included Lord Yarmouth, who soon became the prince's closest companion. They wined and dined together whenever the prince was not swooning at Lady Hertford's feet in the oval drawing-room, which is today Gallery XXII at the Wallace Collection. This is what the prince had to say about him in a letter to Lady Hertford, in which he calls him Francis:

> ... nobody when he pleases (I have never seen him but when did so please) can command either a higher or more pleasing manner than he does, and his style of conversation is most truly delightful, as his sense and information and the accuracy of his judgement and his discrimination is really quite wonderful, and he is indeed in point of talent very superior to all the young men of the rising generation at least to any that I know....

But despite his hectic life with the prince Lord Yarmouth continued to write touching letters to Mie-Mie, complaining that he never heard from her. He gave her news of her ageing father, the Duke of Queensberry, who, he said, never went out, 'being deposited in his window every morning and is removed at night. He cares I believe for nobody on earth but yourself and believes a revolution is so near (that he) is in dread of not ending his days quietly....'

With his letters he sent her tooth-brushes, powder, an Eton

grammar and a black shawl. She sent him chocolate. Nevertheless, despite these presents, he had given up all hope of persuading her to come to live in London. He did not forget his children in his letters and showed concern about Richard's education, foreseeing that he would have to come to England soon – hence the Eton grammar.

On 30 March 1809 he wrote: 'I hope Beauchamp's education is sufficiently attended to to enable him to continue his education here when he is older, born to a great situation in this country the important part of his education must be here.'

In the same letter he said that he had sent her a parcel containing a book of Indian field-sports 'which I wish you to give from me to Mr de Talleyrand'. It was a surprising present for the Foreign Minister who all his life preferred the salons to open-air pastimes.

Mie-Mie's refusal to leave Paris still vexed him and he concluded the letter, 'I hope you find Paris as agreeable as it was. On that subject I never say one word except to hope that when we meet it may be in good humour. God bless you.'

Mie-Mie's father, the duke, who was well over eighty, died in December 1810. Old Q., whom Thomas Raikes described as 'a little sharp-looking man, very irritable, and swore like ten thousand troopers', left an immense fortune; but his will, to which he added thirty-five codicils, was as difficult and complicated as his character. However, it was clear the Yarmouth family were the chief beneficiaries and Mie-Mie now became a very rich woman no longer dependent on her husband. He left her £100,000, his two houses in Piccadilly, the stables and a house in Richmond. Her daughter and her younger son, Henry, were given £50,000 and in an important codicil were left the residue of the estate. Old Q. left nothing to Richard, the elder son, who, he presumably assumed, would inherit the Hertford fortune one day. He did not forget Lord Yarmouth either, in accordance with his promise when he married Mie-Mie, and left him £50,000.

Meanwhile the prince, at the age of forty-eight, had become Regent and the break with Mrs Fitzherbert was complete. Lady Hertford at fifty was the unchallenged favourite, receiving the prince and the royal dukes at her house in Manchester Square.

The stiff formality of these receptions has been well described by Miss Berry. In March 1811 she wrote in her journal:

Went about eleven to Lady Hertford's. We did not get in till near twelve, when the Regent had not arrived from dinner at Lord Cholmondeley's. He came soon afterwards, while we were in the outer room, and we saw the whole ceremony. A circle was immediately made, and the Regent, the Dukes of Clarence, Cumberland, Cambridge and Gloucester, were all in it at the same time. The Regent looked wretchedly, swollen up with a muddied complexion, and was besides extremely tipsy – gravely and cautiously so. I happened to be a good while in the circle; and he at last gave me a formal grave bow, with Kensington legible on it.

In general, he speaks much less, both to men and women, than he did – it is the fashion of the day with him. Did not get away from Lady Hertford's till very near two o'clock – the Prince still there.

The Hertfords went from strength to strength. The marquess was appointed Lord Chamberlain and Lord Yarmouth Vice-Chamberlain, but in Parliament and in the country there was talk of the sinister, unseen influence behind the throne. Cartoons by George Cruikshank ridiculing the Regent and the Hertfords appeared in the Press. Lady Holland, the Whig hostess, not only blamed the Hertfords for putting the Regent against the Whigs but also complained bitterly that Lord Hertford had 'debauched away' her French chef, Morel. But intimacy with the Regent meant sharing his unpopularity to the extent of being insulted in public. Lady Hertford had once to be rescued from the mob by Bow Street Runners and the house in Manchester Square was stoned and the windows smashed.

Away from Manchester Square, in the Regent's circle of intimate friends, Lord Yarmouth was known as 'Red Herrings' or 'Bloaters' on account of his red hair and whiskers and the fishing industry of the town whose name he bore. He was more amusing company than Beau Brummell and the other dandies who claimed to be the prince's friends. He was witty and clever. He could write Greek and Latin and was a discerning collector of works of art. Indeed, he had considerable influence on the prince who, despite his tipsy revelling, was also a collector. The money he was spending on Carlton House and his Pavilion at Brighton was denounced as mad extravagance, but he was forming magnificent collections of pictures, furniture and china which he was to leave to his successors. The Regent trusted Lord Yarmouth's judgement, who in many cases actually bought paintings and objects on his behalf.

In this way two Rembrandts, now at Buckingham Palace, and other fine paintings of the Dutch School, as well as furniture and porcelain, came into the royal collections. The Regent showed his gratitude by giving Lord Yarmouth Hoppner's portrait of himself when Prince of Wales, which he had bought from the painter's widow, to join Gainsborough's famous portrait of the love of his youth, the actress Mrs Robinson or 'Perdita', which he had given to the 2nd marquess. Both are in the Collection today.

When his son Richard reached the age of fourteen Lord Yarmouth again raised the question of his being sent to school in England, stating firmly that it was time he ceased to be tied to Mie-Mie's apron-strings. He clearly had Eton in mind. But Mie-Mie stubbornly refused to let him go. She raised every sort of argument against his being sent to a public school, pleading that his health would not stand it and quoting in support of her arguments the Abbé McNulty, who appears to have been giving the young Richard lessons at home.[1] Once again Mie-Mie got her way and Lord Yarmouth was forced to give up his plan to send his son to Eton. Writing from London on 28 November 1814 he said: 'It was certainly my wish to have had Beauchamp pass some short time at a public school.' He was prepared to give way to her views respecting his health and the progress of his education and he had been persuaded by the Abbé McNulty and others that a public school 'is no wise suited to him'. However, he was not in favour of a smaller school and therefore had been looking for a suitable tutor of impeccable character and trustworthiness. At last he found the right man.

His choice was a young man named Demainbray,[2] whose father, now a professor at Kew Observatory, had been one of the Prince Regent's tutors and also taught astronomy to the king. He hoped that Mie-Mie would agree but realised she was almost certain to raise new objections.

'I hope you will make the arrangement agreeable to Beauchamp.... Beauchamp is an English gentleman. He should know

[1] Later in life he suffered from attacks of asthma which he may have had as a child and which could have been the reason why Mie-Mie feared for his health if he was sent to school in England.

[2] Stephen Demainbray had taught science to George III when Prince of Wales. When Kew Observatory was built in 1768 the king appointed him to be director.

at least as much of England as he does of France ... that his education should be more attended to and that the almost total ignorance of the learned languages and inaccuracy of accent of his (then) own [*sic*] would be very bad things.'

He suggested Richard should come to England to stay a few months with Demainbray in Wiltshire, after which he would be delighted for him 'to spend as much time as can be spared from serious study' with her. Finally, he begged her not to regard this as a personal 'fancy' on his part 'but as one of deep importance to Beauchamp'. Mie-Mie did not give way at once and the next year Richard was still with his mother in Paris.

The final victory over Napoleon and the Allied occupation brought the English back to Paris. Many of them called, perhaps out of curiosity, at No. 1 rue Cerutti to see the wife of the Prince Regent's great friend, the woman who had lived in Paris throughout the period of the Empire, and seen the emperor's return from Elba, the woman who could claim to have had Junot and Duroc as her lovers. The result was that Richard, for the first time in his life, met a number of English people. His father arrived and took an interest in him and introduced him to his friends. The question of his going to school in England must again have been discussed.

Lord Yarmouth did not stay in Paris. We do not know whether he took Richard back with him to England to spend the period in Wiltshire with his tutor as he had suggested. However, we do know that Richard was in Paris in 1816 because early that year he was the victim of a swindle when playing cards with two young English officers. They claimed that he owed them large sums of money which they were counting on his father to pay. But Lord Yarmouth had enough experience of gambling to know how to deal with swindlers. He refused to pay and saw to it that they were court-martialled. After this Mie-Mie had to give in and Richard went to England to live with his tutor and started regular studies.

The young Richard hated England. He missed his mother and was homesick, as we can see from letters he wrote to her from Kew Lodge, Richmond. Mie-Mie wrote frequently to him but unfortunately none of her letters has survived.

His first letter, dated 25 October 1816, was written from Dover to tell her that he had arrived in England. He seems to have gone first to London where his father took him to a play. In a letter dated 7 November he promised Mie-Mie, who was in Brussels, 'I shall write you all that has happened since I am in England.' By 11 November he was complaining of the cold and explained that he did not write because he was never sure where she was. When she was 'safe in Paris' he would let her know everything 'that has happened to me since the miserable day that has separated us'.

Lord Yarmouth tried to be an understanding father during these first difficult days away from home and took him shooting in Kew and Richmond. He also wanted to take him to dinner with Montrond and General Flahaut, 'which party I shall hait [*sic*] more than I can say'. Richard was not happy with his father, partly because he kept him short of money. 'What do you think of £50 instead of £125?' he asked Mie-Mie.

Describing life at his tutor's, he said he had 'damnd [*sic*] four hours work a morning and a couple of hours history of a night after dinner, then prayers and then you may go to bed'.

On 15 November he wrote to tell Mie-Mie that he had heard that Stanhope, one of the officers who swindled him in Paris, had been cashiered for fraud and added, 'I must say I am not sorry.'

On 20 November he asked his mother to give his love to Fanny (his sister Frances) and Henry, and to thank the former for writing to him and 'put the latter in a state of mind to write to me'.

On 23 November, his fifth letter in the month, he was worried because she had not gone back to Paris.

Only one letter to Mie-Mie written in December has survived. Dated 3 December, he thought it 'very odd your staying so long in Brussels' and complained that he had been fifteen days without news. He begged her to write a little more often because 'it is the only enjoyment I have in this damnable country'. More cheerfully, he continued, 'I have bought such a Parrot as you never saw coming from the Antipodes.' His money problems had apparently been solved because he said he paid 'a good deal of money for him'. Was this purchase the first indication of the passion for collecting which was to occupy his whole life later?

In the same letter he also told Mie-Mie that she must do something about his brother's education. Lord Henry Seymour was now nearly twelve years old and clearly Lord Yarmouth, bearing in mind the difficulties he had to overcome before Mie-Mie would agree to Richard going to England, was beginning to worry about Henry. Richard urged his mother, saying that his father had complained to him, to try to make Henry learn how to read and write, pointing out that there were many Englishmen in Paris who could teach him. It would seem that Lord Yarmouth's concern was fully justified.

By the following February the letters show that he was no longer homesick and was beginning to enjoy himself. On 12 February he told his mother: 'I have been to four balls last week at Richmond.' (He may have gone to Paris for Christmas, which would explain the gap in the correspondence.) His letter of 22 February described how he went shooting with the Duke of York, Count Munster and his father, and that he was in London for the queen's drawing-room. The shy, homesick boy was fast becoming a young man about town. 'You cannot conceive how I am liked here, my dear mother. All the girls are in love with me (I say this entre nous, but don't let it pass the sacred limits of the family), I have dinners, parties and balls almost every night.'

The letters were becoming less frequent. In March he was dancing from eleven until six and by May, when the letters end, there was no more talk of work but only of parties and balls. Lord Yarmouth complained to Mie-Mie that his tutor had no control over Richard and allowed him to go to London whenever he pleased. The bird had flown from Mie-Mie's nest. Young Richard had become an Englishman and, now taking after his father, was set upon enjoying himself.

Lord Yarmouth, however, did not give up. He was determined that Richard's education should be completed and if he had not gone to Eton he would go to Oxford. In April 1818, when he was just eighteen, he went up to Exeter College and in his holidays he worked as an attaché at the British Embassy in Paris. The next year, despite his youth, he became a Member of Parliament, sitting for County Antrim, one of the family seats.

Lord Yarmouth by this time had become a close friend of John William Croker, the essayist and Tory M.P., whose abilities had attracted his attention early in his parliamentary career. In December 1818 they were at Brighton together.

'Yarmouth, the most good-natured man alive, has dragged me down here for a few days' relaxation and exercise,' Croker wrote to the Speaker, Charles Manners-Sutton. They went riding together during the day and at night they dined with the Regent at the Pavilion, where Lord and Lady Hertford were guests. According to Croker, dining with the Regent was not always so amusing. He called the dinners 'dull enough' and complained that with eighteen or twenty people at table they were too large for society and not quite crowded enough for freedom, 'so that one is on a sort of tiresome good behaviour'. Croker records an occasion when the Regent poked fun at Lord Hertford when he refused the boar's head, saying it was the only kind of bore Lord Hertford was not fond of. 'This is good,' wrote Croker, 'because Lord Hertford has a real passion for persons whom everybody else considers as bores.' The next year Croker, having failed to secure a seat in Parliament for Dublin University, was elected for Yarmouth, Isle of Wight, with the help of the Hertford family.

But the Regency was nearing its end and with it went the ascendancy of the Hertfords. At the end of January George III died in his eighty-second year without recovering his sanity, and Croker noted with awe at the funeral 'the death-like appearance of old Lord Hertford's fine but feeble figure tottering in before the coffin, and looking almost as if he was going to his own grave'.

Worse was to follow. The new fifty-seven-year-old king grew tired of Lady Hertford and began to see more and more of Lady Conyngham. Young Richard, now in the army, summed up the situation accurately when, after seeing the king riding with Lady Conyngham in Hyde Park, said: 'By God, grandmother must learn to ride, or it is all over with us.' He was right. Very soon the king was passionately in love with Lady Conyngham, although she had been married for twenty-seven years and had four grown-up children. Lady Hertford took it very badly and poured out her sufferings with tears and anger to Princess Lieven, saying that the new love was ridiculous because of the difference in the ages of the two. 'I had great difficulty in keeping a straight face at this point of the story,' Princess Lieven wrote to her brother. 'She is sixty-three and Lady Conyngham forty-five....'

As with the Hertfords, the king's passion included the husband and the children, and when Lord Hertford handed in his resignation as Lord Chamberlain the king tried to appoint Lord Conyngham to the vacant post in his household. He was much put out when the government resisted this move. But Lord Hertford was ageing rapidly and cannot have cared very much. However, he did his best to obtain a dukedom. On hearing that the Marquess of Buckingham was to be made a duke, he wrote to Lord Liverpool, the Prime Minister, from Sudbourne on 2 January 1822:

I have just been assured it is His Majesty's intention to raise the Marquess of Buckingham to the rank of a Duke. I therefore feel it due to myself and to my family to request your Lordship to submit to His Majesty that nearly thirty years ago my father was promised by Mr Pitt, on the part of the late King, that should His Majesty ever consent to increase the number of Dukedoms, his name should be included and stand next to that of Lord Buckingham, to whom a similar promise had already been given.

During the time he held 'high and confidential office close to His Majesty', he said, he 'studiously avoided' any reference to this subject 'lest I might be thought anxious to attain for my family an honour His Majesty seemed to confine to the reward of splendid public services'. But now, on learning about Lord Buckingham, he felt very differently 'and I hope your Lordship will be ready to support with your advice my prayer for an equal favour'.

Lord Liverpool replied on 4 January, saying that neither the king nor he had knowledge of any promise being held out to Lord Hertford's father or himself respecting an English dukedom. He added that no family is entitled to rest their pretensions to new honours on 'what may have passed in conversations either with the King or his Minister' and pointed out that it was usual whenever a promise or expectation had been intended that this should be given in a letter. The Marquess of Buckingham, he went on, submitted more than a year ago a letter from Mr Pitt to this effect and even a promise of this nature is not necessarily binding on succeeding kings.

Lord Liverpool sent a copy of his letter, which put an end to Lord Hertford's hopes, to the king, who replied admiringly from

Brighton on 5 January: 'The King feels most sensibly the delicacy of Lord Liverpool on this occasion, and most highly approves of Lord Liverpool's answer.'

In March Princess Lieven wrote to her brother: 'Lord Yarmouth is awaiting with indecent impatience the death of his father, but it should be said in his defence that the poor old man has become quite childish.' He died in June that year. He left the house in Manchester Square, the scene of his wife's triumphs, and all its contents to her for as long as she lived. She was now the richest widow in England but, still resentful of the king's behaviour, the dowager marchioness set herself to regain her position in society. Her receptions and fêtes at Manchester Square were more brilliant than ever and all the women in London who hated the 'Vice-Queen', as Lady Conyngham was known, were on her side. She outlived the king by four years and died a determined old lady at the age of seventy-four.

Richard now became Lord Yarmouth and in a letter to Mie-Mie after his grandfather's death, in which he gave her details of his will, he has this to say about his father, now the 3rd Marquess of Hertford: 'Dearest Mother I must go down to my father who talks to me *very kindly* now for the Estate is so arranged that he cannot sell a chair or cut down a tree the size of my little finger without my consenting to it.'

But the new marquess was not at all put out at being dropped by the king. With the money his father had left him he decided to devote himself to Tory party politics. His control of eight pocket boroughs was important for the Tories when they needed to find a seat for some unexpectedly defeated member of their party. Leading Tories, including the Duke of York, the Duke of Wellington, Lord Eldon and Sir Robert Peel, were entertained lavishly in London or invited to shooting parties at Sudbourne, his country house in Suffolk. Croker, in a letter to Peel, once described one of these parties.

I know not that I can tell you anything more important than the state and disposition of the company in the midst of which I snatch a moment to write to you. In the large room, Mrs Horace Seymour and Lady Anne Beckett are sitting on a sofa and discoursing of last season's balls and concerts. Mrs and Miss Orby Hunter in two contiguous armchairs are reading out of one red book the fate of a clerk 'for the issue of exchequer bills'. I am writing at a round table, very much interrupted by questions from all the ladies on subjects which I know nothing about. Lord Hertford is lying on a sofa and nursing a gouty knee, which has disabled him this last week; today he walked out for the first time and shot $4\frac{1}{2}$ brace of birds.

In a little middle room, lately created, or rather, lately opened to the larger room, the Duke of York, the Speaker [Manners-Sutton], Henry Baring and Evelyn are playing at whist, as the same party did last night, or rather this morning, till half-past two; the Speaker smarting under the recollection of his losses at Lalworth, which are renewed and aggravated by having lost fifty pounds last night – but I believe they have tonight lowered the stake. As a set off, however, I ought to state that he has won a crown of me.

In a still further room, Mr Orby Hunter is spelling out John Bull, while Huskisson, Lord George Seymour, Horace, and 'Chin' [Sir Alexander Grant] are playing at whist for 6d. a point and 2s. 6d. a bet.

You have our whole party and their present occupations, and you need not be told what their probable employments and amusements are for the whole day.

The Orbys only arrived to dinner today. If they had not been asked to meet the Duke [of York], 'all the fat would have been in the fire' – I quote the host's own expression.

The shooting is very indifferent for Sudbourne shooting, though there are certainly birds enough for sport. We were out in four parties today. D. of Y. killed about 8 brace, Col. Cooke (whom being gone to bed, I forgot in my enumeration) killed 7 brace, Grant 9, Huskisson 3, and I zero.

But the 3rd marquess, unlike his father, had no intention of devoting his life to public service or seeking an important position in politics. By the general election of 1826 he had handed over the management of most of his affairs to Croker. The next year he was sent on a special mission to St Petersburg, the bearer of the Order of the Garter to the Tsar, Nicholas I. This was an occasion for him to indulge his passion for lavish display and the Russian court was astonished by his magnificence and his wealth. But an attack of gout did much to spoil the pleasure of his stay in Russia.

Back in London he moved into Dorchester House, an enormous residence in Park Lane where the Dorchester Hotel stands today, and kept a cow in the park opposite. Not satisfied with this house, he ordered Decimus Burton to build him a splendid villa in Regent's Park designed especially as the setting for the most costly fêtes and entertainments. From now on, this man of genuine if wasted talents was to devote the rest of his life to pleasure, and earn for himself the name of 'the Caliph of Regent's Park'.

Hertford Villa, as the house was first called, was not far from Albany Cottage, a pretty villa that his friend Thomas Raikes had had built in Regent's Park, but it was much grander and larger with a spectacular portico of eight huge, free-standing, Corinthian columns. The roof was tent-shaped with gilt pinnacles covering an enormous room where the Caliph staged his extravagant and costly entertainments on a scale that only crowned heads could afford. Tiers of boxes, as in a theatre, made up one wall of this large room. They were reached by a concealed staircase and were allotted only to specially favoured guests. Enormous numbers of people were invited to the lavish fêtes which lasted until the early hours of the morning, and they were waited on by a hundred servants all in Hertford livery.

In the garden he set up Roman antiquities which he brought back from his travels in Italy. The most important was the Meta, one of the two cone-shaped marble columns which stood at each end of the Circus Maximus, round which the chariots raced, which he had bought in Rome in 1829. He also bought Roman statues and columns to make a colonnade in the garden, while in the park his cows were given the luxury of drinking out of sarcophagi.

A few years after the villa was completed Lord Hertford was able to achieve one of his childhood ambitions. As a boy, he had been taken to see the famous clock of St Dunstan's. The hours were struck by giants, thought to be King Lud and his sons. He had been so amazed by it that he announced there and then that when he grew up he would buy it. In 1830 the church was pulled down because it blocked Fleet Street and the present church was built on what had been the graveyard behind. This gave him the chance to buy the clock. He paid £210 for it, and had it repaired and the figures repainted. He had a special campanile built in his garden and set the clock upon it. Then he changed the name of his villa to St Dunstan's.

The villa enjoyed a different sort of fame when in 1917 it

became St Dunstan's Institute for the Blind, founded by Sir Arthur Pearson as a training centre for blind soldiers and sailors. In the twenties St Dunstan's was empty, but from 1935 to 1936 it became the home of Lord Rothermere. He returned the famous clock to St Dunstan's in Fleet Street where, after three hundred years of life, its giants still strike the hours. In 1936 the villa was bought by the millionairess Barbara Hutton, who pulled it down and replaced it with Winfield House, now the residence of the United States ambassador in London.

Chapter Three

Mie-Mie had just turned fifty when the news of her father-in-law's death reached her in Paris. She was at last the Marchioness of Hertford, but she and her husband had lived apart for so long by mutual consent and force of circumstances that their marriage counted for little. Although neither partner had ever completely abandoned the other, more often than not the main purpose of their rare meetings had been money matters or the need to settle questions arising from property they had inherited. But if Mie-Mie's interest in money was to become almost an obsession as the years went by, she had another, more laudable side to her character. She was a loving and devoted mother. When she had left England she had insisted on taking her children with her, although Richard was not yet three and her daughter only a year older, not only because she had no intention of going back to live in England but quite simply because she could not bear to be parted from them. Through war and peace she had kept her children with her and even added to the family, although her third child, as we have seen, was not her husband's.

Only a woman of great character and determination, as Mie-Mie was, would have contrived to live freely in Paris while the Emperor Napoleon marched his all-conquering armies from one end of Europe to the other. After all, she was a foreigner and, to make it worse, from a country which was in a state of war with France. But her natural self-confidence coupled with her Latin wit and vivacity had made her extremely popular with the French from the very first day she had arrived in Paris. She made friends easily and was an incorrigible flirt but, despite this, she managed to keep her women friends. She had the added advantage of wealth and a title, and during the magnificent years of the Empire she was seen everywhere. After all, she could claim among her lovers the Marshal of the Palace, General Duroc.

She had always been close to her children and more especially to her daughter, Frances Maria, who in April 1821 had married the Marquis de Chevigné, an officer in the bodyguard of Louis XVIII. For months Mie-Mie had been completely taken up by her daughter's romance and arrangements for the marriage. In her concern for her daughter's happiness she had not the time or the inclination to reflect on her new position and title. Then suddenly her happiness was cruelly shattered. In November, barely six months after her wedding, Frances Maria died.

Her loss could not have come at a worse time for Mie-Mie. She was in late middle age and without her daughter it seemed that life held nothing more. The gaiety and splendour of the Empire and the excitement of the Hundred Days were memories. There were no more lovers and those of her friends who were still alive had become dull with age. The daily companionship of her daughter had replaced the gay parties and flirtations of the past. Mie-Mie, who loved to have young people around her, was heartbroken at the loss of her daughter.

In 1820 the young Lord Yarmouth had bought himself a commission in the 10th Hussars. From the fragments of letters to his mother that have survived we learn that he was frequently ill, suffered from nose-bleeding and was always catching colds. This suggests that he was never strong and that Mie-Mie's fears for his health when his father wanted him to go to school in England were not without foundation. Also he had a bad fall from his horse in 1820. He wanted to leave the army and wondered if Fanny, his sister, would lend him some money. He wrote that he had many things to tell Mie-Mie about his 'being a little, that is to say very much in love. It is a great folly but I cannot help it. . . .' The following year he was still in the army and had again been 'very ill', his excuse for not writing. He said the cold barracks had given him a sore throat and a cough.

One day in 1824 Lord Yarmouth brought home to Mie-Mie a little fair-haired English boy, only six years old, called Richard Jackson and asked her to bring him up. This little boy, who had been brought to Paris from London by his mother, Agnes Jackson, was his son. Richard had met Agnes Jackson when he was only seventeen and still Lord Beauchamp. She was eleven years older than he and when the boy had been born in London on 21 June 1818 he had been given his mother's surname but called Richard after his father. Agnes Jackson was the daughter of Sir Thomas Wallace whose mother, Mrs Frances Dunlop, *née* Wallace, had been the patroness of Robert Burns. Her father was Sir Thomas Wallace of Craigie and when he died without a male heir Agnes's father had assumed his grandfather's name and called himself Baronet of Craigie Castle, Ayrshire. Agnes was the child of his second wife, Isabella, and had been born in 1789.[1] In 1808 she had married Samuel Bickley, a member of Lloyd's and a man of some importance in the City. She had two children by him. Sometime after the birth of her second child in 1810 she became separated from her husband and adopted the name of Jackson.

Having found Lord Yarmouth in Paris Agnes left his son and his nurse with him and went back to London, where she must have returned to Bickley because she bore him two more sons in 1830 and 1832. Perhaps this was the reason she brought Richard Jackson to Paris and left him with his father.

After four years of the gay life of a young army officer it is most surprising that Lord Yarmouth accepted the child and decided to bring him up himself. It was far more customary for the children of such extra-marital liaisons to be brought up discreetly by foster-mothers. Furthermore, why was he so sure that the boy was his son? And did Mie-Mie know who he was? It may well be that it was she with her maternal instincts who decided to keep him and bring him up. Whatever the reasons, when she saw the boy she loved him and, despite the possible scandal, she took Richard Jackson into her home. She called him 'cher neveu' and he called her 'tante Mie-Mie'. They became deeply attached to each other and he was to live with her until she died.

Neither Mie-Mie nor Lord Yarmouth ever gave the slightest hint of their true relationships – grandmother and father – to the

[1] The date of her death is not known, but her second child, Wallace Bickley, went to Australia when he grew up and founded a family in Perth. His descendants are living in Australia today.

young Richard Jackson and for a long time mystery surrounded his origins. There was even the unlikely suggestion that Mie-Mie was his mother. Apart from the fact that she already had a son named Richard, she would have been forty-seven when the baby was born.

We do not know whether Lord Hertford was aware of the existence of Richard Jackson before he was brought to Paris. It seems likely that he would have known of his son's affair when he was so young, and may even have arranged that he should become an attaché at the Embassy in Paris in order to break it. After that he was far too busy with his own pleasures to worry about his son's adventures and there is no evidence that he played any part in Mie-Mie's decision to take their grandson into the family. He was rapidly losing all interest in politics in England and since his return from St Petersburg was spending more and more time abroad, relying on Croker's letters to keep him informed. He was fast developing a contempt for society after having been for so many years one of its leading figures. His passion for buying pictures often brought him to Paris where he would probably have called on Mie-Mie. He may have seen Richard Jackson but not Lord Henry Seymour, whom he always studiously ignored.

Lady Blessington, in Paris at this time, described his state of mind accurately. They were old friends and, after saying that she found him as amusing and original as ever, she goes on to say:

> He has great natural talent and knowledge of the world, but uses both to little purpose, save to laugh at its slaves. He might be anything he chose, but he is too indolent for exertion, and seems to think *le jeu ne vaut pas la chandelle* [*sic*]. He is one of the many clever people spoilt by being born to a great fortune and high rank, advantages which exclude the necessity of exercising the talents he possesses.

She had been away from London for some time and calls him Lord Yarmouth. She had probably forgotten that he had succeeded to the marquessate, but it is quite clear that it is the 3rd marquess of whom she is speaking. Surprisingly, she adds that despite his wealth he was 'wholly free from arrogance and ostentation'.

Early in 1828 he too undertook the responsibilities of a guardian, although of a very different nature and in very different circumstances from those which his wife had accepted. His old friend Admiral Sir Richard Strachan begged him, as he lay dying, to be the guardian of his three pretty little daughters, Matilda, Charlotte and Louisa. The choice of Lord Hertford caused considerable comment in London because Lady Strachan, many years younger than her husband, had for several years been Lord Hertford's principal mistress. No attempt had ever been made to hide their relationship and she was often a guest at Sudbourne without her husband. After the admiral died Lady Strachan and her three daughters came to live with Lord Hertford in his London house and travelled abroad with him. They also brazenly wheedled large sums of money out of him which they spent on fine clothes and jewellery. They went to Naples where they all lived in the most lavish style, impressing the Neapolitans with their wealth and magnificence. There no one complained about his morals and he believed the climate was good for his gout. He began to spend more and more time in Italy, chiefly Naples or Milan, and less in Paris because it was awkward for him to appear in public with Lady Strachan in the city where his wife lived.

In April 1829 his gout was so bad during a visit to Rome that he was forced to use crutches to get about, but it did not stop him going to a reception to meet the Grand Duchess Helena of Russia. Nor did it stop him buying statues and columns for the garden of his villa in Regent's Park. Referring to these purchases, which included the Meta from the Circus Maximus, he told Croker in a letter that he had caught 'marble-mania'.

But despite the fine clothes, the jewels, the presents of money, Lady Strachan began to tire of her situation, and felt she needed a real husband. First she bought herself the Italian title of Marchesa Salza and, armed with this, set out to find herself a husband. It was not long before she had given herself to a persistent suitor with the extraordinary name of Pisollili. Lord Hertford was furious at being abandoned in favour of 'a monstrous adventurer'. The result was that he altered his will and she lost the fortune he had left her several years before when her husband was still alive, and was given instead the income from a trust fund with the following spiteful explanation: 'Aware of the infamy of my successor's character, I wish her to be as little as possible in his power. Tho' he will of course, rob her each quarter, yet, when she may quit him, she will be independent and he will have no temptation to shorten her days.'

The three daughters were growing up and they all found themselves foreign husbands. Matilda became the Countess Berchthold, Louisa the Princess Ruffo and Charlotte, the last to marry, became Countess Zichy-Ferraris. She remained in scandalous attendance, so to speak, on Lord Hertford after her marriage, and she and her conniving husband lived with him for long periods, exploiting him without mercy to the extent of many thousands of pounds.

There seems no doubt that insanity was slowly driving Lord Hertford to the depths of depravity. According to Croker, he believed that there was hereditary madness in his family and often talked about it.

Mie-Mie's apartment in the rue Cerutti, now the rue d'Artois, was much too small now that young Richard Jackson and his nurse had joined her household. Her nineteen-year-old son Lord Henry Seymour was still living with her, and the boy's father, Lord Yarmouth, was in the habit of arriving unexpectedly during the course of his travels. After searching around the neighbourhood, she decided to buy a large house on the corner of the boulevard and the rue Taitbout. This she was able to do with the money left to her by Old Q. The house had previously belonged to the Russian millionaire Count Demidof, whose son Anatole was to marry Princesse Mathilde Bonaparte, daughter of Napoleón's youngest brother, Jérome, King of Westphalia. The Demidofs owed their immense fortune to an ancestor, a poor blacksmith who repaired a gun for Peter the Great and presented him, as well, with a pistol of his own invention. As a reward he was given land in the Urals which proved to be rich in iron ore. Here he built a foundry and manufactured cannon, thus becoming an early Russian counterpart of Krupp.

Mie-Mie installed herself and Richard Jackson on the first floor of the new house and sent Lord Henry upstairs to live in a flat of his own on the second floor. The old flat in the rue d'Artois was kept for when Lord Yarmouth came to Paris. This wise and practical arrangement enabled her to keep her sons close to her without restricting their freedom in any way.

At first Richard Jackson must have found all this very confusing, even frightening. His mother had left him with a man he had never seen before in a strange town where everyone spoke a different language. Then he had been taken to live with an old lady whom he was told was his aunt. The rooms, the furniture, the streets and the people were all strange to him. Only his nurse was familiar. But Mie-Mie seems quickly to have overcome his timidity and made him feel he was loved. She was genuinely glad to have the little boy to look after, gave him all her time and grew to enjoy his company. He, on his side, seems to have been a child of unusual charm and good manners, and by the time the move to the rue Taitbout took place the bond between them was complete. They were very happy together: Richard Jackson had found a new home and had settled down.

To the excitement of the move to the new house was added the discovery that on the ground floor was the Café de Paris, the smartest restaurant in Paris. From their windows young Richard could watch some of the best-known people going in and out of the restaurant. Mie-Mie also loved watching the crowds in the fashionable boulevard below. Indeed, this may have been one of the reasons for buying the house. Now that she seldom went out, she may have felt less cut off from life if she could watch the elegant society people with their carriages and fine horses.

One can imagine Mie-Mie, with Richard Jackson at her side, his head pressed against the window, watching the arrivals at the Café de Paris. The *habitués* were nearly all well known – the Baron Louis de Montbrun, the Comte Ludovic de la Tour du Pin; officers such as the Commandant de Bougainville, the Marquis de Saint-Vallier, the Comte de Barral, the famous and redoubtable swordsman, and the Marquis du Hallay-Coetquen; and well-known journalists such as Nestor Roqueplan of the *Figaro* or the famous Docteur Veron of the *Revue de Paris*, the future *directeur* of the Opéra. Soon Richard Jackson knew them all by sight and would notice if one of them failed to arrive. We have no details of his more serious education, but presumably he had lessons at home and would soon have been speaking French fluently.

In 1830, when he was twelve, the revolution that was to force Charles X to abdicate broke out. During the afternoon of 27 July, the first day of the 'Trois Glorieuses', the barricades went up not far away from the rue Taitbout in the quartier of the Bourse, at the Palais Royal, the place Vendôme and the rue St Honoré. In the evening the army intervened. By the following morning the people in the eastern half of Paris were in the streets in open revolt and the shooting began again. Then the army went over to the citizens and the next day Paris was in the hands of the revolutionaries. Young Richard must have seen and heard a great deal of the fighting from his window. Mie-Mie was anxious, for this was different from what she has seen and lived through under Bonaparte. The abdication of Charles X meant the end of the Bourbons, and perhaps also the stability of their life in Paris. Uncertain as to their future, Mie-Mie, Lord Yarmouth, Lord Henry Seymour and Richard Jackson decided to leave everything and flee to Boulogne where they hoped to find a boat to take them to England. As a precaution, Mie-Mie sewed thousands of francs in notes into her skirts.

When they arrived in Boulogne Mie-Mie got in touch with her husband. Lord Hertford's advice was that they should stay where they were. He, who lived in daily fear of revolution in England, apparently told them that the country was on the brink of a revolution far worse than anything that might happen in France. They therefore abandoned their plan to go on to England and remained in Boulogne until things had settled down. Then they all returned to the Paris of Louis-Philippe.

The barricades, the Paris mob, the shooting and the flight to Boulogne must have made a big impression on the young Richard Jackson. Even more important, as a result of the flight he must have realised for the first time that he had a family. There were many family conferences at the rue Taitbout before they all left for Boulogne. He may even have heard talk for the first time of his grandfather, Lord Hertford, and even of his great-grandmother, the old dowager Lady Hertford, still living in the house in Manchester Square, which one day would be his own. In Boulogne, where they all lived together, there must have been talk of other members of the family – the Seymour-Conways, the Hertfords. Probably he asked questions about them without realising that they were his blood relations. What would he think about them at the age of twelve? Did he find the Hertfords as extravagant, arrogant and selfish as we consider them today? Undoubtedly not. To him they must have seemed grand and exciting. He was beginning to take an interest in those around him and seek a personal relationship with them. He was beginning to grow up.

Chapter Four

THE ADOLESCENT RICHARD JACKSON was naturally very much influenced by Lord Henry Seymour, his unacknowledged uncle, who lived in the same house. He was thirteen years older than Richard and was a well-known dandy with a reputation for daring. He had a table permanently reserved for him at the Café de Paris, the sign of a boulevard notable. He was also immensely rich, having inherited the residue of the Queensberry Estate when his sister died. Richard adored him and Lord Henry for his part was sincerely fond of the boy and taught him to fence and ride.

Despite the fact that he had been born and brought up in France and had no wish to go anywhere near England, Lord Henry had an English love of sport and physical exercise, so much so that he installed a gymnasium in the stable loft in the courtyard at the rue Taitbout and there he boxed and fenced with his friends. He had a reputation for great strength and often his servants were told to put on the gloves and box with him at the risk of getting a black eye. At his country house at Neuilly there were large stables where he could indulge his passion for horses and horse-racing. He was also the leading spirit in a group of rich men who had formed the habit of meeting to ride together in the long, tree-lined avenues of the Bois de Boulogne.

The Bois de Boulogne was at this time completely surrounded by a wall and to reach it they had to go out of Paris by the Étoile barrier and then down a road with waste land on either side, on which in later years the opulent houses of the wealthy would be built to make today's Avenue Foch. This group of horsemen included such well-known names as the Comte de Vaublanc, the Comte Walewski, Comte de Castello-Field, Baron de la Bastide, the banker Charles Laffitte, Ernest Le Roy, the composer Auber, the novelist Eugène Sue and the horse-dealer Crémieux. Amongst these men Lord Henry, despite his Latin parentage, was considered completely English and the model sporting English gentleman. Their favourite riding place was over a gallop roughly on the spot where the stands at Auteuil race-course are today. They called it 'le mille de Drake' after Stephen Drake, another horse-dealer. Here they used to race their horses, making bets among themselves.

This racing and betting among friends soon led to more organised race-meetings in the Bois de Boulogne, which quickly became very fashionable occasions. Lord Henry was the leading spirit and the leading owner. He was the acknowledged authority on all racing matters and he introduced English thoroughbreds into France. In 1833 he decided that the time had come to put racing on a more organised footing. He persuaded his friends of the need for a body to administer racing and encourage the breeding of bloodstock, and he founded the Société d'encouragement pour l'amélioration des races de chevaux en France. He was elected president of this society at a secret ballot and under his influence the committee adopted Newmarket rules. In doing so he was following in the footsteps of the man who was supposed to be his father, who had organised similar race-meetings at Verdun when he was Napoleon's prisoner twenty-odd years before. When Lord Henry organised the society's first meeting under Newmarket rules at the Champ de Mars in May 1834 there were already more than fifty members, and the rules were so strict that poor Alfred de Musset, who wanted to join, was blackballed because he was unable to ride.

When the society became too big for its rented room at the Café de Paris it moved to less frivolous premises on the boulevard and became the elegant Jockey Club, on the English model. As he got older Lord Henry had become a quick-tempered, vain, argumentative man. He was not pleased if he did not get his way in all matters and he had many quarrels in his racing career and was always finding reasons for resigning from the Jockey Club.

There was another side to Lord Henry Seymour. He also led a wild Bohemian life which gave rise to the legend that he was the leader of the noisy boulevard revellers at carnival time. He became known as Milord l'Arsouille, which might be kindly translated as Lord Ruffian. He was certainly not responsible for all the rowdy behaviour and scandals that were attributed to him and he denied it all his life. The real Milord l'Arsouille, although nothing could persuade the crowds that they had made a mistake, was not a lord at all but a certain Charles Le Battut, curiously enough more English than Lord Henry Seymour since his father had been an English chemist of very limited means who had persuaded a Breton friend to give his name to a son born out of wedlock.

But more important than Lord Henry's boulevard reputation, although he and his friends may have played many pranks on innocent people, is the fact that he included artists among his friends and, like a true Seymour, which he was not, was interested in works of art and collected paintings. He bought pictures by contemporary painters whom he knew such as Robert-Fleury, Decamps, Eugène Isabey, Ary Scheffer, as well as several horse studies by Géricault. Some of the fine Boningtons now in the Wallace Collection were originally bought by him. He also owned Watteau's *Harlequin and Columbine*, and the Holbein self-portrait miniature, the most important miniature in the Collection.

It is possible, therefore, that it was Lord Henry Seymour who first interested the boy who was to become Sir Richard Wallace in painting and painters. He probably took him to visit them in their studios; and he would have come to know Lord Henry's private collection in the upstairs apartment in the rue Taitbout.

In 1834 the old dowager Lady Hertford died in London. Her funeral attracted large crowds and William IV sent all the royal carriages as a gesture to the woman who had been the favourite of his brother. Mie-Mie had little love for her mother-in-law, who had always looked down on her as being unworthy of her son, and it is doubtful if the news caused much sadness in the rue Taitbout. Her son, the 3rd marquess, was in Italy with the Strachan family when his mother died, so in the absence of her only son and daughter-in-law she was buried by other members of the family. She had already given her son most of her jewels and in her will she left him some fine French furniture, mostly Boulle, which he had bought for her, and a bust of his father, but nothing, of course, to Mie-Mie whom she disliked.

After his mother's death Lord Hertford went back to London and began to go out in society again. Having two houses of his own, he decided to let her house in Manchester Square to the French government and in 1836 it became the French Embassy. His father's return to London seems to have been the signal for Richard's father, Lord Yarmouth, to leave London for Paris. This time he showed every sign of settling there and one of the first things he did was to buy a house in the country. It was no ordinary house, but a little château in the Bois de Boulogne known as Bagatelle. It had been rebuilt by the Comte d'Artois, the future Charles X, who had bet Marie Antoinette that in sixty days, while the court was away at Fontainebleau, he would turn it into a fairy palace for her amusement. The work was finished in sixty-four days – and on the queen's return he gave a magnificent party for her as he had promised, in the newly furbished Bagatelle. Since then it had passed to Louis-Philippe, who decided to sell it. Thomas Raikes, who was living in Paris at the time, describes how on 9 October 1835 he called on Lord Yarmouth and 'found him surrounded with plans and designs of architects. He has just bought Bagatelle, in the Bois de Boulogne for 313,100 francs'. According to Raikes, Lord Yarmouth saved it from being demolished by outbidding a company of housebreakers, which he calls the 'Bande Noire', at the sale. This company made a business of buying old châteaux for the sake of the materials with which they had been constructed, particularly the lead pipes.

Having bought Bagatelle, Lord Yarmouth immediately plunged into a major programme of costly alterations and repairs, for the house had been standing empty for many years. His principal preoccupation was with the bedrooms. The ceilings of the upstairs rooms were very low and he did not hesitate to raise the roof, thus radically altering the original appearance of the château as designed by Bélanger. The result was two good bedrooms with windows replacing the skylights. He also spent money restoring the park which had been laid out for the Comte d'Artois by the Scottish gardener Thomas Blaikie. Raikes was taken to see the new purchase after the work had started and he has left an enthusiastic description. Having noted that Lord Yarmouth was building greenhouses and planting trees, he goes on to say:

There is a large steam-engine which supplies the house, the offices, the park, and cascades with water from the Seine; and the whole premises are so undermined with arteries of leaden pipes, in which the metal (as in those times) was so prodigally used, and is now so valuable, that it in some measure accounts for the anxiety the company called the Bande Noire had to make the purchase.

The dry rot has unfortunately made its way into the house, and it has become necessary to lay down new floorings in all the rooms, both below and above, which is the more to be regretted as it must injure the beautiful painted ceilings of the principal apartments. We detected some remains of the fresco paintings in the boudoir, which were done by the orders of the Comte d'Artois, and form a great contrast to the present devout habits of Charles X. [The frescoes had been painted in 1777, in his gay youth, before he became pious to the extent of bigotry after the death of a favourite mistress in 1805.] When completely restored by the present proprietor it will be the most beautiful fairy retreat in France, at only a quarter of an hour's drive from the capital.

The quarter of an hour was surely an exaggeration.

About the time that he bought Bagatelle Lord Yarmouth seems to have been seriously caught up with a young girl, half-French, half-English, who was living in Paris, and whom he deceived disgracefully. She was the daughter of a professor and called Louise Suzanne Bréart. With the promise of marriage Lord Yarmouth persuaded her to elope with him to London where they were 'married' in what she believed to be a legal Church of England wedding. Not until two months later did he tell her that the ceremony had all been play-acting and that the clergyman had been his valet in disguise. This was some time in 1834. Mademoiselle Bréart must have loved him because despite this monstrous deception she never married and remained faithful to him all her life. She adopted the name of Madame Oger and was installed in an apartment close to his, at No. 6 rue Laffitte. Although he was not faithful to her he always went back to her; she was his hostess when later he went to live at Bagatelle and she was remembered in his will. There was also Amelia Idle, whose husband had been a friend of Lord Yarmouth at Oxford. George Idle's wild life resulted in his early death in Paris, whereupon Lord Yarmouth consoled his widow. She too had an apartment in Paris and he gave her a regular allowance. In his will he left her the surprisingly large sum of £12,000 a year without any explanation.

By 1837 Lord Yarmouth seems to have lost interest in the progress of work at Bagatelle and went off to London.

Richard Jackson was now a young man of nearly twenty. After a youthful wish to join the navy had been vetoed by his father, he seems to have been attracted by the Bohemian world where he made his friends among the artists and writers whom he had first met with his uncle. However, he still lived with Mie-Mie and dined with her nearly every night, often joined by Lord Henry Seymour. They were a very united trio.

Although she was now sixty-six Mie-Mie was still a fascinating and vivacious little woman. When there were guests she would always put on the same yellow dress and a bird of paradise plume in her black hair. She stooped slightly, and with her long nose and very large hands and feet she must have looked rather witch-like. But all this was offset by a most beautiful speaking voice which no one ever forgot. After her sons, her only interest was money and she speculated heavily on the Bourse. In the end it became her obsession and she persuaded Richard Jackson to join her in some not always successful gambles in stocks and shares.

Always restless, Lord Yarmouth did not stay long either in London or Paris, and in July 1838 he was off again with Raikes to take the waters at Carlsbad. He seems to have been genuinely concerned about his health. Leaving Paris at three o'clock in the morning they reached Épernay for dinner, where, with the austerity of the waters at Carlsbad ahead, they drank two bottles of champagne for dinner. Raikes noted smugly: '... it is always right to drink the wine grown in the country....'

Then they moved on to Venice where in October they heard that Lord Hertford had been taken ill in Milan. They hurried there and found him very unwell, but being cared for by a German doctor in whom he had great faith. While in Milan they made use of Lord Hertford's box at La Scala where, in Raikes's view, 'the ballet was brilliant in decoration but feeble in dancing. The singing wretched.' After a week Lord Hertford was 'quite convalescent' and they left Milan for Turin, travelling through the night, stopping to eat white truffles for dinner, as Raikes, always a good gastronomic correspondent, noted. They arrived at Turin at seven o'clock in the morning. They did not get back to Paris until the last day of November. Here at last Lord Yarmouth settled, for he had reached a turning-point in his life. Sir Robert Peel is known to have had a high opinion of his abilities and to have thought that, with his money and position, he had the makings of a Prime Minister had he decided to stay in politics. But, like his father before him, Lord Yarmouth renounced such a promising future. He even refused the offer of the Embassy in Paris. He preferred to live in Paris without the responsibilities of being the British ambassador.

It is difficult to explain the Seymours' sudden disdain for public life and position when they were half way through their careers. Was it laziness, or too much money, as Lady Blessington had thought when she had seen Lord Yarmouth's father in Paris? Perhaps it was a little of both. Perhaps Lord Yarmouth did not want to live in London when the mad debauchery of his father's later years became a public scandal. Whatever their reasons were, it is certain that *he* wanted to live in Paris where he had been brought up. For a wealthy bachelor no city in the world was gayer, freer and more pleasant to live in.

So he settled down in the rue Laffitte, finished the work on Bagatelle, and started collecting works of art. In 1841 he made his first recorded purchase at a public auction. He paid 385 francs for a Fragonard, *The Schoolmistress*, which was being sold by the Comte Perregaux, the banker who had kept his father supplied with money when he was interned at Verdun. The artist's son is supposed to have been the model for the small boy in the painting. It seems nothing today, but at the time it was considered an extraordinary thing to do because eighteenth-century French painting had been out of favour since the Revolution.

From that day on Lord Yarmouth was to devote his life and his considerable fortune entirely to collecting. In continuing the family tradition he was not only a true Seymour but he was to become the greatest collector of them all.

Chapter Five

LORD YARMOUTH'S DECISION to make Paris his home meant that for the first time since they had grown up the two brothers, or, rather, half-brothers, were both living permanently in Paris. To French eyes they must have appeared as two very eligible, titled, wealthy Englishmen. Although Lord Henry Seymour, with his dark hair and exuberant Latin manners, was considered so typically English by his friends in Paris, he would not have looked very English in England. Lord Yarmouth, on the other hand, although he prided himself on his perfect French, was and looked the complete English nobleman. He was a big man, very tall, with fair hair, and an aristocratic, almost disdainful, manner. Although the brothers were often seen together, they had different friends, and their devotion to their mother, whom they visited every day, was the only real bond that united them.

In his comfortable apartment on the corner of the rue Laffitte Lord Yarmouth settled down to live entirely for his personal pleasure. The faithful Croker handled all his political and parliamentary responsibilities so that he could forget that he was a Member of the House of Commons. His favourite club, the Union, which he preferred to the Jockey, was almost opposite. He was a passionate card-player and there he liked to play for high stakes with his friend Lord Granville, the British ambassador, and later with a group of very rich men which included the Baron James de Rothschild and the Comte Greffulhe who played whist for such high stakes that their game was known as 'la grosse partie'. Lord Yarmouth, who was an excellent dancer, was invited to all the society balls in Paris and more than one Parisian hostess must have dreamed of him as a son-in-law. But neither the daughters of the best families in France nor in England were to his taste. The permanency of marriage does not seem to have appealed to him. Instead, he installed two mistresses in their own apartments in Paris, and he had numerous adventures with other women. At bottom he was still a Regency rake and found the leading actresses and ballerinas of the day more exciting than the daughters of the nobility.

Despite this idle, selfish way of life, Lord Yarmouth nurtured his great passion for beautiful works of art and craftsmanship and his desire to own them. In his father's houses he had lived with and learned to admire fine French furniture and Sèvres porcelain. He was beginning to buy both eighteenth-century French furniture and decorative objects. Such things were not fashionable at the time and it was not until twenty years later that the Goncourt brothers drew the attention of the French to their neglect of eighteenth-century French art. But Lord Yarmouth's choice of these masterpieces was instinctive and his taste was sure. It was a real love to which he also brought hard-earned knowledge. It is difficult to identify the furniture and other objects he owned in the early 1840s, but many of the fine pieces in Manchester Square today must have been in his possession then. The search for rare, exquisite pieces, and he wanted only the best, now became his main interest until he died. Few people realised that he was a serious collector because Lord Henry Seymour often acted for his brother at public auctions. Lord Yarmouth was developing a dislike of publicity which was to become an obsession later in life.

Lord Henry, on the other hand, became the subject of a great deal of unpleasant publicity when, largely due to his quarrelsome nature, he was the central figure in a racing scandal which ended with his selling all his racehorses after long and bitter actions in the lawcourts. It all began when his mare Jenny failed to win the Prix du Jockey Club at Chantilly on 18 May 1840. Lord Henry had counted on winning the race and is said to have backed his mare to the tune of 90,000 francs. But after a false start Jenny was, to everyone's surprise, beaten into second place by a filly named Tontine, which had previously only won a modest race at the Champ de Mars. There had been rumours that Tontine was not a three-year-old French filly at all, but a four-year-old English mare named Herodia which had been brought over from England and substituted for Tontine at an auberge near Caen.

This rumour was supported by a lad named Biggs who had formerly worked for Monsieur Aumont, the filly's owner, but who was now employed by Lord Henry. Lord Henry was furious at being beaten and lodged an angry protest immediately after the race. The course committee at Chantilly held a hurried meeting and, not wishing to be involved, declared itself incompetent and referred the protest to the *commissaires* of the Société de l'encouragement. It was a major scandal. No bets were paid and the prize-money was held back. It was not an easy case, involving as it did the founder of the society, but finally, after some weeks during which time Jenny had run in a race at Versailles and again been beaten, the *commissaires* found against Lord Henry. As was to be expected, Lord Henry was furious, refused to accept their judgement, and said he would sell all his racehorses and sue Aumont in the courts. No one believed him, but he was as good as his word. When he started an action against Aumont he had to give up going to the Jockey Club because members turned their backs on him. His horses were put up for sale at his stud at Neuilly in October. The sale lasted four days, but bidding was slack because old friends, whatever they felt about his behaviour, could not bring themselves to buy his horses. The result was that he still owned horses the next year and on 16 May won the Prix du Jockey Club for the fourth time in six years with a horse called Poetess. But that was the end. He lost his case against Aumont and appealed. When the appeal failed to settle the question whether Tontine was Herodia, he sold the remainder of his horses in disgust and gave up racing forever, and at the same time warned Richard Jackson never to have anything to do with the Turf. It was a sad end for the man who had done so much for racing in France. His great ambition had been to win a race in England with a horse born and trained in France. It would have been a wonderful revenge for the way the Seymour family had treated him and his hopes of achieving this were centred on a horse named Oak Stick, but he was thwarted when Oak Stick had an accident and was unable to run at Goodwood.

His break with the Jockey Club was final and, instead, Lord Henry started going to the Petit Cercle, a club founded by his old boulevard friends. It met most conveniently in rooms at the Café de Paris. Its rules laid down that members should go to bed every night at 2 a.m; never play cards; and never discuss politics. Smoking was allowed in all its rooms, which suited Lord Henry who was an enthusiastic cigar-smoker, and it was a great place for good billiards players. Here everyone was very lively and there were few quarrels. Members included Alfred de Musset and two well-known Englishmen, Major Frazer and Captain Gronow. The latter was a friend of Mie-Mie and was always called Nogrow because he was so small.

Lord Yarmouth, typically, seems to have avoided being involved in his turbulent brother's row with the Jockey Club, but his easy-going Paris life was nevertheless soon to be interrupted. His father, still at Dorchester House, had not long to live and he would be forced to return to London to face the duties and problems of succession. He had last seen his father when Lord Hertford had come to Paris on his way to Italy in August 1840 accompanied by Croker, who had been so worried about his health that, at some inconvenience to himself, he had decided to travel with him.

'I shall be more at my ease about him when I leave him in company with Lord Yarmouth,' he had written to Peel the day before they left London.

The night they arrived they had dined with Raikes, who was still living in Paris. He also was struck by Lord Hertford's state of health and noted afterwards: '... he is much altered for the worse, and his speech is so indistinct that I could not understand a word he said'. There is no record of whether Lord Hertford saw his wife, but it is not likely because relations between them had long since ceased. He must have been in a pitiful state because Croker extended his stay from a week to thirteen days. Lord Hertford was loth to let him go and persuaded him to travel with him as far as Fontainebleau. It was the last journey of this inveterate traveller. When he returned to England he had to be carried from the boat at Ramsgate.

By the next year he was almost a complete invalid, living in the library and sleeping in the dining-room in immense, empty Dorchester House. By January 1842 this man of taste and talent, who had been a friend of the Prince Regent, a leading figure in society, the bearer of the Order of the Garter to the Tsar of Russia, was a debauched physical wreck waited on by foreign servants and prostitutes. When Raikes called to see him at this time he found him in bed with gout 'in addition to his other infirmities'.

Lord Yarmouth manifested no desire to comfort his father during his last days; he even claimed to have been unaware that his father was seriously ill until he received a letter from Minny Seymour. The little girl who had unwittingly contributed to the Prince Regent's passion for Lord Yarmouth's grandmother was now a woman of forty-four and married to Colonel the Hon. George Dawson-Damer, a son of the Earl of Portarlington. She must have written to Lord Yarmouth to warn him that his father was dangerously ill, because in February 1842 he wrote to her: 'I had no intimation of Lord H's illness. The moment I received it I sent for a passport and prepared myself to start the next morning.' He says her letter came as a great surprise and went on: 'I am very unwell and perfectly incapable of travelling'. But he was saved from having to try because he tells her that the morning after he received her letter he got a letter from 'himself'. So he never went.

After complaining that none of the letters he received mentioned the nature of his father's illness and that he had no news of her, he ended the letter by saying, 'I am dull and miserable and see nobody and go nowhere, Paris is very empty, everybody going to the German waters'.

It is impossible not to wonder how much truth there was in these last sentences. Certainly he did suffer probably from asthma and had been to Carlsbad himself, but how often did he plead illness to avoid having to do disagreeable things? His other remaining letters are full of references to his bad health and the dullness of his life. Was he, unknown to himself perhaps, developing a horror of humanity which was to lead to a misanthropic old age?

Lord Hertford died suddenly on 1 March 1842. He was in his sixty-fifth year. Croker had been sent for and was present when he died. But his son and heir was still in Paris and four days later wrote to Mrs Dawson-Damer to tell her how surprised he had been to hear of his father's death. The day before Lord Hertford died Raikes had written a letter which, Lord Yarmouth says, so alarmed him that he would have set off immediately if he had not been unwell himself. He says he had been in bed for two days.

But in the end he had to go. He was now the 4th Marquess of Hertford and his father could not be buried until he arrived. Wellington, Peel, the Prime Minister, Lord Lyndhurst and the Lord Chancellor were among the many prominent men who attended the funeral of the man they called the Caliph of Regent's Park.

The 3rd marquess had no intention of being quickly forgotten after death. He left a will that was a monument of calculated spitefulness, even for those days when wills were used to unleash, from the safety of the tomb, all the contempt and hatred of relatives and friends that had been nurtured in secret for years. His will had been his passion for a long time. He had thought a great deal about it and relished the disappointments it would cause. As the years went by it grew longer and longer. In dull moments when travelling abroad he would think of some new addition to the discomfort of some unfortunate relation. In the end there were thirty-five codicils and the whole document took four hours to read. It disposed of a fortune of some two million pounds, but the complications were endless because many of the codicils contradicted one another or cancelled paragraphs in the body of the will. The Lord Chancellor summed it up when he said the will 'seemed to have been prepared with the express object of benefiting the legal profession'.

Croker was one of the unfortunate executors. He had never received any remuneration for all his services to the late marquess, it being understood that he would be remembered in his will, and he was in fact left a total of £21,000. An additional 100,000 dollars in the Virginia United States Bank was left to him in a codicil that was not correctly drafted, so although he took his claim to court Croker never got the money. The late marquess, who had lived in constant dread of revolution *à la française* breaking out in England, had deposited money in banks in Paris, Frankfurt, Vienna and Naples. It was before the days of numbered accounts in Switzerland.

His wife Mie-Mie was not mentioned in the will at all, but large sums of money were left to the Strachan family. The three daughters of his old friend received a total of £220,000, the lion's share of which – £100,000, St Dunstan's and all its contents – went to Countess Zichy, the former Charlotte Strachan who had lived on him like a parasite for years.

His many mistresses were all remembered; even his mistress when he was interned in Verdun in 1803 was given a pension of £100. He had intended to leave the Star of the Order of the Garter to Peel but had later revoked the bequest. His diamond Order of St Anne of Russia, which he had been given in St Petersburg, was left to someone described as Lady Strachan's French maid, but who was in fact another of his many women.

Disraeli was very interested in the will and on 14 March wrote to Mrs Disraeli:

Hertford's will is still the subject of endless tales. ... He left his star of the Order of the Garter, in costly brilliants, with a long panegyric to Peel, as the saviour of the country and all that and the legacy was afterwards revoked. I suppose his ghost smelt the Income Tax. ... The Zichy had £150,000 because she saved Lord Hertford from being poisoned by her mother. ... The new Lord cut off his mustachios, saying: 'There never was a Marquess of Hertford with mustachios.'

It is not surprising that the Seymour family were indignant. Many large bequests expected by members of the family had been revoked and they were left with nothing. Lord Yarmouth, the residuary legatee, inherited the property and estates, but there was less money for him than he might have expected from his father. He was given the option of buying his grandmother's jewels for £10,000; otherwise they would go to Countess Zichy, who was already in possession of them. He refused to pay, nor did he ever forget. Many years later, when at a public function he saw her wearing some of the pearls, he took the opportunity of pointing to the studs in his dress-shirt and telling her that he was wearing mother-of-pearl while she was wearing grandmother's pearls.

The executors had great difficulty in settling the estate. They found that large sums of money were missing and all attempts to get accounts from Countess Zichy were rebuffed. Then a missing package containing 100,000 francs was found amongst the belongings of Nicholas Suisse, the French valet of the dead marquess. He had already been left money in seven different codicils adding up to more than £20,000. 'Nicholas Suisse, my head valet, an excellent man', was how Lord Hertford had described him in one of the codicils. Suisse declared that the money was a gift from his late master. Knowing this to be a lie, Croker, with the agreement of the new marquess and the other executors, decided to prosecute, although he must have known that a public trial would mean the most sordid revelations about the last days of the late marquess.

The trial opened at the Old Bailey in the summer and, as expected, a sensation was created by the revelations of debauchery as one prostitute after another went into the witness-box. It became clear that Suisse had been employed by the 3rd marquess to procure women for him. There was a back entrance to Dorchester House by which they were let in at night and left in the morning. A woman named Henriette was in the house when he died. A young Frenchwoman, Angeline Borel, with whom Suisse had been planning to escape to France, defended him. She said that for seven or eight years she had been dining with the marquess at Dorchester House and sleeping with him afterwards. Not only that, but Croker himself had been present at one or two of their dinners. Under cross-examination Croker admitted that this was so, but that Mademoiselle Borel had appeared to him more like a nurse. He added, however, that rather than be seen with her he had refused to stay in the carriage with the marquess on one occasion when he had been told they were going to Clarges Street to pick her up.

The action failed. The jury acquitted Suisse on the grounds that the money was his reward for handling what his counsel described as these 'delicate transactions'. The new Lord Hertford was much criticised for allowing the trial to have taken place at all and thus having his father's name dragged through the mud every day in the popular Press. But he did not seem to care. He could not bear to think of Suisse getting away with the money. Later, Suisse was arrested and tried again in Paris, but again he was acquitted.

It took a long time for the sensational trial to be forgotten but more lasting fame was in store for the wicked marquess. Three famous novelists used him as the model for characters of extravagant life and behaviour. In *Vanity Fair* Thackeray chose him for his Marquess of Steyne, who had a back door at Gaunt House for late-night visitors. In *Coningsby* Disraeli, who had known him as a friend, based his Lord Monmouth on him. He was also famous in France where, it is said, Balzac used him as the model for the rich Lord Dudley in *La Fille aux yeux d'or*.

While waiting for the trial of Suisse to come up Lord Hertford stayed at Dorchester House and began to fulfil his duties as the 4th Marquess of Hertford. He took his seat in the House of Lords. In April he went to the queen's levée and the following month he attended a fancy-dress ball at Buckingham Palace. When he started having alterations made to his father's house in Piccadilly people began to wonder if he intended to make London his home after all. But once again they were to be proved wrong. When the trial was over he began to think about going back to Paris. The indefatigable Mrs Dawson-Damer seems to have tried to make him think seriously of getting married before doing so. In September he wrote to her: 'You say you have found a Marchioness likely to suit. I wonder who she is?'

But his curiosity cannot have been very deeply aroused, for he goes on to say that the fact that she is twenty-five years younger than he creates an insuperable difficulty. No more questions were asked about this young lady who might have become his marchioness.

In fact, he had already made up his mind to return to Paris, for a few days later he wrote again to Mrs Dawson-Damer: '... if I go back to Paris, which is very probable for I am a little too miserable in this enormous house quite by myself and London quite to myself in the bargain.'

Chapter Six

WHILE HIS FATHER WAS AWAY IN LONDON burying the 3rd marquess and Lord Henry Seymour was quarrelling with the members of the Jockey Club, Richard Jackson made up his mind to be somebody else. He decided to call himself Richard Wallace, the name under which he was to become famous. As if in an attempt to make the name official, he even had himself baptised in the name of Wallace at the Anglican Church in Paris, opposite the British Embassy in the rue d'Aguesseau. The ceremony took place on 21 April 1842, if not in secrecy, in extreme privacy. It seems there were no witnesses present and he gave as the name of his parents only the single name Wallace with no address. To the certificate of baptism, which is today in London at St Catherine's House, Kingsway, the Rev. George Lefèvre, who baptised him, added the somewhat despairing note: 'No further information can be obtained.' It is unlikely that he was told that the young man he had just baptised had a mistress and was the father of a son nearly eight months old. And so Richard Wallace was, so to speak, 'born' in his twenty-fourth year. Although he still lived with Mie-Mie and was her devoted companion, he was in fact also leading a life of his own. His mistress was Julie Amélie Charlotte Castelnau and they had met when she was selling scent in a shop on the boulevard much patronised by the young Bohemians of the day.

Unfortunately we do not know why Richard decided to change his name; even later in life he never gave any reason. He must have known by now that Lord Hertford was his father, and that he was therefore entitled to the name Seymour. But Lord Henry was perhaps the obstacle there. One doubtful Seymour was enough. Why did he then choose Wallace as his name? Perhaps, as his mother was descended from the Wallaces of Craigie Castle,

Ayrshire, he preferred the historic name of Wallace to the assumed name of Jackson. If he could not publicly claim to be a Seymour he could claim to be a Wallace.

Then why did he not take the usual steps to change his name? Baptism, which is not a method of changing one's name, merely meant that the name Wallace was registered officially in the church records. Was this all he wanted? Or was there a more urgent reason? Was Mademoiselle Castelnau, the mother of his child, pressing him to marry her? She was a Protestant and if she wanted to be married in church he would have had to produce evidence that he had been baptised. If he did not know whether he had been baptised, and had no means of asking his mother, the simplest solution was to be baptised. But why the secrecy and the refusal to give information about his parents? It may have been through fear of his father, whom he knew would oppose the marriage, if he had not already forbidden it. Lord Hertford, himself unmarried, was away in England, and Richard may have been planning to get married in his absence. If this was his plan it failed for some reason. Whatever the truth of the matter, Mademoiselle Castelnau had to wait nearly thirty years until Lord Hertford was dead before she was married to Richard Wallace.

On his return to Paris in 1843 Lord Hertford, for the first time, began seriously to interest himself in Richard – and it was not too soon. He had not noticed it, but the 'cher neveu' had suddenly grown into a man called Richard Wallace who was leading a carefree existence with a group of Bohemian friends. He was also frequently in debt, sometimes as the result of rash speculation on the Bourse in partnership with Mie-Mie, who despite her great age was still obsessed with making money. After Lord Hertford had come to Richard's rescue and paid his debts on more than one occasion, he decided it was time to put an end to this extravagant way of life. Richard needed an occupation and must be taught to manage his own affairs. Lord Hertford therefore took him to work for him as his secretary with the responsibility of keeping his accounts, and gave him only a modest allowance. It was the start of a daily association which was to last until Lord Hertford's death, and the beginning of the apprenticeship of Richard Wallace as the keeper of the great collection.

Lord Hertford was by now a completely dedicated collector and he was rich enough to be able to compete with anyone. There was nothing to stop him from surrounding himself with the finest examples of the works of art he loved so deeply. So he left the lawyers to argue about his father's will and returned to Paris to seek out his own treasures. His friends in London were disappointed and exasperated by his refusal to settle in England now that he had succeeded to the title. He was still in his early forties and in his new position he was expected to play a leading role in the public and political life of his country. The popular Press had never been friendly since the trial of Suisse. *John Bull* openly rebuked him for living 'so continually abroad' and thinking only of 'his personal tastes and caprices'.

To understand Lord Hertford's motives at this crucial period one must also attempt to understand his baffling character. He was much more than the rich idler of outside appearances. In private, where few people saw him, he spent many hours in study. Thus, he brought to his collecting not only intelligence and taste but great expert knowledge. He already possessed an important library of books on the ornamental arts. For many years he had been following sales of works of art all over Europe and receiving their catalogues. He made careful notes in them in his own hand and kept them for future reference. In this way he grew to know what to look for and learned to recognise the work of the master *ébénistes* and *fondeurs-ciseleurs*. He knew the history of many of the privately owned works of art which he was to buy later. It was difficult to deceive him. He could spot a copy and he would never buy unless he was sure of the work's authenticity.

This way of life, the solitary pursuit of beautiful things, fitted in admirably with that strain of aloofness in his nature which with the years became one of his dominant characteristics. He shunned prominence; he did not care for other people's views; and, in fact, he hated being forced to take any notice whatever of other people.

It is impossible to identify with any certainty what Lord Hertford already owned at this period, but it seems probable that the foundation of the collection had already been laid by the time Richard Wallace started to work with him as his secretary. His enthusiasm for eighteenth-century French painting was not new. As Lord Yarmouth, he had bought two Watteaus for 180 francs in 1828, and these were probably in his collection, although they cannot be identified today. Fortunately, after 1843 Lord Hertford's purchases of paintings are known, because sales of pictures were always recorded in more detail than furniture. For example, at the Paul Périer sale in 1843 he bought eleven pictures, which included two Bouchers, for less than a quarter of the price he paid for one Prud'hon. The same year he bought four Boningtons in Paris. During 1844 the account-books kept by Wallace show that 13,575 francs were spent on works of art, bought by Lord Henry Seymour on his brother's behalf.

When France's long war against Abd-el-Kader in Algeria spread to Morocco, Tangier was bombarded by the Prince de Joinville and by the middle of August the Moroccan army was defeated by Maréchal Bugeaud. Lord Hertford seems to have been alarmed by this and considered leaving Paris for his mother's sake. In a letter to Mrs Dawson-Damer written in September 1844 he talks of his mother and his fears for the future in France. As usual, he starts by complaining of his health: he feels, he says, as if he were 'going to *make* an *illness*', then goes on: 'We have been very War like here and I really thought at one time it was all up with peace and Paris – and I had prepared to take my old mother over as she cannot live without me and I cannot live without her. Now things seem more quiet for the moment – I cannot help thinking it will not last long. . . .

For a man who had the reputation of having no feelings it is a touching revelation and certainly true.

In 1845 he went to Rome, telling Mrs Dawson-Damer that it was because he had a bad cough. Here he bought ten pictures at the sale of Cardinal Fesch, as well as furniture, sculptures, tapestries and decorative objects. But again there was to be an interruption to his pattern of life and this time it came from Ireland.

Lord Hertford was one of the largest Irish landlords. He had inherited 66,000 acres of estates around Lisburn in Ulster from which he derived his chief source of income, £60,000 a year. After the potato famine the Devon Commission of Inquiry had blamed absentee landlords for many of Ireland's troubles and, since his father had never once visited his Irish estates, he thought it would be advisable for him to go over and show himself to his tenants. The idea must have been distasteful to him, but his worried agents in Antrim may have made an urgent request. He stopped in London on his way to Ireland and made a point of going down to Drayton Park to call on the Prime Minister. It was a well-chosen moment. Sir Robert Peel, alarmed by the Irish situation, was about to repeal the Corn Laws, which meant abandoning protectionism. A split in the Conservative Party was anticipated and support from Lord Hertford would be of great help.

In Ulster a big welcome was waiting for him. It was an event to receive a visit after all those years from the Marquess of Hertford in person. There was more than curiosity in his tenants' desire to see their landlord in the flesh for the first time. For his part, he did his best for Peel by playing the role of the model landlord, despite his aloofness. He declared he had come for a long stay and even went so far as to promise to build a house where he would spend his summers. But country life in Ireland was not to his taste. He made a noble effort, but after five weeks he could stand it no more and went back to London. He never returned and never built his house there.

Surprisingly, he seems to have been very pleased with his visit to Ireland and when he got back he wrote to Mrs Dawson-Damer to tell her that he had had 'a most Prosperous Irish expedition and hope and believe I did much good especially to myself, as I find there are places in the world where I may gain a little by being known'.

One of his first acts on his return was to call again on the Prime Minister, who had promised to recommend to the queen that she should confer upon him the Order of the Garter. Had there been a bargain at Drayton Park? If it was his reward for going to Ireland he did not have long to wait, for he was invested at Windsor Castle in January the next year. It was the last Garter that Peel had the power to recommend and its gift to Lord Hertford provoked the most violent criticism in the Press, both of Lord Hertford and himself.

It was while Lord Hertford was staying at Dorchester House that he took the important decision to use his grandmother's house in Manchester Square to store his English collection, which consisted mainly of pictures. The house was to be kept always ready for him and a housekeeper and staff were engaged. He owned another house in Berkeley Square which he also arranged should be made ready for his use. He did not bother to visit the two country houses which he had inherited, Ragley Hall, the Seymour-Conway family seat in Warwickshire, and Sudbourne Hall in Suffolk. They were shut up and left in the charge of caretakers. He had done his duty in Ireland and now all he wanted was to go back to Paris to be free to live as he pleased.

He was in London again, however, in August 1846, this time staying at his house in Berkeley Square, where he received a letter from Mie-Mie in Paris telling him that she had escaped miraculously 'from a terrific accident'. She fears that he will be alarmed, and continues: 'I know all you will say but that doesn't signify, as I shall not hear it.'

It appears that before going to bed she was boiling some milk, for the next morning, which 'exploded' in her face. She thought she was blinded and had felt her way to Wallace's bedroom and woken him 'with the agreeable news of having put both my eyes out'. She was in great pain and 'Richard' washed her face. Her eyelids were blackened and she was dreading seeing Dr Chermside, who came the next morning.

Fortunately for Lord Hertford, it was just at this time that a number of important collections, in England as well as on the Continent, were being dispersed. He had always kept himself informed of every approaching major sale and now, with his knowledge, he could choose the rarest and the most beautiful among the works of art for sale and with his wealth few could bid against him. In fact, prices for works of art were low compared with what they fetched later in the century. For example, whereas he paid only 385 francs in 1841 for his first Fragonard, in 1865 two quite small panels were to cost him more than 30,000 francs each. An exception was Sèvres porcelain, which was still much prized and fetched high prices.

Lord Hertford seldom bought from dealers because he did not like paying their commission. Most of his purchases were made privately or in the salerooms after making careful inquiries and, if possible, seeing for himself what might interest him. He could be present at a sale, but he would always bid through an agent who would be instructed not to reveal the name of his client. And so, piece by piece, almost in secrecy, the Collection was assembled. With his means he could have bought an entire collection but, confident of his own taste and judgement, he preferred to make his own choice. French art of the eighteenth century had been completely rejected since the Revolution, so that his enthusiasm for it was both original and surprising. Nor was he narrow in his taste, for he also admired and bought fine paintings of all the European schools. In that year, 1846, he bought in London the famous Rubens, *The Holy Family with St Elizabeth and St John the Baptist*, which was painted for the oratory of the Archduke Albert, Regent of the Netherlands: he also acquired a Murillo, *Adoration of the Shepherds*, which had formerly hung in the Capuchin Convent in Genoa. Paintings by Murillo were highly prized in the 1840s and fetched very high prices. The next year he bought in Paris *The Lady with a Fan*, one of Velasquez' few portraits of someone not in Spanish court circles.

All this time Richard Wallace was his secretary and constant companion. He knew every detail of Lord Hertford's collections and recorded every purchase. As time went by he was given more responsibility and began to act for Lord Hertford in the way that Lord Henry Seymour had represented him in the past. He travelled for him to inspect and report on specific works of art and Lord Hertford began to value his judgement; after all, he had taught him all he knew. At no time, however, did he give any hint that Richard Wallace was his son. In his household and in the world of art-sales he was always known as 'Monsieur Richard' and he never called Lord Hertford anything else but 'Sir', although no association between father and son could have been closer.

About this time Lord Hertford was almost forced to leave the rue Laffitte. The building in which he had his apartment was to be sold and a prospective buyer called early one morning while Lord Hertford was still asleep. The story goes that when his valet woke him up he demanded angrily, 'Ne suis-je pas chez moi?' A servant was sent to tell the man to go away and inform him that he would be buying the building himself. With that he turned over and went back to sleep. In this way he became the owner of the entire building at the corner of the rue Laffitte and the boulevard des Italiens. Such were the lengths to which he was prepared to go to avoid being disturbed by other people.

But owner or not, he was soon going to be forced to move by political events which were to bring about the end of the reign of Louis-Philippe. On the afternoon of 23 February 1848 a riot broke out over a political banquet that had been banned. Fifty demonstrators were killed on the boulevard des Capucines and overnight the riot became a revolution. The next day the shooting continued, and as the rioters approached the Tuileries the seventy-four-year-old Louis-Philippe hurriedly signed an act of abdication. Then, undetected, he drove off in a *fiacre* across the place de la Concorde to Saint-Cloud and from there he fled to England. It was the end of the July Monarchy.

At the rue Taitbout there was consternation. Mie-Mie had been frightened by the shooting, which had been very close. She had seen Bonaparte, Louis XVIII and Charles X come and go and knew what shrieking, violent Paris mobs were like. When they burned down the Rothschild château at Suresnes she decided, old and ill as she was, that it was time to go to England. She did not want to face the uncertainty of the Second Republic.

Lord Hertford agreed to take his mother as well as Richard Wallace and Lord Henry Seymour. But for once he was unaccountably short of French money for the journey and had to wait until a messenger arrived from England with a wad of notes from Coutts' bank. Finally they got away, but they had to leave everything behind. Nobody was allowed to leave France with any heavy luggage and the government had put an embargo on plate and furniture. Bearing in mind that Lord Pembroke, who had tried to get his property out, had had everything destroyed when the mob stopped the carts and set them on fire, Lord Hertford did not try to move any of his possessions.

Incredible as it seems, Richard Wallace also left behind Mademoiselle Castelnau and his son. Lord Hertford probably refused to take them.

As in 1830, when Charles X had abdicated, they headed for Boulogne, but this time they crossed the Channel at once. When they arrived in London they moved into the Berkeley Square house. They were given a great welcome by their neighbour Lady

Jersey. So in her seventy-seventh year, tired, old and bent, Mie-Mie found herself back in London after an absence of just over forty years. For Richard Wallace it was, so far as we know, his first visit to London since his mother had taken him as a child to Paris.

Whatever worries Lord Hertford may have had for the safety of his valuable works of art in Paris and at Bagatelle, they did not stop him collecting. No sooner had he arrived in London than he started buying pictures as if nothing had happened. On 5 May he was at Christie's where he bought seven pictures at the sale of Casimir Périer, Louis-Philippe's former minister. A week later he acquired seven more at the William Wells sale, again at Christie's. From these two sales alone the Collection was enriched by two Rembrandts, a Velasquez, a Van Dyck, a Canaletto, a Murillo and a Greuze, not to mention the seven other paintings. However, not all the members of the family at Berkeley Square were as happy as he was and there were some who were wishing they were back in France.

The first to return was Lord Henry Seymour. He was always made to feel an intruder by the Seymour-Conway family and now that his racing days were over he had nothing to interest him in England. The news from France was, after all, not so alarming, so he decided to go back as far as Boulogne. Nor did he go alone. With something of his old Seymour spirit he took with him a twenty-one-year-old blonde, blue-eyed daughter of a clergyman named Ellen Stevens. On arriving in Boulogne he installed her in a house on the boulevard Saint-Beuve and as she was unmarried she called herself Mrs Minchin. She played the piano well and had a pleasant singing voice. Lord Henry did not intend to be lonely, bored or unhappy in Boulogne. In case the political situation in France should look dangerously like revolution again, he bought a steam-yacht which was kept in the harbour ready to take him back to England in a hurry if necessary.

Events in France remained calm and Mie-Mie began to feel a yearning to return. It was not long before she and Richard Wallace joined Lord Henry. The three of them settled down in a wing of the Hôtel des Bains, where they were to stay for six years.

Chapter Seven

Having seen Mie-Mie safely installed in the Hôtel des Bains, with Richard Wallace to look after her, Lord Hertford returned to Berkeley Square. He would go over to Boulogne from time to time to spend a few days with his mother when she asked for him, but London was the centre of his interests at the moment. As a result of events in France, a number of important French collections were being put up for auction in London salerooms and he did not wish to miss one of them. So settled did he seem that once again people began to wonder whether, after all this time, he had finally decided to stay. They felt even more certain when Madame Oger arrived from Paris and was given a house in Half Moon Street. Lord Hertford let people think what they liked. He never revealed his plans to anybody and all we know is that this period marks the beginning of his most active years as a collector.

He employed as his agent Samuel Mawson, the Berners Street art dealer, and fortunately many of his letters to him have survived. They not only tell us a great deal about Lord Hertford's taste in pictures and his methodical approach to collecting but in addition they reveal that behind the aloof, disenchanted exterior of the marquess there is a human being with a certain acid sense of humour and more than a little charm.

The first of these letters is written from Boulogne when he was on one of his visits to his mother in September 1848. He warns Mawson that he may not be able to get back in time for the Duke of Buckingham's sale at Stowe on 15 October, which he had very much wanted to attend. He had clearly been studying the catalogue and knew what he wanted.

'I think I must have "The Unmerciful Servant" by Rembrandt and hope the price will not be so unmerciful as the subject – but you know that I place all confidence in you and depend on your kindness on this occasion. . . .' He goes on to say he is 'very anxious' to have the *Sybilla* by Domenichino 'as much for the frame as for the picture' and wants as well 'the little Murillo, the "Conception of the Virgin" ', if the price is reasonable. 'Pray have the kindness not to mention to anybody that you buy on my account. I am very anxious my name should not appear.'

He ends the letter by giving Mawson instructions as to how he will communicate with him during the bidding if he is able to be there.

'In the event of my being in time for the sale, you would see me there, and my hat would play the same part it has already acted in similar circumstances.'

What these prearranged signals with his hat were the letters do not reveal, but they were, of course, in keeping with his passion for remaining anonymous. One cannot help wondering how many people were hoodwinked, for the marquess was a very big man who could never pass unnoticed. Nevertheless, noticed or not, the signalling seems to have been successful because Mawson secured all three pictures for him. There was competition for the Rembrandt and no doubt there were some hat signals before it was knocked down to Mawson for £2,300. The Domenichino cost him 690 guineas and the Murillo only £58.16s. All three are in the Collection today. The so-called Rembrandt is now called *The Centurion Cornelius*, which was its earliest known title, and the Murillo is called *The Assumption of the Virgin*. The Domenichino is no longer in the frame which interested Lord Hertford, but the Bartolommeo Veneto portrait in the collection has a fine Renaissance carved frame dated 1543 which may have been the original frame of Domenichino.

At the same sale, which lasted several days, Lord Hertford also bought furniture which included a set of eight early eighteenth-century Italian carved state chairs, probably Venetian, and a monumental eighteenth-century French astronomical clock. (Twenty-four years later two of these chairs were used by the Prince and Princess of Wales, the future Edward VII and Queen Alexandra, at the opening of the Bethnal Green Museum.) He probably went to Paris in October when he bought a Murillo, which had once been in the Spanish royal collection. This he did through Laneuville, one of his agents in Paris, and it is unlikely he would have bought the picture without seeing it.

In France the provisional government had restored order: the Second Republic had been born and a National Assembly was to be elected. In London Prince Louis Napoleon was waiting for the moment when he could return to France, this time to stay. When on 17 September five departments elected him to represent them in the National Assembly he judged his hour had come. On 25 September he arrived in Paris and two days later the Citoyen L. N. Bonaparte took his seat in the Assembly. By the end of the year he was elected President of the Republic. The Citoyen Bonaparte became the prince-president and moved into the Elysée.

Lord Hertford knew the future Napoleon III well. He had met him at the house of his father's friend Lady Blessington when he was an exile in London. He must have met him also at the Dawson-Damers where one night after dinner the prince had astonished his hosts by promising that he would return their kindness one day at the Tuileries.

It was at Lady Blessington's also that Louis Napoleon had met Miss Elizabeth Ann Howard, the great love of his life, who followed him to Paris and was now living in a house close to the Elysée. His star was in the ascendant. He was already in the Elysée and was on his way to the Tuileries. As for Lady Blessington, her extravagant life with the irresistible Comte d'Orsay had ended in ruin. Early in 1849, unable to pay her debts, she had fled to Paris with d'Orsay, leaving Gore House, where she had entertained the literary and fashionable world of London, to be sold with all its contents. In Paris she saw Louis Napoleon again, this time at Miss Howard's house. Although she was sixty and penniless, she had kept her Irish wit and when the prince-president asked her if she was in Paris for long she replied: 'Yes, sire, and you?' But for her it was not to be. A few weeks later she died of a heart attack.

The sale of her house and property in London took place in May shortly before she died. Gore House stood near where the Royal Albert Hall stands today. Lord Hertford bought a portrait of her by Lawrence and a portrait of her niece Miss Nellie Power, in coloured chalks, by Landseer. He also noticed and bought a pair of bronze fire-dogs with eagles by Gouthière that had been at Malmaison. Although he did not like the Highland stags, he was becoming interested in Landseer, who was to be knighted the following year, as we see in the letter he wrote from Paris in 1852 to Mawson, who had told him about some Landseers that were coming up at Christie's: '... I cannot say whether I should like the Landseers as I have not seen them. I like his dogs better than his deer, and it appears there are none in the two pictures in question....'

He did not buy either picture and a month later wrote to thank Mawson for details he had sent him of another Landseer which had been sold a few days previously. 'By your account of it I think it would not have suited me. I should like to have a picture by that master but it must be *first-rate* and a pleasing subject. Perhaps we may find one one day.' Some years later he bought three, two of which he kept: one of dogs and the other a Highland scene without deer are still in the Collection. The third, entitled *The Prize Calf*, he sold later.

By 1850 there must have been doubts about Lord Hertford's intention to settle in London because his visits to Paris were becoming more and more frequent. There he was a member of Louis Napoleon's intimate circle and would spend many informal evenings with him at the house of Miss Howard. When official duties permitted it was easy for the president to visit his mistress without being noticed. Her front door was in the rue de Cirque, but the back gave on to the avenue de Marigny, on the other side of which was the Elysée garden. The president had only to let himself out by a door in the wall of the garden, cross the road and go into Miss Howard's house by the back door. The beautiful Elizabeth Ann was accepted as his official mistress and they were seen together in public a great deal. Almost daily they would meet in the Bois to ride together. Life was coming back to Paris again and Lord Hertford was too much of a Parisian to be able to leave it for long.

In Boulogne Mie-Mie, Lord Henry Seymour and Richard Wallace were still living in their wing of the Hôtel des Bains. Despite the differences in age they were a devoted trio. They had lived together for so long in the rue Taitbout that to be reassembled in Boulogne must have seemed perfectly natural. Lord Henry could always visit Mrs Minchin, and we can only hope that Richard Wallace occasionally went to Paris to see his son and Mademoiselle Castelnau, or that they spent some time with him in Boulogne. Unfortunately, we are not told anything about Wallace's relations with his mistress or his son during this period. Did Lord Hertford disapprove of their seeing each other?

Life in Boulogne was not dull at this time. It was both fashionable with the English and popular with the French so that in a sense it was almost an Anglo-French town. Thackeray visited there and for two years in succession Charles Dickens rented a villa, where he wrote large portions of *Little Dorrit* and *Hard Times*. The theatre was bilingual. Both English and French companies presented plays, and even the great Rachel did not think it beneath her dignity to leave Paris to perform there. So the old Marchioness of Hertford and her son and grandson were not lacking for friends or entertainment.

They seem also to have been active in charitable work on behalf of Boulogne's fishermen and their families. Aware of the dangers of sea-fishing, they bought a lifeboat for the town and subscribed to a fund to reward acts of outstanding heroism in cases of shipwreck. Lord Henry noticed that the fisherfolk had no fresh water so he built them a fountain of drinking water. Was it this that gave Wallace the idea for his famous gift of fifty fountains to the city of Paris twenty years later? If Mie-Mie was ill or she asked for him, Lord Hertford would leave everything and go at once to Boulogne. Often he would sit up all night by her bedside. His devotion to his mother contrasts strongly with the selfish, disdainful side of his nature which he so often showed to the rest of the world. She had not long to live and it may be that they all remained in Boulogne because its climate suited her.

Wallace was probably under instructions to report regularly to Lord Hertford on Mie-Mie's health. One of his letters written from Boulogne has survived and it shows how he was looking after Mie-Mie like a nurse. It is interesting also to note that, whereas Mie-Mie always wrote in English, Wallace wrote to Lord Hertford in French.

On 17 January 1853, '6½ hrs. du soir', he wrote: 'Mme la Marquise s'est trouvé très bien après votre départ. . . .' For dinner, he goes on to say, she had a little soup, some fish and the wing of a roast chicken ('Elle a fait ce repas avec plaisir.') and went to sleep almost immediately afterwards. Then in great detail he tells how Mie-Mie woke up and he gave her a cup of tea. She was not so well and at 2 a.m. they decided ('nous avons déterminé') that she should take a pill, after which she slept until 7 a.m. He adds that he thinks the medicine weakens her. She did not get up and dress until half past one and since 5 p.m. she has been in the drawing-room and at this moment is sleeping with her feet on a hot-water bottle. Tomorrow he hopes to give him 'd'excellent nouvelles de notre chère malade'.

He signed the letter: 'Votre bien tout dévoué. R.W.'

In June 1850 Lord Hertford in London began to write codicils to his will, five of which he wrote without the advice of his lawyers. One on which they did advise him, however, made provision for a little girl named Seymourina Suzanne Vincent, who was his child by Suzanne Oger and had been born on 14 May 1846. When she was two he had arranged for her to be legally adopted by Frederick John Cuthbert, an Englishman who had been persuaded by Lord Hertford to say that *he* was Seymourina's father. From that time on Seymourina added 'Cuthbert' to her name.

To understand Lord Hertford's will we must go back to the year 1837 when his father, the 3rd marquess, was alive and he was still Lord Yarmouth. Sometime in the course of 1837 he entered into an agreement with his father that, if the 3rd marquess revoked the deed to the Irish estates and settled them on him as his son and heir, he in his turn would make a will leaving the Irish estates to his brother Lord Henry Seymour. His father probably wished to provide for Lord Henry but feared litigation from other members of the Seymour family if in his will he acknowledged Lord Henry as his son. The following year, after a family council in London, Lord Yarmouth and his mother had each made a will. In his will he left the reversionary rights of the Irish estates, after payment of his debts, to Lord Henry Seymour. In the event of his brother leaving no children, he left the Irish estates not to Francis George Hugh Seymour, the heir to the title and the entailed estate, but to another cousin, Sir George Hamilton Seymour, who was then British minister at Brussels. At the same time he left £30,000 invested in British public funds other than

Irish in trust for 'Richard Jackson (son of Agnes Jackson) now of the age of twenty or thereabouts, and residing at No. 1 rue Taitbout, Paris'. No mention that Richard was his son.

It was this will, untouched since he had made it as Lord Yarmouth in 1838, that Lord Hertford decided to change by a codicil, made without legal advice, which reads as follows:

I hereby revoke the bequest contained in my will of the residue of all my real and personal estates to my brother, Lord Henry Seymour, and to reward as much as I can Richard Wallace for all his care and attention to my dear mother, and likewise for his devotedness to me during a long and painful illness I had in Paris in 1840 and on all other occasions, I give such residue to the said Richard Wallace now living at the Hôtel des Bains, Boulogne-sur-Mer, in France, and whose domicile previous to the Revolution of February 1848, was in my mother's house, rue Taitbout No. 3, formerly No. 1, absolutely.

Again no mention that Richard Wallace, formerly Richard Jackson, was his son.

Why Lord Hertford suddenly decided to revoke his bequest to Lord Henry in favour of Richard Wallace while his brother was still alive we do not know, because after writing this codicil he put the will away in his desk, locked the drawer and never mentioned what he had done to anybody. Perhaps he thought his mother had not long to live and knew that in her will she had left half of her considerable fortune to his brother. Or did he think that he might die? He was never strong and in the codicil he mentions a 'long and painful illness' and wanted to be sure the Seymours got nothing of his. He had no love for his family. There was also now the Collection which had not existed when he had made his original will, and which was now the chief interest of his life. Had he already decided that Richard Wallace was the one person he could trust to keep the collection together and look after it when he was dead? He may have feared that his family would split it up and sell parts of it. Whatever his reasons, the fact that with his passion for secrecy he had written the codicil himself, instead of entrusting it to his lawyers, later cost Richard Wallace £400,000.

Having dealt with his will, satisfactorily as he thought, he went back to collecting in earnest and in the next two months acquired some pictures of major importance. First there was the famous

Salvator Rosa, *Apollo and the Sibyl of Cumae*, which had once belonged to Cardinal Mazarin. It was the largest and the finest of three Salvator Rosas that came up at Christie's in July 1850 when the Earl of Ashburnham sold ninety-one of his pictures. Mawson bought it for £1,785 and at the same sale he also secured a Gaspard Poussin. The next month he bought eleven pictures including two Van Dycks, two Rembrandts, a Rubens and a Hobbema at the sale of paintings from the collection of King William II of Holland. At this time Hobbema was very much in fashion and his paintings fetched higher prices than any Rembrandt. It was not until the 1860s that paintings by Rembrandt began to command high figures.

In Paris things were soon going to be very different. There was an atmosphere of conspiracy now when the little group of friends met at the house of Miss Howard in the shadow of the Elysée. Louis Napoleon was plotting the *coup d'état* which would take him to the Tuileries, and Lord Hertford, who followed the fortunes of his friend very closely, was certainly informed of what was being planned. In fact, it is most likely that Lord Hertford was among those who gave money to help to finance his bid for power. Miss Howard gave her lover her fortune, 300,000 francs, raised by selling her horses, pawning her jewellery and mortgaging her houses in London. Louis Napoleon's cousin, Princesse Mathilde, to whom he had once been engaged, also pawned her diamonds to help him. The day finally chosen was 2 December 1851 – no day could hold more promise for Bonapartist ambitions, for it was the anniversary of the coronation of Napoleon I and the day of his victory at Austerlitz. The sun of Austerlitz smiled for his nephew too. All those likely to oppose his ambitions, republicans and royalists alike, were swiftly arrested; the Assembly was dissolved and an uprising in Paris stifled before it could spread. Exactly one year later to the day, Louis Napoleon was proclaimed Emperor Napoleon III with absolute powers. In one year the prince-president, who had been elected for ten years, had transformed himself into an hereditary emperor.

In the intervals between Lord Hertford's visits to his mother he found time to write to her very frequently, whether he was in Paris or London, and she to him. Some of Mie-Mie's letters from Boulogne have survived and show clearly the deep attachment each had for the other. She still started her letters with 'My dearest Beauchamp' as she had when he first left her to go to school in England. She obviously adored him and his devotion to her was sincere.

In her letters she tells him about her health and asks him to buy for her things she could not find in Boulogne. Gloves, for example–'real *gants de Suède*'–which had to be men's size: 'I mean men's gloves you know my hands are immense and I hate everything that is tight.' She even wrote to him when he was staying at Compiègne with the emperor.

One letter dated 24 December 1852 was delivered to him there two days later, although it was a Sunday. 'My dearest Beauchamp–I am really overpowered with your goodness in writing me such constant and long letters. . . .' She tells him that he seems pleased and she thinks his existence must be very agreeable since 'you have everything and no thought or trouble which I conceive to be the perfection of life'. He had bought her a wheel-chair because she had said the weather was dreadful and she had rheumatism so that she never moved 'but in your admirable chair, which I frequent very much'.

But Mie-Mie was wrong about his trouble-free life. There was trouble brewing for him in Ireland. She did not know that he had also received at Compiègne a letter from his agent in Lisburn telling him that at the recent elections his candidate had been defeated because his tenants voted for the opposition candidate, and that the agent had been assaulted.

Lord Hertford wrote back on 22 December saying he did not care about the result of the election and if his tenants wanted to show their independence he could do the same, and he agreed to his agent raising some of the rents.

When the agent announced his intention to raise the rents the indignant tenants got together and arranged to send a deputation to Paris to put their case before Lord Hertford in person.

The idea of having to receive the representatives of his tenants filled him with horror and on 11 January he wrote to his agent from Boulogne telling him to stop the deputation from coming because 'they derange without being of any use'; it could all be settled in writing. In any case, he was not in Paris and 'owing to my mother's very serious illness I often sit up all night' and he was not inclined to be disturbed in any way. Therefore, there was no question of him receiving any deputation.

But the tenants were not to be put off so easily and it seems they came to Paris, because in a letter written to Mie-Mie in June from Paris he complains about the bother and problems of owning property and says he has been 'much bothered with my deputation and have only been able to get rid of it by fresh sacrifices and they will not be the last'.

At the end of his letter he seems to be trying to persuade her to return to Paris, which he tells her continues perfectly quiet and it is more than three years since there was the vestige of a disturbance. Paris is extremely full and very gay, 'your boulevard is impassable all the evening and I always look up at your window with the regret of knowing you are not there looking at the merry mob below....'

During the course of the year 1851 Lord Hertford bought four Bouchers at one sale. Although art experts scoffed at his taste, he was beginning to build up his collection of paintings by the protégé of Madame de Pompadour. Indeed, by the time he died it had become the most important collection of Bouchers in the world. The next year, 1852, with Bonapartism very much in the air, he bought a painting which had been carried off by Napoleon's commander Marshal Soult after the Spanish campaign. It was one of a series of eight panels depicting scenes from the life of St John the Evangelist by the Spanish painter Alonso Cano, who painted them during the first half of the seventeenth century as an altarpiece for the nuns of Santa Paula in Seville. Marshal Soult had taken three of the eight panels in 1810, and after his death they were included in the sale of his works of art. It was at this sale that Lord Hertford bought the *Vision of St John*, which had been the lower right-hand panel of the altarpiece. The two others were bought at the sale by the Duc de Galliera and are now in the United States in the Ringling Museum of Art at Sarasota. The five other paintings which completed the altarpiece have been lost. This is an example of works of art being preserved by looting.

During this time Lord Hertford was also buying some of his finest pieces of eighteenth-century French furniture, clocks, candelabra, Sèvres porcelain and tapestries. Unfortunately, there is much less documentary material surviving to help identify these objects; nor are there many sales catalogues, bills or receipts which might reveal when and where he acquired them. It is known that he bought furniture in England, for example, at the Stowe sale and later at the sales of both the Earl of Pembroke and the Earl of Shrewsbury, but most of his purchases of furniture at this time were being made in France and remained in France with him. For years he had been following sales and knew who owned the finest furniture. Many of the pieces he bought may first have caught his discerning eye in private houses and years later he secured them at the sales that followed their owners' deaths. It may well be that he already possessed some of his greatest pieces such as the chest of drawers from Louis XV's bedroom at Versailles, the 'dragon' chest of drawers by Cressent, the outstanding roll-top desk, known as the 'Bureau du Roi Stanislas', the 'Avignon' clock and the wall-lights from Marie Antoinette's card-room at Fontainebleau.

But that was not enough. So great was his passion that he asked permission from Napoleon III, Queen Victoria and the Duke of Buccleuch to make copies of particularly superb pieces of furniture in their collections because he saw no possibility of his ever being able to own them and he admired them so much.

He asked Napoeon III to allow him to copy the roll-top desk known as 'le Bureau du Roi Louis XV', now at Versailles. Permission was given, but it was stipulated that no moulds should be taken from the original bronzes, the models for which had to be sculpted. His copy was made in Paris by Dasson and cost Lord Hertford 90,000 francs. The desk is decorated with pictorial marquetry and when the copy was made its marquetry was carefully matched to the faded original as it was in the 1850s. Today the marquetry of the copy has faded too, so that it differs considerably from the original.

Another piece of furniture he admired enough to have two copies made was the writing-table made by A. C. Boulle in about 1715 for the Elector of Bavaria. It was then in the possession of the Duke of Buccleuch, and it was purchased by the Louvre in 1951. The writing-table supports a cabinet with drawers on which rests a clock. Lord Hertford insisted that his copies, which were made in London by John Webb of Cork Street, should be exact in every detail, but he never intended that they should pass for the originals. In his copies of this desk he had the arms and crests of the Elector Maximilian replaced by the Seymour-Conway arms, and the monogram H with a marquess's coronet was substituted for the elector's M. One has survived at Hertford House in the Collection. The whereabouts of the second copy was unknown until 1977 when it suddenly turned up in a sale in California. It has since disappeared again.

Other copies that he had made included the Provence cabinet at Windsor Castle, the astronomical clock at Versailles, and a medal-cabinet in the Bibliothèque Nationale, but these are no longer in the Collection. He also owned a copy of a Caffieri chimney-piece at Versailles.

During these early days of the Second Empire Lord Hertford was never away from Paris for long. His friendship with Napoleon III meant that he was invited to the formal Tuileries receptions and the Château de Compiègne, the royal residence the emperor preferred to all others. In January 1853, less than two months after becoming emperor, Napoleon III married Eugénie de Montijo. The following June Haussmann, who later demolished much of the centre of Paris to build new avenues and boulevards, was sworn in as Préfet of the Seine. Paris was on the threshold of a new and unrivalled splendour. It was the overture to the Fête Impériale and Lord Hertford was not going to miss the performance.

Since his return to England he had been carrying out extensive alterations to the house in Piccadilly which he had inherited from his father. Suddenly he gave orders for the work to be stopped, even though the new staircase was far from finished. One story is that he had had a disagreement with the parish over the drainage and had refused to give way. He closed the house to annoy them, and because the staircase was not finished he declared the house uninhabitable and refused to pay the rates. Whatever the reason, he left the house with no staircase and once again returned to Paris.

Chapter Eight

IN THE SUMMER OF 1855 people from all over Europe flocked to Paris to see the splendours of the Second Empire. It was the year of the Exposition Universelle, opened by the emperor on 15 May. Queen Victoria, accompanied by Prince Albert, visited it in August and was dazzled by all she saw and not a little charmed by Napoleon III. The new Court of the Tuileries was more lively than St James's or Potsdam, St Petersburg or Vienna, and it radiated festive opulence. It was the empire of the crinoline and dancing to the music of Offenbach, while fireworks lit up the night sky. The Empress Eugénie was the centre of all this elegance and ostentation, the dictator of feminine taste and fashion.

The excitement was so infectious that even Lord Hertford could not resist it. He allowed the rigid pattern of his self-centred life to be drastically altered when he agreed to become chairman of a committee set up to judge certain categories of exhibits submitted for inclusion in the Exposition Universelle. It can only have been as a result of personal pressure by the emperor that he consented to take on what was the nearest thing to work he had ever known in his life. He wrote to all his friends complaining of the hours it involved and that he got no sleep because he had to get up so early to be in time for his committee meetings. To Mawson he wrote:

Only think of my being at the Champs-Elysées every morning at 10 o'clock. Hard work for an old fellow who has very different habits. ... I am obliged to get up every morning between 6 and 7 o'clock to be at the Exhibition in proper time to preside over a group composed of four classes. I remain there almost all day doing my work, and as I am not accustomed to this sudden activity I am very tired and in consequence neglect my own affairs.

He told Mrs Dawson-Damer that he had to get up at eight o'clock to be there at ten: a slightly different story, but despite his protests he went every day and carried out his duties most conscientiously.

In England, meanwhile, his father's old friend the Countess Zichy had decided to sell the contents of St Dunstan's, in Regent's Park. Lord Hertford wrote to Mawson asking him to attend the sale of his father's possessions for him as he had 'no time to spare' and enclosed a list of three paintings he wished him to buy. He was anxious to have a portrait of George IV as Prince of Wales by Hoppner. This was understandable because it had been given to his father by the prince, who had bought it from the painter's widow in 1810. One of the other pictures he wanted was a landscape by Ruisdael – 'what you think it is worth and a little more'. Mawson bought the Hoppner portrait but not the Ruisdael. In a letter written to Mawson after the sale to thank him for buying 'my caprices', we discover that he wanted the Ruisdael for purely sentimental reasons: 'I rather regret the landscape tho' an indifferent picture because it was in my room when I was a boy, a *few* years ago. What prices people give now for all these old affairs. It is ridiculous.'

Presumably when the 'little more' than what the Ruisdael was worth had been exceeded Mawson had stopped bidding, and somebody else had secured the picture for what Lord Hertford considered was a ridiculous price. Was it sour grapes? It looks like it because that year he spent £6,000 buying Sèvres at the Bernal sale at Christie's, attracting at the same time a good deal of publicity.

It is interesting to note that Lord Hertford was not at all interested in antiquities. Mawson was not instructed to bid for the Meta, or any of the marble statuary that his father had brought back to St Dunstan's from Italy. The Meta, with a sculptured relief of racing chariots on its plinth, was bought by the Earl of Lonsdale and taken to Lowther Castle where it remained until 1947. It was Lot 2332 at the Lowther Castle sale that year and was described in the catalogue as 'The Olympian Meta'. Its present whereabouts are unknown.

Meanwhile, in Paris work on the preparations for Queen Victoria's visit did not prevent Lord Hertford from acquiring two particularly fine and unusually large Bouchers, which had once belonged to Madame de Pompadour and were in her sale after her death in 1766. Entitled *The Rising of the Sun* and *The Setting of the Sun*, they were originally painted by Boucher as designs for tapestries to be made at the Gobelins factory, but according to the story, when La Pompadour saw the paintings she begged King Louis XV to let her have them instead of the tapestries. This story was confirmed in 1949 when the paintings were cleaned and it was discovered that *The Rising of the Sun* had been painted, as is usual for tapestry cartoons, entirely in grisaille and later overpainted in colour. *The Setting of the Sun*, however, shows no sign of grisaille painting, having been painted in colour from the very beginning, which suggests that *The Rising of the Sun* was finished first and that when Madame de Pompadour saw it she asked for both paintings although the second had not been completed. Lord Hertford bought the two for 20,200 francs at the sale of the Baron de Comailles on 2 August. Today they hang on the Grand Staircase at Hertford House. Boucher, it is said, considered them his finest paintings.

Sixteen days later Mie-Mie, Lord Henry Seymour and Richard Wallace must have been among the thousands who watched the arrival of Queen Victoria at Boulogne in the royal yacht *Victoria and Albert*. The town was full of English people. Ten thousand are said to have crossed the Channel the day before in seven specially chartered steamers to see their sovereign arrive in France, and a British naval squadron had been anchored off Boulogne for some days.

The weather was perfect, but Queen Victoria was late and it was already two o'clock when the shining white, brand-new royal yacht came alongside the jetty. Enthusiastic, cheering crowds lined the streets of Boulogne as the queen drove to the railway station, where the imperial train was waiting to take her to Paris. The sight may have caused Mie-Mie to think that perhaps it was time she went back to Paris now that there was no longer any danger from rioting. The real reason may have been that she knew she had not long to live and wanted to be near Dr Robert Chermside, the British Embassy doctor who had always been close at hand because he had an apartment in her house in the rue Taitbout. Whatever the reason, the decision was taken that autumn and in November, after six years at the Hôtel des Bains, the trio returned to Paris where No. 3 rue Taitbout was waiting for them exactly as they had left it.

But Paris was not the same: changes were to be noticed everywhere. Haussmann had already begun to pull down some of the old houses and narrow streets in the centre of the city. The Champs-Elysées was becoming the new fashionable district. Thérèse Paiva, one of the most fabulous adventuresses of the Second Empire, who had been born Esther Lachmann in the ghetto of Moscow, had bought a piece of land there on which she was having built the extraordinary house which is today the Travellers' Club. Mie-Mie must have noticed the early stages of the building as she drove by on her way to see Lord Hertford at Bagatelle. She must also have noticed the big changes in the Bois de Boulogne which, while she was away, had become the property of the City of Paris and was now being turned into a public park. Many new trees had been planted and men were digging the lakes and landscaping the ground. This new development had not pleased Lord Hertford who, fearing his privacy would be disturbed, had, with the help of the emperor, bought land in the Bois so as to make his large garden even larger and keep the undesirable public well away from Bagatelle.

Lord Henry Seymour noticed changes in his cherished boulevard which did not please him at all. It was now crowded with people from the provinces and even foreigners, brought to Paris by the railway. People he had never seen before strolled on the boulevard and, more shocking still, they invaded the Café de Paris so that it was crowded with strangers. There was nobody there whom he knew and he was not very happy. He installed Mrs Minchin near him in the rue Godot-de-Mauroy and visited her every afternoon. The quick-tempered gentleman-sportsman had become, alas, too fat to ride and was now a terrible tyrant. He was consumed with jealousy and sent written instructions to her every morning telling her how she must pass each minute of her day. The clergyman's daughter did not always accept his tyranny meekly and they had frequent and violent quarrels. One of the most bitter concerned a dog of Lord Henry called Don Juan which he had asked her to look after when his mother was ill. Mrs Minchin sent the dog back complaining that it had made messes in her house. Lord Henry, beside himself with rage, denied the charges against his dog's behaviour and for some time the couple exchanged abusive letters and stopped seeing each other.

Richard Wallace returned to find changes too. He must have been surprised to find his son Edmond was no longer a little boy. He was now fifteen years old but, all the same, Wallace left him with his mother, and went back to live with Mie-Mie and Lord Henry Seymour in the rue Taitbout. The trio remained united and took up their life exactly as before.

One reason may have been that Mie-Mie, now eighty-four, was getting weaker every day. One night at the very end of February she was so ill that Lord Hertford sat up with her until the early hours of the morning. When he got back home he realised his mother had not long to live and wrote down his concern on a piece of paper which he put in an envelope, writing on it: 'Souvenir about my mother. H. 28 February 1856.' Inside he had written:

'I have just returned from my poor dear Mother who is unfortunately very ill and in bed since a couple of days – I am very uneasy and miserable.

'Rue Laffitte 2 (night of the Mi-Carême) 28 February 1856. 3½ o'clock in the morning. H.'

Mie-Mie lingered on for two days and died on Sunday, 2 March. The details of her death we know from Lord Hertford himself. In her drawing-room two days after her death he again poured out his grief on paper:

'Most Melancholy details and souvenirs of my poor dear excellent Mother.

'Paris, rue Taitbout 3, 4 March 1856.'

That was what he wrote on the envelope after he had written the following on heavily black-edged paper:

My poor dear and most excellent Mother was suddenly attacked with pain in her side which did not however prevent her from beginning her little dinner with us, on Tuesday 26 February 1856 – She most unfortunately grew worse and worse and expired on Sunday the 2nd of March/56 at exactly 10 o'clock in the morning – Henry, Richard and myself were by her bedside and I held her hand a moment before or at the time when she closed her dear and precious eyes for ever without a sigh or any pain. Chermside came into the room at the fatal moment.

May the Almighty God bless her I humbly and fervently pray.

H.

In my poor dear mother's drawing-room – Tuesday 4 March 1856 rue Taitbout 3 with Henry and Richard.

In another envelope he put a lock of Mie-Mie's hair with the note: 'My poor dear Mother's hair cut off on Tuesday, 4 March 1856 at ½ past 11 o'clock (morning) on her deathbed. May God bless her. H.'

Mie-Mie was buried the next day, 5 March, at Père Lachaise cemetery next to her daughter. The only mourners were her two sons and Richard Wallace.

The day after the funeral, at rue Laffitte, Lord Hertford was again driven to pour out his feelings on black-edged paper. It was as if he wished to record, in what were in fact introspective letters to himself, his feelings before they faded with time. They were a sort of self-portrait of his misery. This time he wrote:

The burial of my most excellent and beloved Mother took place yesterday Wednesday, 5 March 1856.

We left her house at ½ past 8 o'clock in the morning for the sad and painful ceremony, that was performed by Doctor Male, Chaplain to the Embassy.

May God have received her soul in Heaven.

Rue Laffitte 2, 6 March/56
H.

On the envelope into which he put it he wrote: 'My dearest, dearest departed Mother – 6 March 1856'.

Mie-Mie's death passed unnoticed in English society. London had forgotten the old marchioness who had lived almost exclusively in France for fifty years. She had come to Paris in the time of the first Bonaparte and had become more French than English. In recent years she had been seen in public very seldom and all that people could remember was a curious, bent old woman, looking like a witch, with a reputation for avarice.

But for each of the three men who followed her to Père Lachaise she had been for as long as they could remember the central person in their lives. To Lord Hertford she was the parent with whom he had lived and been brought up while his father came and went. Then at an age when most mothers have had enough of bringing up young children she had brought up his illegitimate son. Lord Henry, who had lived with her all his life, owed everything to her. His real father had never shown the slightest interest in him and it was Mie-Mie who had persuaded her husband to make him a Seymour and an Englishman. Richard Wallace also had been brought up by her and made a member of the family. She was his grandmother, although it was never admitted. She had taken him into her home when he might have been sent to foster-parents and she loved him as if she were his mother. In return, all three had given her their unswerving devotion, even in old age. Few mothers could boast such love and affection.

Lord Hertford was so overcome by her death that after the funeral he shut himself up and refused to see anyone for three weeks. Even the trusted Mawson who happened to come to Paris was sent away when he called.

When it came to writing wills Mie-Mie was very different from the Seymours. Her will was short, only two pages, and untouched since the day she had made it in London after the family council in 1838. She had written none of the confusing codicils which the Seymours always added to their wills. Her property, which included the two houses in Piccadilly which she had inherited from Old Q., she simply divided equally between her two sons.

The unity of the family circle was broken by the death of Mie-Mie. The two brothers began to drift apart, seeing less and less of each other, while Richard Wallace divided his time between them and eventually became their only link. There was still no question of his living with Mademoiselle Castelnau and his son.

Lord Henry too was genuinely upset by his mother's death and his general health began to deteriorate. In August, on the advice of Dr Chermside, he went to take the waters at Aix-la-Chapelle, but the cure did not do him much good. He came back in low spirits and his temper was not improved by frequent attacks of gout which kept him a prisoner in his room. He was also horrified to learn that the Café de Paris, now deserted by its old customers, was going to close for lack of clients; and he deplored the increasing number of new shops and other signs that commerce was taking over the boulevard.

Meanwhile, Lord Hertford's collection continued to grow. In 1859 his picture purchases alone included two Rubens, two Watteaus, a Van Dyck, a Velasquez and a Titian. Storage was becoming a serious problem. Every available attic in his Paris house and at Bágatelle and Lord Henry Seymour's now empty gymnasium were full of furniture, pictures and cases of precious porcelain. It was the same in the two houses in London. But a corner of the veil of secrecy which had kept these treasures hidden from the eyes of the public was soon to be lifted.

In 1855 Lord Hertford had instructed Mawson to unpack the pictures stored in cases in the houses in Manchester Square and Berkeley Square. Mawson had been acting as the curator of his English collection. Although Lord Hertford had seen little of what was stored in these two houses, he kept careful records of everything he bought – this was probably one of Wallace's tasks – and he knew exactly what was there. An example of this occurred when Mawson reported that while unpacking he had found an empty case. The meticulous marquess looked up his records and replied that he was 'rather uneasy' as case No. 60 ought to contain a painting on slate by Horace Vernet, *The Taking of Constantine*, one of Vernet's Algerian pictures. Mawson must have found it because it hangs in Hertford House today.

Perhaps it was while he was unpacking all these masterpieces that Mawson realised that they ought to be seen by the public. An Art Treasures Exhibition was due to open in Manchester in 1857 and he proposed to Lord Hertford that he should lend some of his best paintings to it. It is a sign of Lord Hertford's confidence in Mawson that he agreed, even though it would involve personal publicity which he so disliked. However, he would be far away in Paris and this may have made it easier for him to consent to what in a sense was an invasion of his privacy. There was a hitch in the arrangements when the committee of the exhibition refused to insure his pictures and it was not until April, barely a month before the exhibition was due to open, that the committee changed its mind and Lord Hertford finally agreed to send forty-four of his pictures.

The paintings, which were among the finest in his collection in England, included four Rembrandts, four Van Dycks, two Rubens, four Velasquez and five Murillos; there was also the Salvator Rosa, a Watteau, two Greuzes and a Poussin. They were hung all together in a special gallery, a privilege granted to no other exhibitor, and they caused a sensation. The *Manchester Guardian* called the Hertford Gallery 'a mine of wealth and excellence'.

The Manchester Art Treasures Exhibition was the first major mixed exhibition to be held in England and for this reason it attracted a large international public. This did not prevent Lord Hertford from having doubts about the wisdom of lending his pictures. When he heard that a madman had fired a gun into the exhibition he immediately wrote to Mawson: 'I hope that his bullets have not passed through some of our pictures.'

When he was told by French people unused to Manchester weather who had been to the exhibition that 'the damp is dreadful', he became convinced that his pictures were being destroyed by the damp and rain in Manchester. Mawson was blamed for everything and received letter after letter complaining and regretting the whole business.

'I cannot say how miserable it makes me having had my finest pictures so stupidly destroyed,' he says, adding bitterly that his consolation will be the honour of having contributed to the glory of the Manchester exhibition.

In another letter he refers to some pictures which were in the house in Berkeley Square and he calls them 'those paintings that remained in the Ark and thereby escaped the deluge'. He is so miserable, he says, that he does not feel disposed to make any new purchases.

There appears to have been a heavy storm or cloudburst at Manchester and rainwater did come through the roof of the exhibition. Lord Hertford was convinced that all his pictures had been ruined. 'Everybody tells me that several of my pictures were destroyed by the water spout.' He believes Mawson does not tell him because he does not want to annoy him and blames him for advising him to send his pictures, 'a most imprudent step'.

Then he found a new cause for worry. He says he is quite

'uneasy' because he read in the paper that 'it is the fashion to steal pictures'.

Mawson seems to have borne all this petulance and panic with great patience. When the exhibition was over and all forty-four pictures were safely back in Manchester Square he wrote to tell Lord Hertford that it was not true that his pictures were all destroyed by water at Manchester, as he would see for himself when he came to London. He also assured him that the Berkeley Square and Manchester Square houses were well guarded against theft and pointed out that the theft he had read about had happened in the country.

Before the panic about the damp, Lord Hertford had said that he did not regret sending his pictures to Manchester because it would give him a chance to see them, but in the end he never went to the exhibition. There was always an excuse and as usual it was ill-health – this time rheumatism and gout. Nevertheless, he confessed to Mawson that he would never forgive himself for not having seen the exhibition: 'My putting off vice often punishes me.'

Ill-health again prevented him from going to England as he had intended in December 1858. He was giving up the house in Berkeley Square and he had planned to go over to be present when the pictures, those he had called the pictures in the Ark, were moved to Manchester Square. He had to be out of the house by Christmas Day, but on 11 December he wrote to Mawson to say he was too ill to cross the Channel and asked him to help Richard Wallace who would be coming to supervise the move.

His brother Lord Henry, although five years younger than himself, was much more seriously ill. In the summer of 1857 he had gone for a second time to take the cure at Aix-la-Chapelle. This time Dr Chermside had accompanied him, but the waters did little for his rheumatism and when he returned to Paris in September he was much exhausted by the journey. Throughout the year 1858 he lingered on, a melancholy figure, seldom able to go out. All his zest for life had gone, although he still wrote letters to the newspapers denying that he had had any connection with Milord l'Arsouille and his rowdy companions. It was a legend that it was impossible to kill.

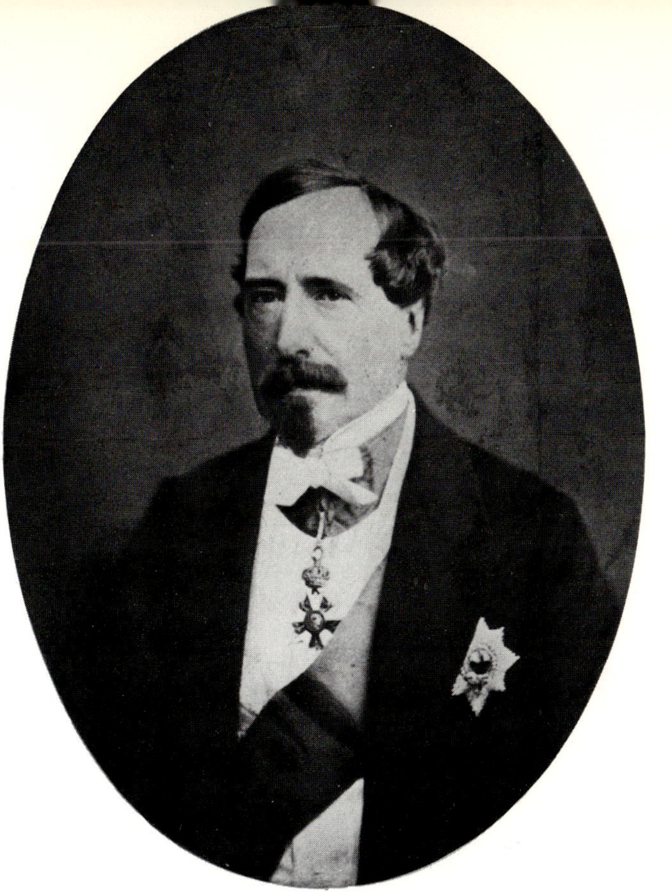

1. Lord Hertford wearing his Garter ribbon and the Legion of Honour.

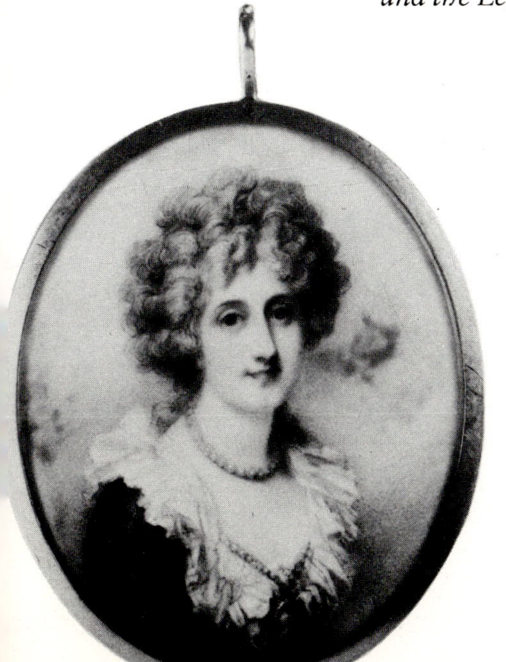

2. Mie-Mie as a young married woman. A miniature by Richard Cosway.

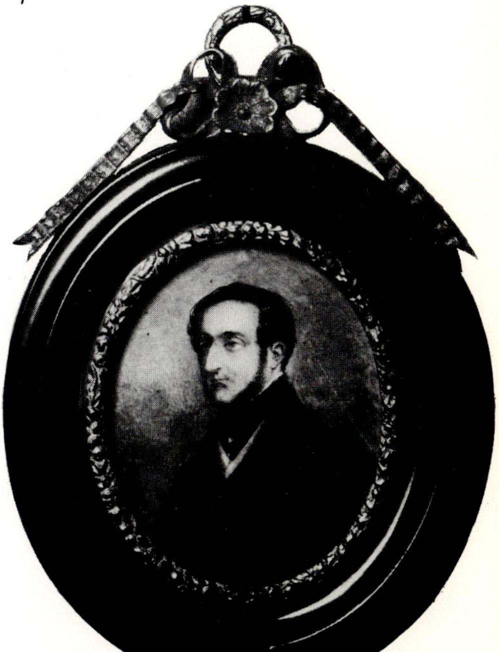

3. Lord Henry Seymour. A miniature by an unknown artist.

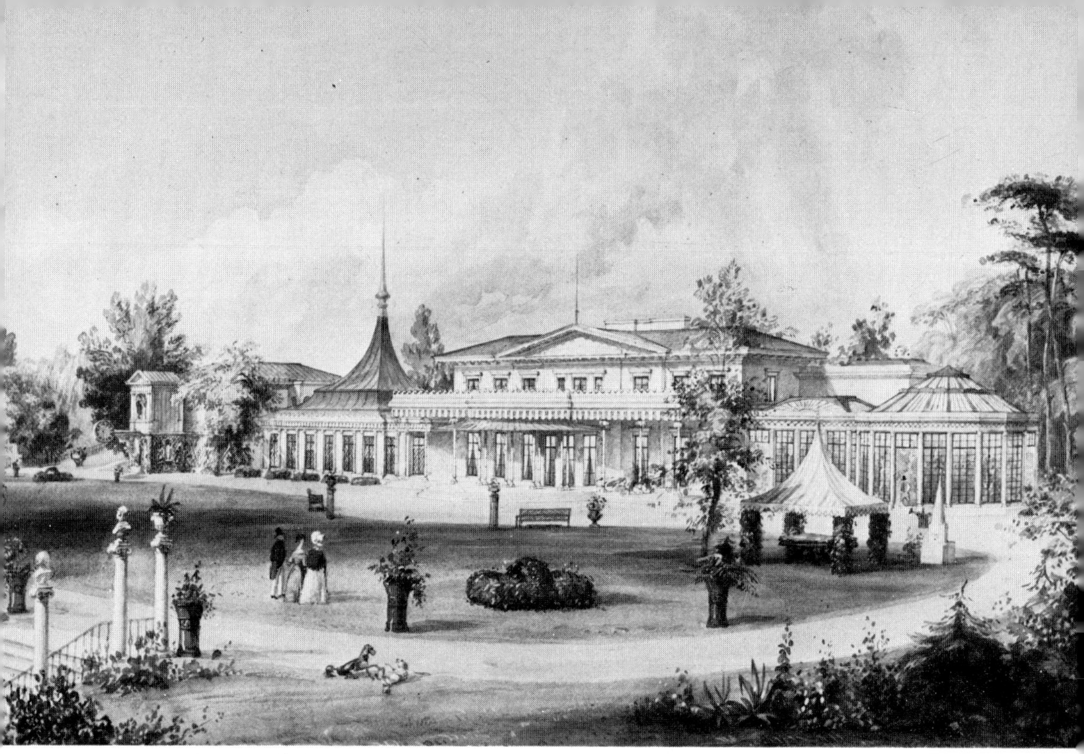

4. *The south front of St Dunstan's. The Tent Room is on the left and on the extreme left is the clock from St Dunstan's Church in Fleet Street. Part of the colonnade can be seen* (bottom left), *while the Meta is on the extreme right.*

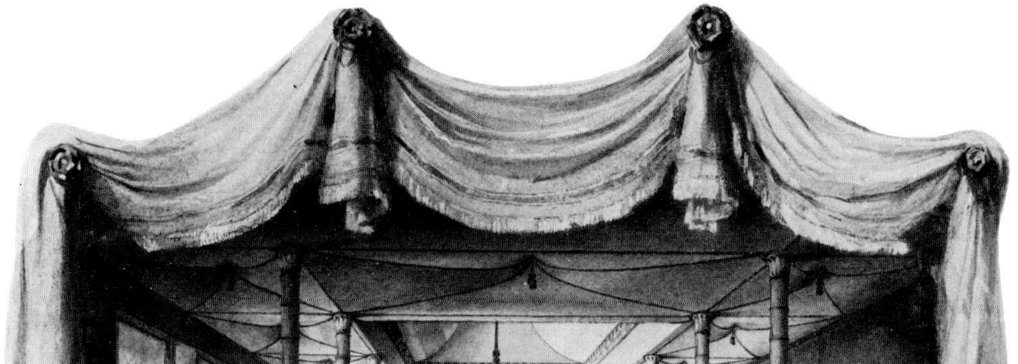

5. *The interior of the Tent Room at St Dunstan's. On the right are the portrait of George IV as Prince of Wales by Hoppner and two large Canalettos, all of which are still in the Collection.*

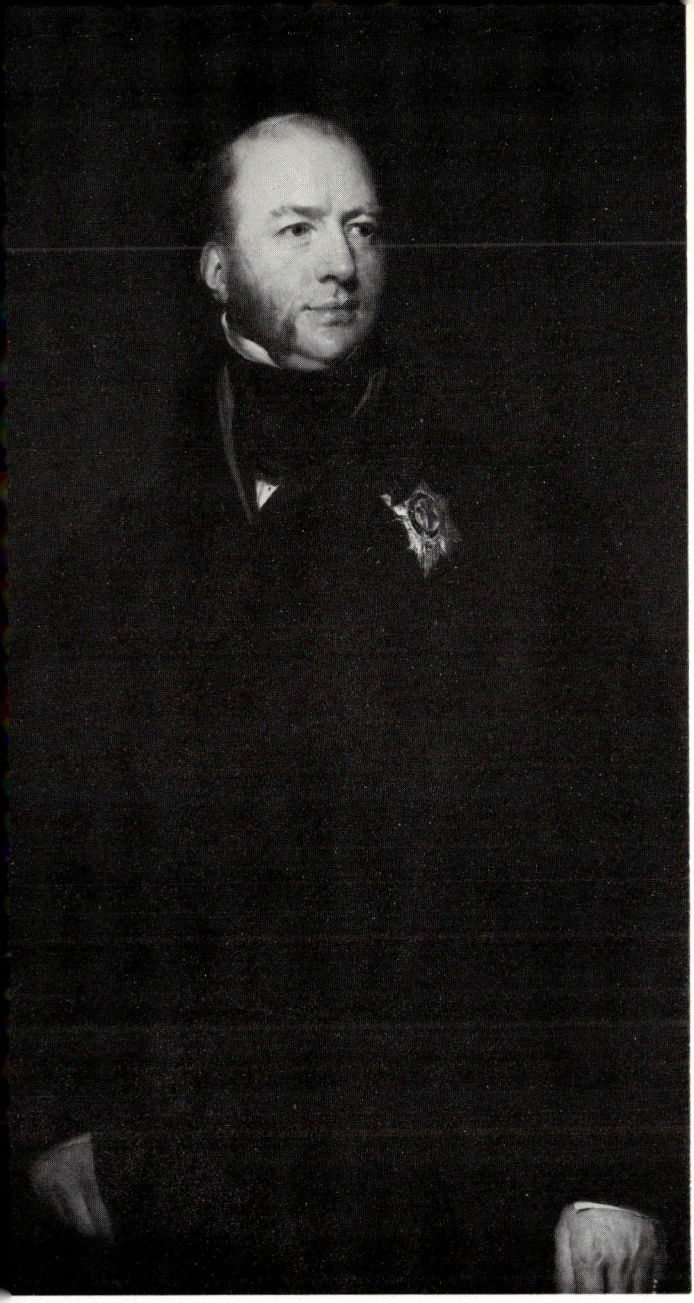

6. The Caliph of Regent's Park: the portrait of the 3rd Marquess of Hertford by Sir Thomas Lawrence, now in the National Gallery of Art, Washington.

7. 'An excursion to R(agley) Hall' by George Cruikshank. The Regent and Lady Hertford are sitting in the carriage which is being driven by the Devil. Lord Yarmouth is leading the way on a donkey as they pass a 'Female Asylum', in the windows of which are the former favourites of the Regent.

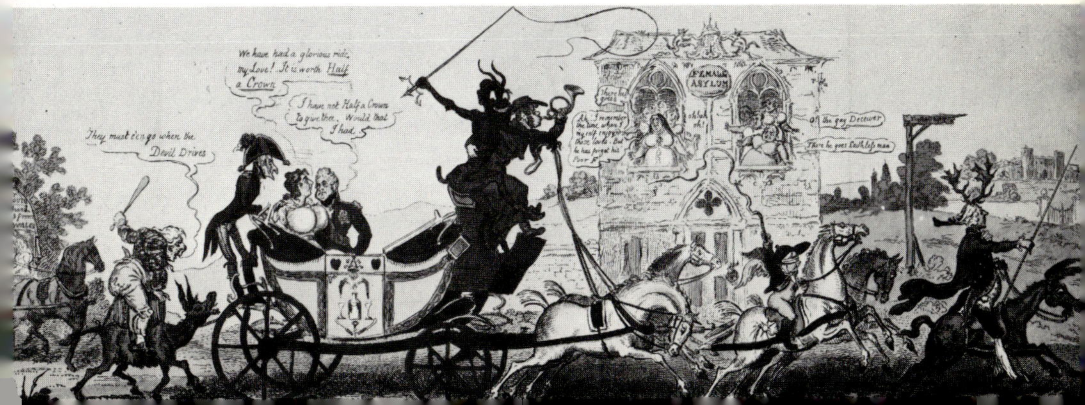

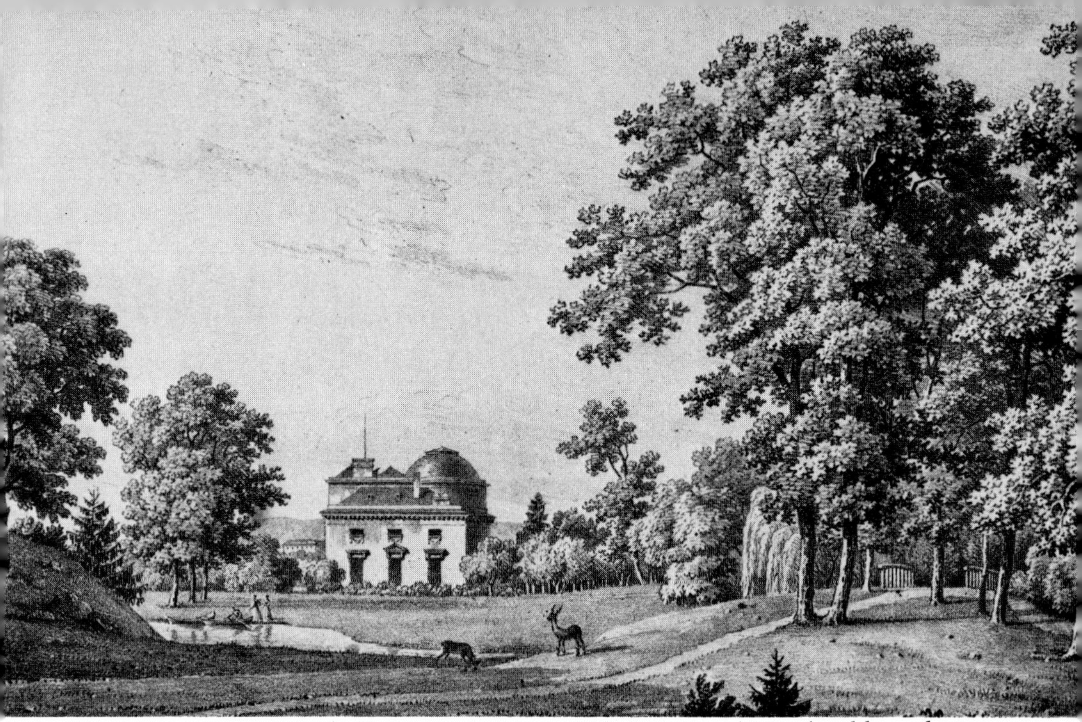

8. Bagatelle as it was in 1818, before Lord Hertford bought it.

9. The entrance to Bagatelle.

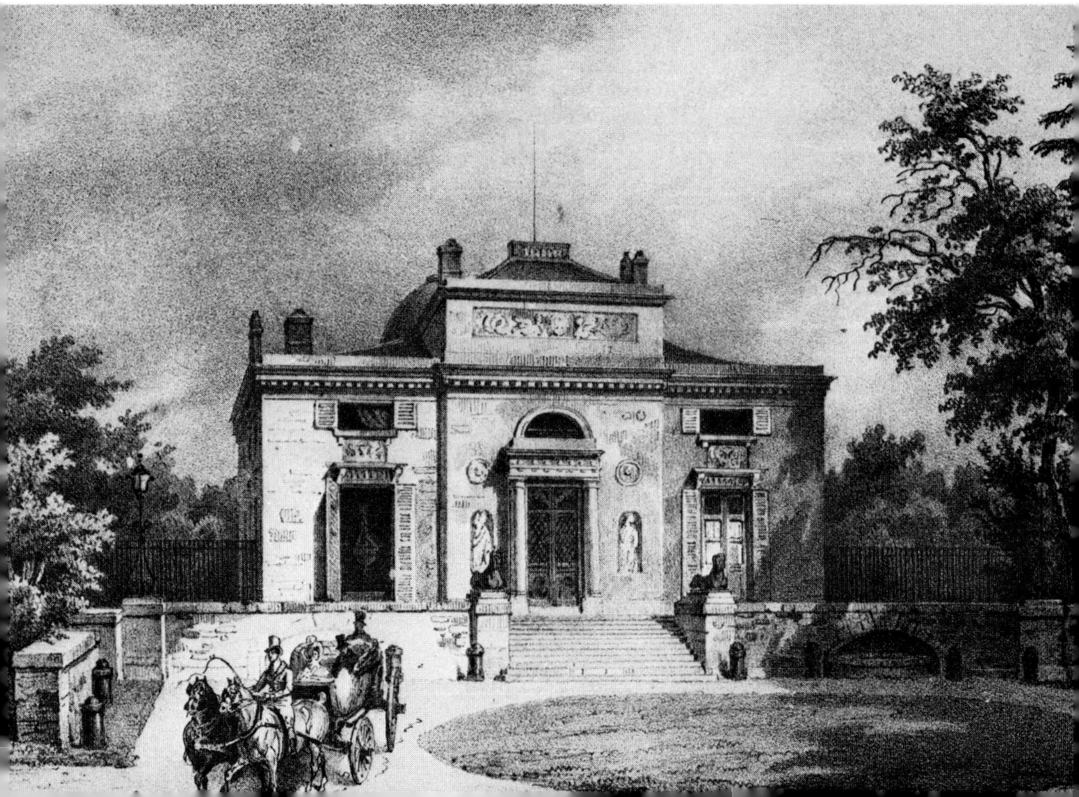

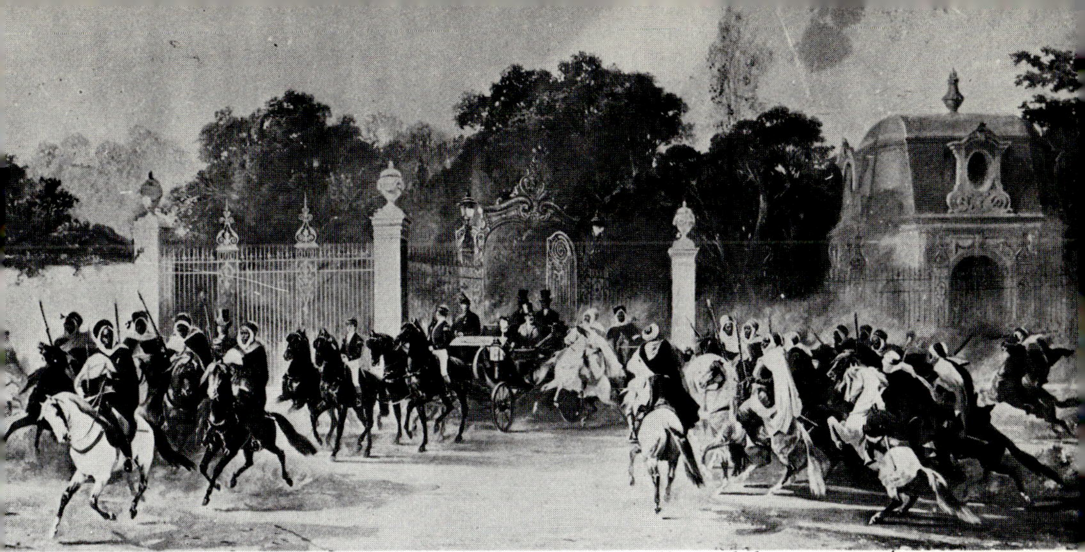

10. *The Prince Imperial driving out of Bagatelle with his escort of Spahis. (From the painting by Alfred Decaen which was in the possession of the Empress Eugénie and which is now owned by the Prince Napoléon.) Lord Hertford had a replica of the painting in his apartment in Paris but its present whereabouts are unknown.*

11. *Lord Hertford and Richard Wallace at Bagatelle. The lady is probably Madame Oger.*

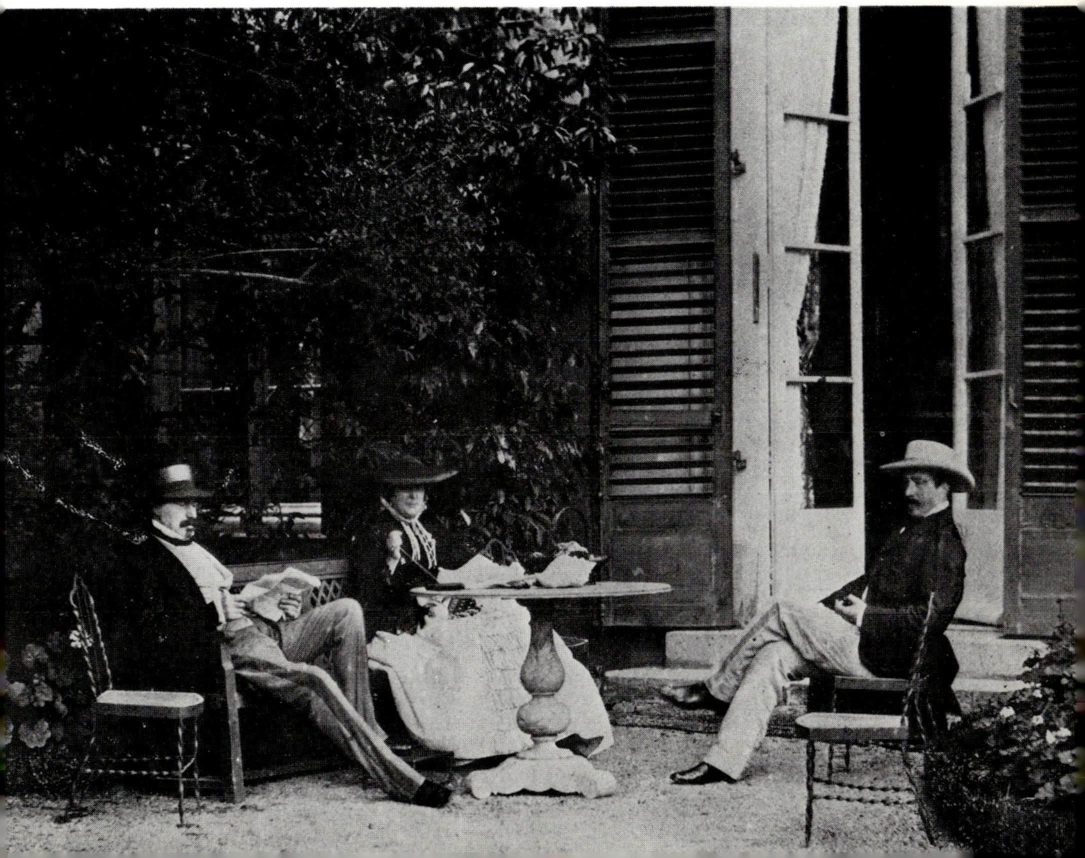

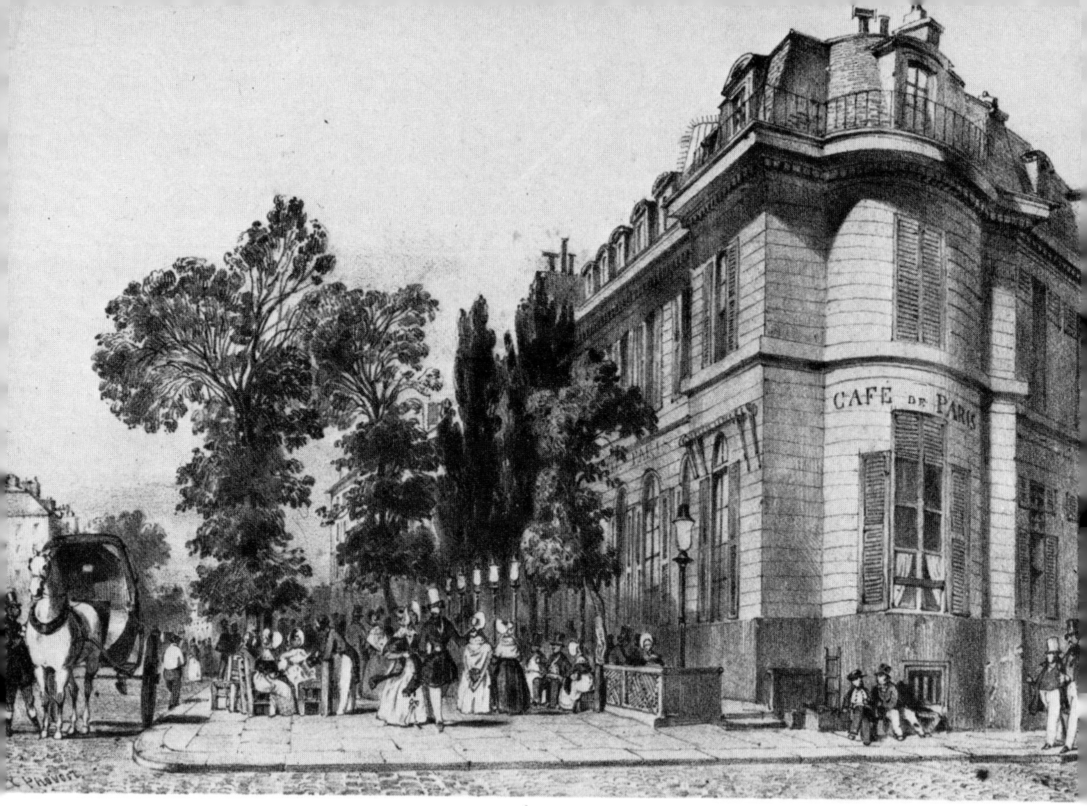

12. *The Café de Paris and Mie-Mie's apartment.*

13. *The boulevard des Italiens as Lord Henry Seymour loved it.*

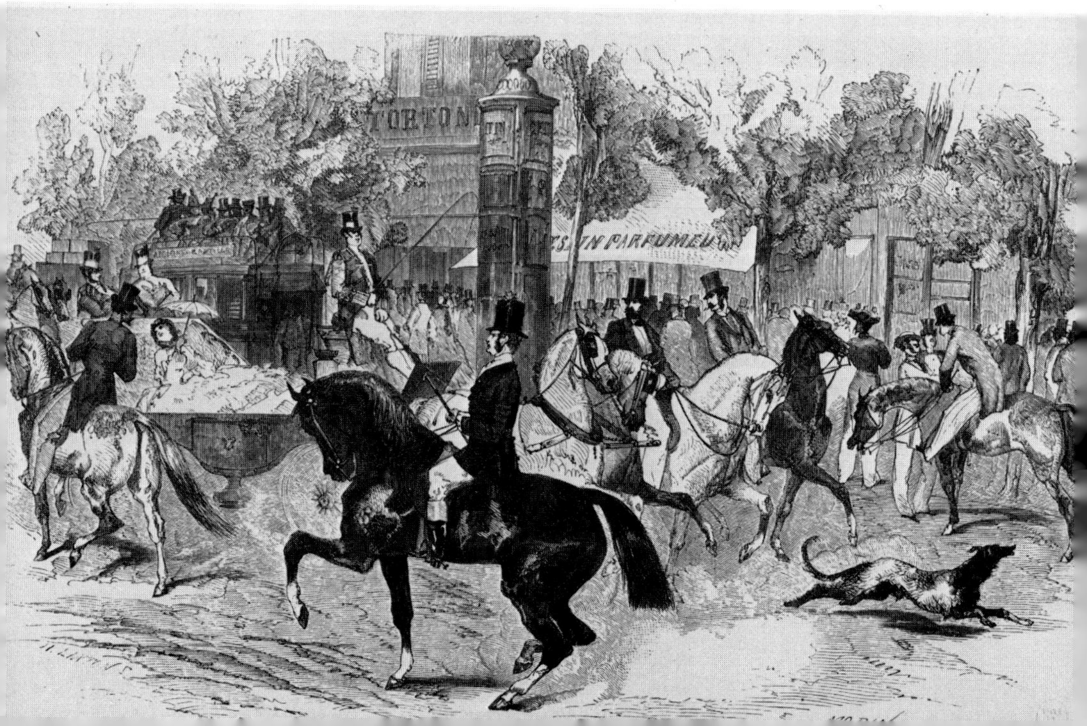

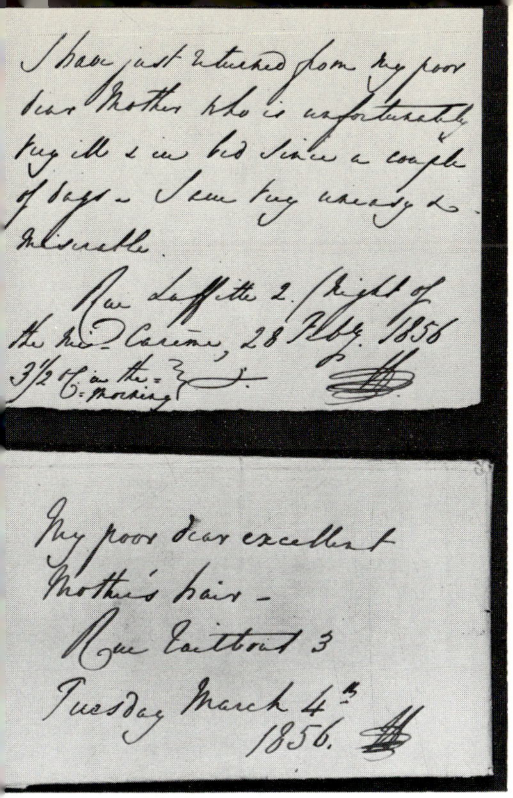

I have just returned from my poor dear Mother who is unfortunately very ill & in bed since a couple of days - I am very uneasy & miserable.
Rue Laffitte 2. (Night of the Mi-Carême, 28 Feby. 1856
3 1/2 o'c in the morning)

My poor dear excellent Mother's hair -
Rue Taitbout 3
Tuesday March 4th
1856.

4. *The note which Lord Hertford wrote when Mie-Mie first became ill, and the envelope in which he placed a lock of her hair after her death.*

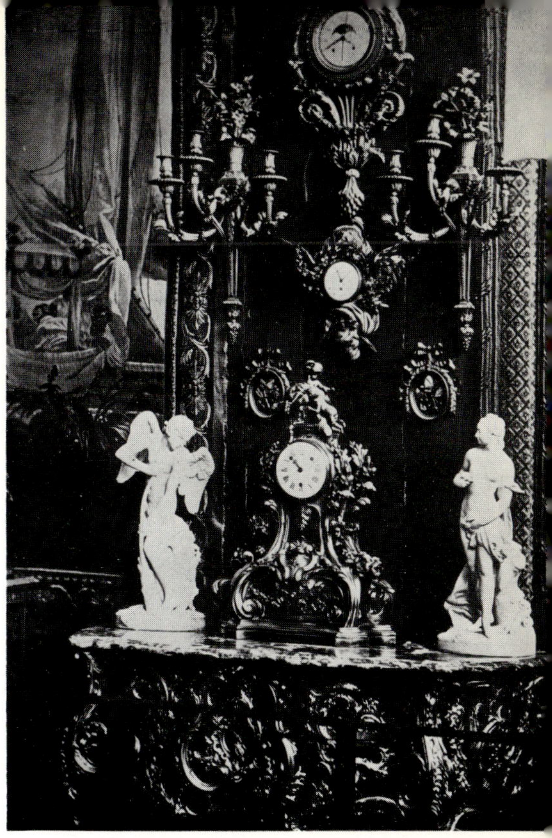

15. *Part of Lord Hertford's exhibit at the Musée Rétrospectif in 1865, showing the Bouchardon statue of Cupid on the left (now in the National Gallery of Art, Washington), and also on the left a corner of a Beauvais tapestry (now in the Metropolitan Museum of Art, New York).*

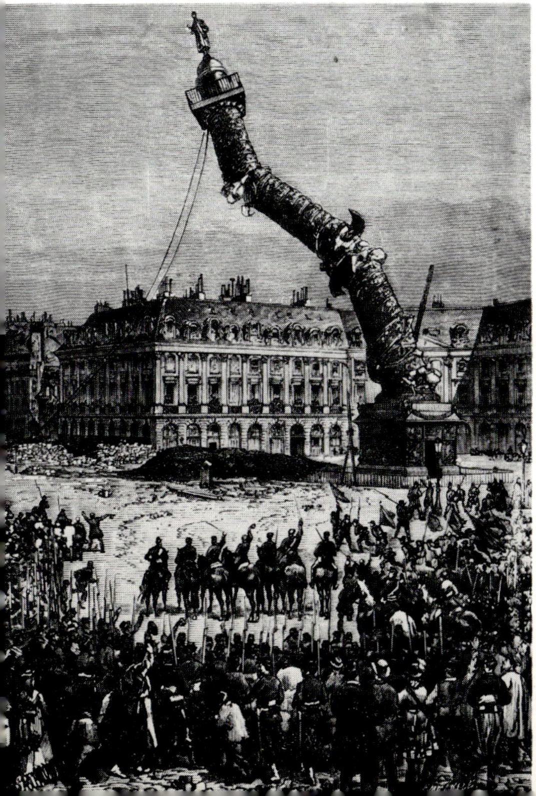

16. *Courbet's triumph – the column in the place Vendôme is pulled down by the Commune.*

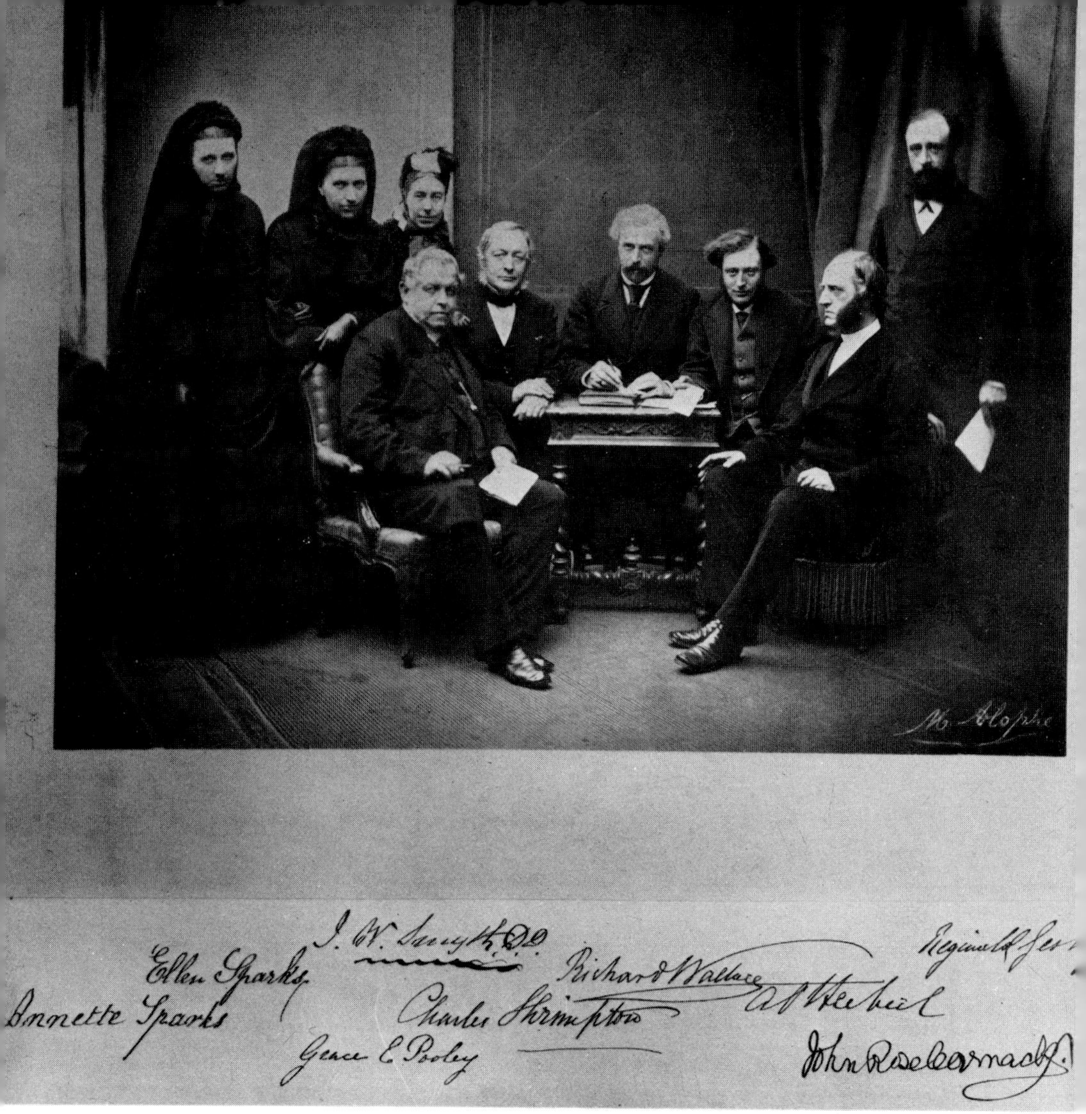

17. *Richard Wallace during the Siege of Paris, surrounded by the committee members of the British Charitable Fund which distributed relief to the needy British.*

On 16 August the following summer the cantankerous old sportsman, whom the French believed so English, died. He was only fifty-four years old. Although the brothers had not spoken to each other since their mother's funeral, Lord Hertford went to see him and was there at the end, having sat up all night at his bedside. At his own request Lord Henry was buried at seven-thirty in the morning in the vault at Père Lachaise beside his mother and sister. The Jockey Club forgot the scandal of the past and sent representatives to his funeral.

Although he had not a drop of Seymour blood he had made an interminable will, like any true Seymour, three years before he died. What his mother had left him went to his brother, which meant that Lord Hertford was enabled to unite both his father's and his mother's considerable fortunes. Lord Henry had always had great affection for Richard Wallace ever since he came to their house as a little boy. To him he left his Watteau *Harlequin and Columbine* and the Holbern self-portrait miniature.

From his will we discover that by Mrs Minchin he had had a daughter who was ten years old when he died. To this little girl he left £24,000, of which a portion was to be used to buy an annuity for life. The sweet-voiced Mrs Minchin was to receive £400 a year on condition she did not marry. But the English clergyman's daughter had not been his only love. Three other children were mentioned in his will.

Lord Henry in his younger days had also been a collector, although on a much smaller scale than his brother. Nevertheless, he owned a number of fine Boningtons and pictures by contemporary French painters such as Isabey, Géricault, Decamps and Delaroche. At the sale which took place the year after his death Lord Hertford bought five of his watercolours by Bonington. The fastidious marquess refused the others because Lord Henry had carelessly hung them on a wall that caught the sunlight and as a result their colours had faded.

However, it was not the pictures, bronzes, sculptures, miniatures, porcelain or armour which excited the interest of the general public at Lord Henry's sale. What attracted the most attention was his enormous collection of cigars. There were in all 14,716 of different kinds.

Chapter Nine

After the death of Lord Henry Seymour Richard Wallace found himself alone in Paris and free to live as he pleased. No longer was he called upon to be the grown-up 'cher neveu' always in attendance on the ageing Mie-Mie and the eccentric Lord Henry. He was forty-one and it was time to start living his own life. Although he had gone back to live in the rue Taitbout with Mie-Mie when they returned from Boulogne, he had begun to make more and more friends of his own. Amongst these friends were some of the contemporary painters in Paris. Of course, he was working again for Lord Hertford, but at the same time he seems to have been determined to be something more than 'Monsieur Richard', the tactful, indispensable secretary.

Perhaps it is not surprising that he started to make a collection of his own. He had been well trained by Lord Hertford and his work for him brought him in daily contact with dealers in art and antiques. It was natural that he should want to exercise his own judgement and taste. He did not seek to acquire exactly the same objects as Lord Hertford, nor did he follow his taste in everything. He bought pictures by his friends Diaz and Meissonier, as well as a Lancret and a Géricault. He also collected oriental objects, porcelain, jade, ivories and Florentine bronzes. He seems to have bought no furniture, not wishing, perhaps, to add to the already acute problems of storage space. He was beginning to establish a reputation of his own as a connoisseur and a discriminating collector.

He still could not avoid running into debt by speculating on the Bourse. Mie-Mie is always blamed for encouraging Wallace in these disastrous efforts to get rich quickly but, whoever was responsible, the fact remains that in November 1856 Lord Hertford had once again to come to the rescue with 271,000 francs to pay his debts. This was a very large sum on top of the allowance of £1,000 a year which he was already paying Wallace. Naturally, Lord Hertford was not pleased and when, not long afterwards, Wallace was again in trouble with his creditors he refused to help. Wallace was therefore forced to sell his collection to raise the money. It was a harsh decision, perhaps, but Lord Hertford had already left Wallace all his fortune as well as his collections in France and England. If he was to be able to look after all this wealth he must learn to manage his own financial affairs. Lord Hertford was meticulous in paying his own debts and he could not bear the thought that Wallace, who was so closely associated with him, should owe money and be unable to pay.

And so the first Wallace Collection was sold a few years after it had been started. Poor Wallace, it must have been a bitter blow. The sale took place in early March 1857 and lasted for two days. One wonders what he must have felt when he saw Lord Hertford buying his best pictures – the Lancret, the Géricault, the Meissonier and the two Diaz. The sale attracted a great deal of attention and to the experts it was clear that, although small, it was the collection of a discerning and knowledgeable *amateur*. It also solved his immediate financial problems, for it brought him in more than enough to pay his debts. But he was not allowed to keep the surplus. Lord Hertford, fearing perhaps that he would soon lose it all again, made him buy a house which had been recently built on the site of the Bains Chinois, a famous landmark in earlier times. Here, in an apartment at 29 boulevard des Italiens, Wallace installed his mistress and his son, Edmond.

Lord Hertford's firm handling of the situation must have had its effect because we never again hear of Wallace being in debt or the marquess having to put up money. Perhaps at last Wallace had grown disenchanted with the Bourse. The painful question of Wallace's debts does not seem to have shaken Lord Hertford's confidence in him as his secretary. He began to trust his judgement and gave him more and more responsibility. In fact, he was becoming a partner in the tireless search for more and more works of art of the highest quality.

One of Wallace's close friends at this time was the painter Ernest Meissonier, whose tiny, very detailed historical genre paintings were becoming enormously popular. Cham, the famous caricaturist of *Charivari*, the satirical revue made famous by Daumier and Grandville, said 'if fleas had money they would all have their portraits painted by that man'. Wallace, it seems, had discovered his paintings on his own and bought the picture which is called *A Sentinel, time of Louis XIII*. It is a full-length portrait of a man with an arquebus on his shoulder and measures no more than 27 centimetres high and 17 centimetres wide. And it was this picture that Lord Hertford bought when Wallace had to sell his collection to pay his debts.

No painter, except perhaps Picasso, has seen his work fetch higher prices, in real money values, during his lifetime. Lord Hertford continued to buy Meissonier's tiny pictures right up to his death. There are sixteen in the Collection today – more than in any other public gallery in the world. Napoleon III admired Meissonier too. He was the first painter to be given the Grand Cross of the Legion of Honour, and in 1859 the emperor had him attached to the general staff of the French army to paint pictures of the Italian campaign. Even more astonishing was his success in England where he was made an honorary member of the Royal Academy. The title Honorary French Royal Academician, which had to be invented for him, gave him the right to put the letters H.F.R.A. after his name. Towards the end of his life he tried to paint large canvases of historical subjects, but they were not successful. It is for his tiny pictures that he is famous.

It was probably Meissonier who introduced Richard Wallace to the beautiful Madame Apollonie Sabatier, better known as 'La Présidente'. Her real name was Aglaé Joséphine Savatier and she had been born in 1822. She had started life as a singer and then posed for the sculptor Clésinger whose famous nude, *La Femme au Serpent*, had caused a sensation at the Salon of 1847. Meissonier had also painted her several times. Her beauty inspired Baudelaire to write for her three of the poems which were later to appear in *Les Fleurs du Mal*. He first sent her anonymously 'Reversibilité' ('Ange plein de gaieté. . . .') on 3 May 1853; eight days later this was followed by 'Confession'. He sent the third poem, 'L'Aube Spirituelle', in February the next year with a note in English, 'After a night of pleasure and desolation, all my soul belongs to you.' After the publication of *Les Fleurs du Mal* in 1857 Apollonie Sabatier offered herself to Baudelaire and he was her lover for a single night. It was a disaster. Baudelaire, whose mistress was a mulatto, liked dark, skinny women because thinness, he said, made them look more naked. Apollonie was a Rubens. His dream was shattered.

At this time Apollonie was the mistress of a rich Belgian financier named Alfred Mosselman. He had come to Paris in the reign of Louis-Philippe with his brother-in-law the Comte Le Hon, who had been appointed Belgian Minister in Paris. He installed Madame Sabatier in a house in the rue Frochot near today's place Pigalle, and it was there that Meissonier must have taken Wallace soon after his return from Boulogne.

She knew a great many artists and writers. Among them was Théophile Gautier who first called her 'La Présidente', and soon she was never called anything else. She was gay and extremely beautiful, with a mass of chestnut-coloured hair. Every Sunday night her most intimate friends would gather at her house for dinner. Gautier was the leading spirit on these occasions. Meissonier and Alfred de Musset went regularly and so did Gustave Flaubert when he was in Paris. She must have liked the fair-haired young Englishman who was a friend of Meissonier because Richard Wallace soon became a close friend and a member of the little group that dined with her every Sunday.

It was not only the conversation and wit of the leading literary figures of the time that drew Wallace to Montmartre. He was falling in love with La Présidente, and when in 1860 Mosselman left her and returned to Brussels she became his mistress. At this point she moved from Montmartre to Neuilly, where he had found for her a little house conveniently near to Bagatelle.

When Mosselman left her Madame Sabatier was forced to sell her possessions in the apartment in the rue Frochot, and at the sale Lord Hertford was able to buy his second Meissonier. It was a picture of *Polichinelle* painted on a panel in one of the doors in her apartment. Wallace must have told Lord Hertford about it and he bought it for 13,000 francs. That panel from Madame Sabatier's door in Montmartre hangs with the other Meissoniers in London today.

For Richard Wallace life was sweet. Lord Hertford was now living almost permanently at Bagatelle – Haussmann's demolitions in Paris may have forced him to seek refuge in the country.

Richard Wallace, therefore, had plenty of time to spend at Neuilly. In all probability Lord Hertford was delighted with Wallace's choice of a new mistress. To settle down with a well-known beauty from the demi-monde who would never expect him to marry her was, after all, exactly what he had always done himself. He may even have hoped that in the arms of La Présidente Wallace would forget Julie Castelnau, whom he had never really liked. And she was far away from Neuilly at 29 boulevard des Italiens, right on the other side of Paris. Wallace, however, this time did not desert the mother of his son, who was now twenty-one and starting to be a soldier. He may have remembered that he himself once wanted to join the navy.

Wallace's relations with Lord Hertford were excellent at this time. The two men had never been closer. Lord Hertford trusted his judgement and sent him more and more frequently on missions abroad to examine and report on works of art that his agents had informed him would soon be coming up for sale, or whose owners wished to sell privately. With advancing years Lord Hertford was becoming more and more of a recluse. It was a long time since he had travelled even as far as England. When he went on his visits to the antique dealers in the streets adjoining the rue Drouot he was always accompanied by the younger man. Wallace was shorter and less forbidding-looking, but both men followed the fashion set by the emperor and had moustaches and small beards. Often there was a third Englishman with them, Colonel Claremont, who had been Military Attaché at the British Embassy since 1855. After 1860 the marquess was reluctant even to visit Paris and remained invisible at Bagatelle. Wallace dealt tactfully with requests to see him or his pictures. Since the Manchester Art Treasures Exhibition there had been an increasing number of requests to visit the collection and a few privileged people in England had been authorised to visit the house in Manchester Square. A carefully selected few were also given permission to see some of the treasures at the rue Laffitte and Wallace would always accompany them. One of these few was Sir Charles Eastlake, director of the National Gallery and President of the Royal Academy in London. We are indebted to Lady Eastlake, who accompanied him, for a charming description of Richard Wallace which she wrote in her diary after the visit:

He took us into an entresol of the tiniest dimensions, looking out on the noisiest part of the boulevard. There Lord Hertford lived for thirty-six years, thinking it a bore to move into his present gorgeous apartments. He made us sit down, with an easel before us, and handed us up a succession of small pictures of great value, which were piled on the floor. I am sure we saw what would fetch £50,000 at Christie's. The young man was most kind, and worked as hard as a drayman lifting heavy frames for our gratification.

It was not the first time Lady Eastlake had met Wallace. She had seen him three years before in Hanover where she had gone with Sir Charles to attend the Stolberg sale. Sir Charles Eastlake was hoping to be able to acquire for the National Gallery two Ruisdaels which he had very much wanted for a long time. When he saw Wallace at the sale he was afraid that Lord Hertford wanted the pictures too and had sent Wallace to bid for them. Lord Hertford would be able to pay more than the National Gallery could afford. But Wallace did not bid for them, and Sir Charles secured them for the National Gallery. It is interesting that Lady Eastlake, who also recorded this incident in her diary, twice called Wallace Lord Hertford's son. To what extent the relationship was generally assumed we do not know, but Lady Eastlake certainly seems to have believed it.

Only the emperor could tempt the marquess out of his self-imposed seclusion. Napoleon III must genuinely have liked this aristocratic if eccentric Englishman. The empress too must have forgiven him for having been a friend of Miss Howard because she numbered him among the closest friends who were invited to the informal weekend parties at Compiègne. With the help of Prosper Mérimée, she went to great trouble to bring a note of gaiety to these occasions. One evening after dinner the Duke of Atholl and his sons danced reels to the music of their own piper. Mérimée was shocked by the savage music and the naked knees in the drawing-room. Jokes at the expense of other guests were not forbidden. One night Mérimée and Morny acted a little sketch which the former had written in which they poked fun at Lord Hertford for 'having a vast fortune and never spending it, beautiful houses in England and never visiting them, fine pictures and never showing them: he is content with a bagatelle'. Lord Hertford was not amused and had to be placated.

Whatever was the basis of Napoleon III's friendship with Lord Hertford, it certainly was not a common love of painting. Maxime du Camp tells an amusing story about the emperor paying an official visit to the Salon the day before it was opened. The Duc de Morny, as president of the jury, conducted him round the exhibition, followed at a respectful distance by the other members of the jury. The best pictures had been hung in the first rooms, but the emperor seemed not to notice them and walked quickly through one room after another without saying a word. Finally he stopped before a very bad picture consisting of a series of white triangles supposed to represent Mont Blanc rising above the other Alpine peaks. He remained a long time in silence, then turning to Morny said that the painter ought to have indicated for comparison the heights of the different peaks. After which 'bonne reflexion', he left.

Napoleon III was a frequent visitor to Bagatelle. Indeed, he arranged for the little Prince Imperial to have his first riding lessons in the paddock where the rose garden is today. Lord Hertford had a kiosk built for the empress to sit in while she watched the little prince trotting round on his pony, and this still stands on the slope overlooking the rose garden.

Chapter Ten

THE YEAR 1865 WAS EXCEEDINGLY IMPORTANT. It started very much as Mérimée had been bold enough, even in jest, to point out, with Lord Hertford continuing to spend a fortune to add to his very large collection of pictures that nobody ever saw. In the short space of two months and a few days Lord Hertford bought thirty-four pictures for a total of 937,620 francs and nearly all of them were major acquisitions. This great burst of purchasing began on 25 March at the sale of the Comte de Pourtalès, where he bought twelve paintings, including one that has since become one of the most famous and popular pictures in the world – *The Laughing Cavalier* by Frans Hals. It cost him 51,000 francs and everyone thought it was a mad millionaire's folly because, although Frans Hals had had a certain success in his lifetime, his pictures had never been greatly admired since his death. *The Laughing Cavalier* had only fetched the equivalent of £15 when it had been sold in 1774. Seventy years later two other portraits by Frans Hals had been sold at the Stowe sale for the derisory sums of seven guineas and eleven pounds and sixpence. Lord Hertford knew all this, but he wanted the painting and was prepared to pay for it even if it was to cost him more than £2,000. It is one of the best examples of Lord Hertford's complete contempt for other people's opinions. When he bought the picture it was called *Portrait d'homme vu a mi-corps*. It was not until after Lord Hertford's death that the picture was given its present name.

At the Prince de Beauvau sale on 21 April Lord Hertford restrained himself and bought only one picture, a Greuze. But he made up for this by buying for 31,900 francs a unique red jasper perfume-burner, mounted in gilt bronze, by Gouthière, which had once belonged to Marie Antoinette.

In May he broke all records with his purchases. At the Baron von Brienen van Grotteslindt sale on 8 and 9 May he bought six pictures including a Rubens, a Hobbema and a Van de Velde. On the last day of May at the Duc de Morny sale he bought fifteen more pictures. Among these were two Fragonards, a Watteau, a Greuze, four Guardis and two Meissoniers. It is interesting to note that then he had to pay more for each Meissonier than for any one of the four Guardis. After this great burst of buying it was presumably Wallace's task to solve the ever more acute problem of where to hang, or store, these new acquisitions.

Prosper Mérimée's little joke about Lord Hertford's large collection of pictures that nobody ever saw was not to remain true for much longer. Eight years had passed since the English had been allowed to see at Manchester some of Lord Hertford's paintings, brought out for the occasion from the great empty house in Manchester Square. Now it was to be the turn of the French to see an unrivalled collection of furniture, tapestries, sculpture, bronzes, porcelain, clocks, covering the whole range of the decorative arts in eighteenth-century France, that had been hidden for years in his houses in France.

An exhibition, conceived specifically to sponsor the decorative arts and called the Musée Rétrospectif, was to be held in the Palais de l'Industrie. A few days after the opening on 10 August 1865 Napoleon III offered to lend his large collection, some five hundred items, of arms and armour and the committee naturally accepted this royal loan. Lord Hertford was one of the first to go to see the emperor's armour after it had been put on display and it appears that he came away so impressed with the exhibition and the admirable manner in which it had been arranged that, forgetting about the damp in Manchester, he offered to lend a large part of his own collection. As at Manchester, he made it a condition that he should have a separate gallery, and once again he was granted this privilege. The committee must have acted quickly because the new gallery containing Lord Hertford's loan was open to the public by the middle of September. It added greatly to the success of the exhibition, which instead of closing in early October remained open until the end of November.

One glance at the catalogue shows that Lord Hertford's insistence that he should be given a gallery to himself was fully justified.

Three hundred and eighty items are listed and it is difficult to imagine how this fantastically rich collection could have been put on display otherwise. There were sixteen tapestries which, of course, demanded considerable wall-space, twenty-five pieces of sculpture and thirty-six items of furniture, some bulky. There were ninety-seven separate pieces of Sèvres porcelain, eleven clocks and many bronzes. Finally, not to be outdone by the emperor perhaps, he included no less than 249 items of oriental armour.

Léopold Double was the only other exhibitor to be given a gallery to himself and he also was showing French eighteenth-century furniture and decorative objects. His collection, although similar to Lord Hertford's and of excellent quality, was much smaller.

Lord Hertford's and Monsieur Double's collections were the only exhibits from the eighteenth century. The remainder of the more than six thousand objects displayed were of the Renaissance or even earlier dates. This shows that in his passion for French eighteenth-century art Lord Hertford had been and still was far in advance of the other collectors. The French Rothschilds, for example, whose contributions to the exhibition were particularly large, sent no single piece of Sèvres. The Second Empire's rich bankers and industrialists had scarcely begun to admire and buy eighteenth-century works of art. That was to come. For years Lord Hertford had been almost alone in this field and the richness of his exhibits was as staggering then as it is today.

Most fortunately for us there exist photographs of Lord Hertford's gallery in the Musée Rétrospectif and this has made it possible to identify for the first time many objects which are in the Wallace Collection today. They also enable us to know with certainty which objects were acquired by Lord Hertford before 1865. Without the photographs this would have been impossible because, in many cases, the brief descriptions in the catalogue could apply equally to several of the pieces of furniture. It is now clear that Lord Hertford already possessed most of his finest pieces of furniture before 1865. We can see also that he sent the jasper perfume-burner that he had only bought in April. Another intriguing aspect of the photographs is that they show us objects which are *not* in the Wallace Collection today. Not one of the tapestries, nine pieces of sculpture, six of the clocks, or many important pieces of furniture, bronzes and Sèvres porcelain, are in Manchester Square. These remained at Bagatelle and in the rue Laffitte when, after Lord Hertford's death, part of his collection was moved to London.

Surprisingly, Lord Hertford also collected oriental armour. He must have been considerably influenced by the Orientalist movement that followed the French conquests in North Africa and which sent romantic painters and writers such as Delacroix and Flaubert to North Africa and Egypt in search of inspiration. We know that at this time he bought many paintings of Arab scenes by Decamps and Horace Vernet, as well as pictures of Egypt by Prosper Marilhat. But until the Musée Rétrospectif it was not known that he had been buying pieces of oriental armour for their elaborate and often sumptuous decoration. One of the pieces he sent to the exhibition was a large ceremonial elephant-cloth of red material, entirely embroidered with gold thread. It gave rise later to the story, completely false, that he kept an elephant at Bagatelle.

Public interest in the exhibition was so great that an enterprising composer from Strasbourg, who was fortunate enough to be named Strauss but had no connection with the famous Viennese family, published a set of dances dedicated to the principal lenders to the exhibition. Among these was a waltz entitled 'L'Idéal' dedicated to Lord Hertford. On the cover to the music were illustrations of a number of Lord Hertford's exhibits. In the centre stood the superb Sèvres inkstand, given by Louis XV to his third daughter, Adelaide, which is in the Wallace Collection today. The composer artfully arranged for his name, Strauss, without his telltale first name Isadore, to be printed in large letters on the cover also. Thus many people must have been misled into thinking it was a genuine Strauss waltz.

The sheer size and variety of Lord Hertford's loan to the Musée Rétrospectif, as well as the superb, unsurpassed quality of each object, came as a staggering surprise to collectors in 1865. It was no secret any longer that Lord Hertford was rich enough to spend vast sums of money every year buying works of art from all over Europe. However much he may have deluded himself, he was known both in London and Paris to be one of the leading collectors in Europe. The Manchester exhibition had revealed his taste in painting and the remarkable quality of his collection. Now the Musée Rétrospectif established him as an expert and connoisseur of every aspect of French eighteenth-century decorative art. Apart from a fondness for Sèvres porcelain, nobody knew much about his taste in other fields until that autumn in Paris. The quality and size of his collection of furniture came as a revelation. Indeed, every work of art that he exhibited at the Musée Rétrospectif showed that Lord Hertford was not only a man of almost unlimited financial resources, but also a passionate and deeply informed collector.

We know that Lord Hertford was by nature secretive, and in making his purchases everything was carried out with the greatest discretion. He had a remarkable memory for any picture or piece of furniture he had once seen and it was difficult to deceive him. He knew all the ways in which furniture could be made to look older than it really was. In May 1853 he sent Mawson a list of items in the catalogue of the Duchess of Bedford's sale which he wanted him to examine 'carefully', adding: 'I should like to know if they are *old* or whether they are imitations or made up half new and half old, as is so often the case here, and I dare say in London also.'

If Mawson's impression was good he was asked to send a 'word' by the telegraph – '*yes* if you approve and *no* if you do not' – no need for lengthy descriptions.

Lord Hertford did not despise modern methods. He must have been one of the first collectors to use photographs which were sent him by the auctioneers and salerooms. In another letter written in 1861 we see how his quick eye could detect the difference between good and bad craftsmanship, even in the imperfect photographs of those days. Mawson had told him about some Sèvres vases and a piece of furniture which were coming up for sale in London. Lord Hertford had already received photographs of these objects and had not been long in making up his mind.

I do not much like the shape of the Louis XVI secretaire [Mawson was told]. They make up these sort of things so *admirably* now that it is very difficult to make out whether they are *pure* and *all* old or not. When one knows where they come from, one can, to a certain degree, be guided, but when the contrary is the case, as far as I am concerned, unless I can *see* the Article *myself*, I am not inclined to purchase, although you know I have a very high opinion of your taste and judgement.

A week later, after the sale, he wrote with undisguised triumph to Mawson: 'You see, the china did not sell well, – indeed it appears the vases were not sold at all – I had some doubts about them – as for the little secretaire, if it had been good, it would have fetched a thousand.'

Clearly it is not an accident that his collection contained so many superb pieces from Versailles or Fontainebleau. He bought them deliberately because he knew that they had once belonged to members of the royal family, and that they therefore had been made by the greatest craftsmen of the time.

In the same year that he refused the Sèvres and the secretaire in London, his flair for good craftsmanship enabled him to buy from a dealer in scrap-iron perhaps his most extraordinary and unique acquisition. It was a magnificent balustrade, twenty-five metres long, of forged-iron and bronze, chased and gilt, which had been made between 1733 and 1741 for the staircase leading up to Louis XV's Cabinet des Médailles in the Palais Mazarin. In the centre of each large panel are the interlaced Ls, the monogram of Louis XV, and sunflowers, the emblem of the kings of France. The Palais Mazarin was pulled down between 1855 and 1862 to be rebuilt as the Bibliothèque Nationale, and the balustrade was sold as scrap-iron when the staircase was demolished. Having bought it, Lord Hertford never did anything with it and it must have presented Wallace with another unusually difficult storage problem. Wherever it was kept, probably in Lord Henry Seymour's old stables, it remained unseen until Wallace brought it to England after Lord Hertford's death. Today it forms the balustrade on the Grand Staircase at Hertford House, and is the finest surviving example of French forged-iron and bronze work of that date.

When it came to buying paintings, Mawson appears to have had Lord Hertford's complete confidence because he was authorised to buy pictures Lord Hertford had never seen. But the letters to him are full of the oft-repeated question 'Is it really good?' He had to be sure that it was a really 'fine work'.

'I do not much like buying pictures that I do not know by sight, but I have the greatest confidence in your taste and judgement,' he wrote about a Wilkie.

When the famous Lancret, *The Italian Comedians by a Fountain*, came up for sale, even though he knew the picture and was determined to have it at any price, he still wanted to be sure.

'Without of course mentioning me,' Mawson was told, 'try to have a look at the Lancret, and tell me what state it is in – I remember it but imperfectly.'

It was only after serious reflection that the decision to buy a picture or a piece of furniture was made. His taste in pictures was both conventional and original for his time. His purchases of Rubens, Murillo, Rembrandt, Hobbema, Domenichino and Salvator Rosa, together with the English portrait painters Reynolds, Gainsborough, Hoppner and Lawrence, represented the taste of an aristocratic English collector of the day. His originality was in his love for the French eighteenth-century painters. The Revolution, followed by the First Empire's craze for the Pompeian, had killed the taste for painters such as Fragonard, Boucher, Nattier, Watteau, Lancret, Pater and the earlier Greuze. Lord Hertford had been almost alone – certainly the only Englishman – in his enthusiasm for these painters. In England the taste for French eighteenth-century furniture and Sèvres porcelain had survived. His father had bought both. Of the painters of the same period, only Greuze was admired in England. His heads of young women in anguish pleased early Victorian taste. Lord Hertford had bought several, but at the same time he also bought Fragonard, Watteau and Boucher when nobody wanted them and prices were low. As we have seen, he bought his first Fragonard for 385 francs in 1841. He had to pay more than 30,000 francs for each of the two Fragonards he bought at the Duc de Morny sale in 1865, the year of the Musée Rétrospectif.

When buying contemporary nineteenth-century French painters Lord Hertford favoured the Romantics, buying paintings by Delacroix and his English friend Bonington, whom he greatly admired. In England he bought Wilkie and Landseer. He was of the generation that admired pictures more for the subject and sentiment than for the manner of their execution. He told Mawson that he liked 'pleasing pictures', meaning pleasing subjects.

'I do not much like the portrait of an old man, however fine it may be; it is not pleasing.'

He once refused a Greuze that a man was pressing him to buy because it was sad. He told the owner he knew the picture and it merited all he said about it. 'It is very fine,' he admitted, 'but I don't like the subject which is extremely sad and it is this reason alone that prevents me from buying it.'

His memory for pictures was infallible. He also told the owner of the Greuze who wanted him to go to see it: 'I think it is impossible that I can have made a mistake – this Madeleine is naked and there is a lion in the background.' If by any chance the picture did not correspond to this description, he would go to see it.

Saintly, bearded figures fasting in the wilderness were not for him: nor were the Primitives. Nor did he ever buy a picture by an Impressionist painter. It is often asked why he did not, and therefore whether he was as discerning as he is said to have been. The question is a false one because the word Impressionist was not invented until four years after Lord Hertford's death and the Impressionist group of painters did not exist in his lifetime. However, because Manet, Pissarro and Renoir were exhibiting their work in the sixties it is necessary to examine the facts.

He must have known about Manet, the best-known of the three, and he would almost certainly have seen some of his work. Manet was for a time a pupil of Thomas Couture, whose work Lord Hertford admired so much that he bought at least five, if not seven, of his pictures. The scandal over Manet's revolutionary style of painting first began in 1863 when he sent *Le Déjeuner sur l'herbe* to the Salon where it was refused by the jury together with nearly three thousand other canvases. To calm the outcry that the refusal of so many canvases had provoked, Napoleon III hurriedly instituted the famous Salon des Refusés, hoping that the public would confirm the verdict of the jury of the official Salon. It attracted 7,000 visitors on the first day, which was not at all what the emperor had hoped, so the art critics were left to attack these painters.

Here *Le Déjeuner sur l'herbe* was first shown to the public and provoked a storm of abuse. The picture at that time was called *Le Bain*. Napoleon III thought it was indecent, a view that was also held by the large majority of the general public, and there is a story, with many variations, that when he saw it he struck it with his riding whip. The critics attacked the painting for its unorthodox technique as well as for the indecency of the subject. The naked woman, in no way idealised, with the fixed stare straight at the viewer was too close to reality. Nudes were supposed to have their eyes modestly averted.

Lord Hertford would almost certainly have agreed with the emperor and the critics, although neither man had anything against nudes. In fact, at the official Salon that very year Napoleon III had bought a seductive nude, *The Birth of Venus* by Cabanel. It is more interesting to note that at the same time as the two Salons, official and unofficial, were open in Paris, Lord Hertford bought in London four watercolours by Turner, the painter who was anticipating the Impressionists.

Two years later, the year of the Musée Rétrospectif, Manet caused another scandal. This time it was at the official Salon for, after a very much smaller Salon des Refusés in 1864, the emperor had not repeated the experiment. In 1865 Manet was exhibiting his most famous nude, *Olympia*, and the outcry was for the same reasons. The realism, the fixed stare and the revolutionary painting offended the public.

Lord Hertford must have seen the early paintings of Pissarro and Renoir at the Salons, and if he went to the first Salon des Refusés in 1863, he could have seen a painting by Cézanne too, but it was not mentioned in the catalogue. Both Pissarro and Renoir were regular exhibitors in the early sixties, but they had hardly begun to adopt the Impressionist technique. He therefore cannot be blamed for not buying Impressionists, since he never saw Impressionist painting as we know it today.

However, it must also be remembered that he did not buy Millet, either. Millet, the ultranaturalist, became as popular in England as Meissonier. Lord Hertford must have known his work because Millet had been exhibiting at the Salon for years. Curiously enough, the same year as the jury refused Manet's *Le Déjeuner sur l'herbe* they accepted one of Millet's most controversial pictures, the famous *Man with a Hoe* (*L'Homme à la houe*) which aroused a storm of criticism.

Lord Hertford was not alone if he considered that Millet's peasants labouring in the fields in sabots were not at all pleasing subjects. Another of his famous pictures, *L'Angelus*, which became one of the most expensive pictures of all time, had been sold in 1859 for 100 francs. It was not the sort of picture that Lord Hertford could ever have admired. He preferred his Meissoniers and if he had ever heard Degas' sneer 'Everything is in steel, except the breastplates' ('Tout est en acier, excepté les cuirasses'), he would not have cared.

Chapter Eleven

LORD HERTFORD WAS NOW SIXTY-FIVE and, although for nearly all his life he had lived in the very centre of the busiest part of the boulevard, the part known today as the boulevard des Italiens, so successfully had he hidden himself from the public eye that all that Paris society, which crowded the fashionable cafés and restaurants on his very doorstep, knew about him was that he was immensely rich and supposed to be excessively mean with money. It is typical that he never sat for his portrait.

He was very different from his brother, Lord Henry Seymour, the sportsman-dandy, who had been a famous figure on the boulevard with his sensational waistcoats and enormous ties knotted with infinite care. Although he was also a member of the Jockey Club Lord Hertford was never to be seen with those noisy sportsmen, nor did he have his table at the Café de Paris. He had always preferred the respectable atmosphere of the Union, favoured by the diplomatic corps, for his card-playing and gambling. He was not, however, antisocial. He had been the friend of successive British ambassadors, and now as a close friend of the emperor was invited to all the official ceremonies and receptions. After all, as a marquess he must have ranked as the senior British resident in Paris quite apart from the fact that he had probably lived there longer than any other Englishman. His large, impressive, quietly dressed and rather sombre figure was well known on the boulevard, but he had never tried to cut a dash with the snobbish members of the Jockey or the literary lions that gathered at the Café de Paris under his mother's windows or Tortoni's on the opposite corner. His distant reserve has been interpreted in different ways by different people at different times, in most cases to his disadvantage. His contemporaries judged him harshly. In England his friends in politics never forgave him for preferring to live in France when, with his wealth and title, he could have played a leading role in Conservative Party politics. In Ireland his tenants had not forgotten the promises he had made to them on his one and only visit. To them now he had become another typical absentee landlord interested only in the rents which they paid him, which were one of the main sources of his wealth. His attitude to them was one of complete indifference. In France his friendship with the emperor was well known and earned him respect, but when, as he got older, he chose to live more and more at Bagatelle and was not seen in Paris for long periods, a legend of eccentricity built up around him.

The Goncourts wrote of his avarice in their *Journal* and said he never invited anyone to dinner. They tell of an unfortunate man who arrived at lunchtime and was given only one cutlet. Doctor Phillips, Lord Hertford's doctor, they say, was told he was lucky when all he got was some *bouillon* after driving out to Bagatelle to see his patient. They are also the authorities for the terrifyingly cynical saying attributed to Lord Hertford: 'Men are evil and when I die I shall at least have the consolation of never having rendered anyone a service.'

Bernard Falk, his biographer, is wholeheartedly convinced that he was essentially selfish and heartless. 'He was a mean and selfish man' is a typical comment.

On the other hand, his friend Charles Yriarte, the art critic who later became Inspecteur-Général des Beaux Arts, wrote after Lord Hertford's death that he was good company, an amusing storyteller, witty and well-read. He maintains that his cynicism was a pose and that his few close friends knew this. His personal tastes, according to Yriarte, forced him to be withdrawn and reserved, although when in society he was always excessively polite and correct. Yriarte also says, however, that he was so indifferent to other people and events that 'he wouldn't even have bothered to draw his curtains to see a revolution in the road outside his windows'. Another story tells how when he was asked if he would allow two acquaintances to fight a duel in the park at Bagatelle he replied he did not care if the two men wanted to shoot each other but he was not going to risk his precious statues.

He can certainly be charged with heartlessness in his behaviour to Mademoiselle Bréart. The promise of marriage and the mock wedding ceremony in London are almost unbelievable pieces of deception, and one can be forgiven for wondering if Lord Hertford had any feelings at all. Nevertheless, she did not leave him and as Madame Oger she bore him a daughter. Nor did he fail to make provision for the child.

The answer is surely that, despite the many women in his life, Lord Hertford's emotions were stirred by only one woman, his mother. His devotion to Mie-Mie was sincere and deep and lasted until she died. All his letters to her from the age of sixteen, when he was sent to a tutor in England, until the melancholy, mawkish notes he wrote to himself after her death as if to record for ever his uncontrollable feelings of grief, testify to this curious strain of sentimentality for his mother alone.

He did not avoid women, but it seems he was never emotionally involved. He was a social success and in his youth, like his father, he had been a great dancer. He had many affairs, starting from his days in Regency England and continuing into the opulent, pleasure-loving Second Empire. The Comtesse de Castiglione, the ravishing Italian whom Victor Emmanuel and Cavour sent to Paris in 1856 to seduce Napoleon III, has left in her diary a fascinating picture of how Lord Hertford behaved with women. He was very polite and correct, she says, was attracted by women and showed it. But it was not for love. Although she called him a mean, stingey man she said his money was the cause of his success with women. She did not find him attractive, if anything she thought he was ugly.

'His appearance is rather gloomy, almost sinister, and he flashes his eyes, like the tyrant in a melodrama' ('... il roule les yeux furibonds, comme un tyran de melodrame').

Despite all this wild rolling of eyes, after her liaison with the emperor had ended she was certainly his mistress and glad to take his money, which she needed badly. There is a legend that he gave her a million francs for the pleasure of one night during which she promised every known form of *volupté*. There is no evidence to support this legend, or the story that afterwards she spent three days in bed.

Disdainful of humanity, he spent his last years in almost total seclusion at Bagatelle. But his unflagging passion for collecting never died. It drove him to go on buying far more furniture, paintings and other works of art than he could ever use, need or even see to admire. In the end it was his only reason for having any contact with the world beyond the walls of Bagatelle.

His increasing ill-health is not sufficient explanation of his desire to remain aloof. In good health or bad it had always been a part of his enigmatic character and became the dominant element from middle age onwards. His contemporaries in France tried to explain it away by calling it eccentricity, but there was never the slightest thing odd about Lord Hertford's behaviour. Everything he ever did and everything surrounding him was extremely correct and formal. The explanation is probably that he was a mental and spiritual dandy, although not a beau or a dandy in way of dressing. In his study of dandyism the French writer Barbey d'Aurevilly, who was living in Paris at the same time as Lord Hertford, gives the clue. Although with the dandy, he says, the accent is often on dress, he is in fact an intellectual, not a physical, being. His indifference to and superiority over the visible world can be expressed by a look. He is an artist. Beau Brummell's work of art was himself. Always withdrawn, distant, dandies were masters of themselves, drunk or sober. They never dared to show enthusiasm for fear of an involvement which would make them inferior. To sum up, Barbey d'Aurevilly says: 'Dandyism is the product of a society which is bored, and being bored does not make anyone pleasant.'

Lord Hertford was no exception. On the rare occasions that he came to Paris he was a spectator, even a *voyeur*. As Gaston Jollivet records in his memoirs of the late sixties, when he and his young friends took dancers and actresses to supper at the Maison Dorée, they could never get the waiters to draw the curtains of the windows of their favourite private dining-room. The rascals had been handsomely paid by Lord Hertford whose shadowy figure could be seen at the opposite window of No. 2 rue Laffitte, peering through opera-glasses at their amorous revels. Jollivet calls Lord Hertford the 'richissisme anglais neurasthénique'.

If Beau Brummell's work of art was himself, then Lord Hertford's was his collection, and this was the secret of the man whom all Paris knew of but few people knew. It was the dandy in him that drove him to avoid close contacts and to refuse all but the very best. It also perhaps goes a long way to explain his love for French eighteenth-century painting which, to quote M. Pierre Rosenberg, Conservateur at the Louvre: '... avoided the unpleasant sights of daily life, in itself not very tempting, not by prudishness, far from it, but by good taste. All suffering was concealed, not because it did not exist, but from fear that its revelation would be indecent and cause embarrassment.'

Lord Hertford's health was failing, but the collecting did not stop even when he was bedridden. In the year 1867 a second Exposition Universelle was organised in Paris, larger and more splendid than that of 1855, which had been the occasion for Queen Victoria's famous visit to Napoleon III. This time it was the Prince of Wales who came from England, and the kings of Portugal, Sweden, Norway and the Belgians also made the journey to Paris.

For the benefit of visitors to the Exposition a two-volume guidebook was published called *Paris-Guide*. In the first volume, devoted to Science and Art, there was a long and important description by the art critic William Bürger of the private collections of pictures in Paris. Although he was not French, Lord Hertford had pride of place, his collection being described before all the French collections.

'The greatest collector in Europe is without doubt Lord Hertford,' wrote Bürger by way of introduction to his article describing in detail the pictures at the rue Laffitte.

Bürger was no stranger to Lord Hertford's collections. He had been one of the privileged few who had been allowed to visit the house in Manchester Square in London, and he starts his article by recalling what he saw there.

'Velasquez and Murillo, Titian and Andrea del Sarto, Claude and Poussin, Greuze and Watteau, Reynolds and Gainsborough, Rubens and Van Dyck, Ruisdael and Hobbema, Terborch and Metsu, Van Ostade and Van de Velde, Cuyp and Wouwermans and Rembrandt.

'Ah, what pictures; all first class,' he exclaims and then adds that he never saw the other palaces and castles 'à Londres and dans le country [*sic*]' which he seems to have believed contained other masterpieces belonging to Lord Hertford which he had not seen.

Bürger goes on to describe what he saw inside No. 2 rue Laffitte, and it is the first description we have of what it contained. Unfortunately, Bürger was interested only in pictures and tells us nothing about the furniture, sculpture, tapestries, bronzes and clocks that he must also have seen.

'In Paris', Bürger says, Lord Hertford has 'more than anything else modern French, old French, Dutch, some Flemish, some Spanish and some English'. The last he describes as 'almost nothing, worth only four or five millions'. Two hundred and fifty paintings were hung in the gallery and the rooms on the first floor, not counting pictures which were all over the house waiting to be hung in a new gallery under construction. Among the paintings which were hung he counted seventeen Decamps, ten Meissoniers, twenty-five Horace Vernets, eight Greuzes, eight Paters, ten Bouchers, six Weenix, four Willem van de Veldes and three Paulus Potters.

When he reached Lord Hertford's bedroom, where for the first time he noticed furniture, Bürger says there was a magnificent bed with a Reynolds portrait on one side and on the other a Greuze painting of a 'jeune fille' with her elbows on a cushion, in a white dress and wearing a feathered hat. This could have been what is believed to be a portrait of the actress Sophie Arnould, of whom Lord Hertford also possessed a bust by Houdon which is now in the Louvre. There were also some Bouchers in the bedroom and a collection of more than two hundred miniatures.

It was in a rotunda which formed the angle of the rue Laffitte and the boulevard that Lord Hertford had hung his favourite masterpieces, notably four Bouchers, which were let into the wall, the Frans Hals *Laughing Cavalier*, a Murillo *Madonna*, a Rubens portrait, a Hobbema, three Greuzes, two Willem van de Veldes, a Watteau, a Prud'hon and a Bonington.

Leading out of the rotunda was the library and 'salon after salon containing furniture and ornaments', and that is all that Bürger has to say on the rest of the collection.

There were several important collections in Paris during the Second Empire. The Duc de Morny, half-brother of the emperor, owned one of the largest but it had been dispersed after his death in 1865. Lord Hertford bought fifteen of his pictures at the sale, including two Fragonards, a Watteau, a Greuze, four Guardis and two Meissoniers. Others had been built up in the last ten years, mostly by French bankers and industrialists, and a few rich foreigners. These collectors owned so many pictures that their houses were, in effect, private museums. Since their pictures were too numerous to be hung in the living-rooms it was the custom of the time to hang them in specially constructed galleries, some even with glass roofs for lighting. The fashion was to hang the pictures in massive gold decorated frames in several rows, one above the other, and so close together that the walls were completely covered. Thick carpets, red velvet, gold decorations and the inevitable palm trees in pots gave a stifling impression of luxury and opulence in these galleries. François Delessert, who lived in a vast house in the rue Montmartre, had a printed catalogue of his 236 pictures which was distributed to visitors and anyone interested.

According to Bürger these collectors preferred Dutch seventeenth-century pictures above all else. Sombre pictures were much esteemed and the yellow-brown Dutch varnish had the effect of making a bad picture look almost like a masterpiece. But all the pictures noted by Bürger were true museum-pieces.

The collection of Baron James de Rothschild was particularly rich in paintings of the Dutch School. It contained examples of Hobbema, Ruisdael, Rembrandt, Frans Hals, Pieter de Hooch, Van de Velde. He also owned a Velasquez, a Luini, a Delaroche and a celebrated triptych by Van Eyck which is now in the Frick Collection in New York. Baron Nathaniel de Rothschild owned Italian pictures as well as the fashionable Dutch. Baron James's son Alphonse, who lived in the Hôtel Talleyrand, owned a Watteau and a Greuze, according to Bürger. Ten Rembrandts were to be seen in the rue de Varenne at the house of the Baron Seillières, as well as Ingres's famous *La Grande Odalisque* which is today in the Louvre. The Count Mnizech owned twelve paintings by Frans Hals.

In the rue de Faubourg St Honoré the Pereire brothers owned so many pictures that they had built on to their house a private museum. There were several galleries and the principal one had a glass roof. They had, of course, a large collection of fine Dutch pictures, but they also had eighteenth-century French pictures, modern French pictures – Delacroix, Léopold Robert, Decamps and Meissonier – and some Spanish painters.

Apart from Lord Hertford's collection, the largest and the most interesting one, in that it was really rich in French eighteenth-century paintings, belonged to Dr La Caze, who lived in the rue du Cherche-Midi.

'It's a museum,' exclaims Bürger as he starts to describe the pictures of all schools. Among the French eighteenth-century painters he lists Watteau, Lancret, Pater, Chardin, Boucher, Fragonard, Greuze, Prud'hon. He raves about the famous *Gilles* by Watteau, now in the Louvre. 'Thirty years ago', he says, 'painting of the eighteenth-century French school was relegated to the pavement outside junk shops, today it is the basis of several distinguished collections.'

The *Gilles*, probably Watteau's best-known picture, was bought shortly after the Revolution for 150 francs by Denon, who was Napoleon's Ministre de Beaux Arts. When he died in 1826 his nephew bought it for 650 francs and sold it a few years later for 1,200 francs to the Marquis de Cypierre. When the marquis died La Caze paid 1,600 francs for it at his sale in 1845. Before the picture went to the Louvre in 1869 La Caze said that he had refused an offer of 300,000 francs from an English collector. He did not name the would-be purchaser, but one cannot help wondering whether it was Lord Hertford. It is an interesting example of the rise in prices of French eighteenth-century painting after it had been rescued from oblivion by men like Lord Hertford and Dr La Caze. When Dr La Caze died he left 272 pictures to the Louvre and 310 to museums in the provinces. Not all were eighteenth-century French, but the Louvre at that time had practically nothing and without his bequest it would today be very poor in painters like Chardin, Fragonard, Watteau, Van Loo and Boucher.

Lord Hertford is referred to again, this time for his collection of armour, in another article in the same volume of the *Paris-Guide* by Albert Jacquemart entitled 'Les Collections d'Art'.

It was very seldom that Lord Hertford's health permitted him to leave Bagatelle. In July 1869 the Goncourts noted in their *Journal* that they had been told by Dr Phillips that he was dying from a particularly painful form of cancer which the 'archimillionaire anglais' had borne for nine years with extraordinary vitality and courage. 'Whether it is for love of money or sheer eccentricity, what an unusual miser is this Lord Hertford,' was their comment. Nevertheless, he continued to buy pictures and that same year he added another Watteau, another Pater and another Bonington to his collection. The sale catalogues were scrutinised as carefully as ever and Richard Wallace, who never left him, passed on his orders to his agents. He decided to engage a secretary to help him with the day-to-day business arising from the Collection and Lord Hertford's property in France and England. His choice was a young man of twenty-four named John Murray Scott, whom he knew because his father was an English doctor living in Boulogne-sur-Seine, not far from Bagatelle. Dr Scott had on occasions been summoned to Bagatelle to treat Lord Hertford when he had bad attacks of asthma, and he had become almost a friend.

Chapter Twelve

THEN CAME THE FATEFUL YEAR of 1870, which was to spell defeat for France on the battlefield and resulted in the collapse of the Second Empire. All that summer the storm-clouds were gathering. When a Hohenzollern prince was put forward as a candidate for the Spanish throne the quarrel with Prussia came to a head. France obtained the withdrawal of the prince's candidature, but Napoleon III wanted an assurance that it would never happen again. King Wilhelm of Prussia tried to ignore the French request when it was submitted to him by the French ambassador, but Bismarck used the occasion to provoke French feelings with the famous manipulated Ems telegram, which falsely presented to the world the encounter between the king and the French ambassador as having been insulting to the ambassador and France. The result was an outburst of anti-Prussian feeling from one end of France to the other. The emperor could not ignore the clamour, and on 19 July France declared war. Nine days later, accompanied by the fourteen-year-old Prince Imperial and a numerous suite, he left to command his armies at the front from the private railway station at Saint Cloud. The emperor, who was ill and often in such pain that he could hardly sit on his horse, was never to return to Paris. The empress, who has been unjustly blamed for pushing Napoleon III into this disastrous war, remained behind as regent.

Across the Seine at Bagatelle Lord Hertford was getting weaker every day. Earlier in the year he had had the strength to add two more Meissoniers to his collection and in April he had bought five pictures at the San Donato sale. A sixth was the famous Greuze *Les Oeufs Cassés*, for which he paid a record price of 129,000 francs. Today it is in New York in the Metropolitan Museum as part of the Vanderbilt Bequest. These were probably the last pictures Lord Hertford bought. However, they were not his last purchase. On 27 May, acting on his instructions, Frederick Davis, the London dealer, bought at the Marjoribanks sale at Christie's a Boulle table, and the corner cupboard and secretaire that had been made by Riesener for Marie Antoinette's apartments at Marly. These two superb pieces of royal furniture, almost certainly his last purchase, passed into his London collection and Lord Hertford could never have seen them. As his condition deteriorated, Wallace must have wished he had Lord Hertford back in Paris, but the doctor would not let him be moved, even to the rue Laffitte. If there had ever been any question of going to England when war became inevitable, there was no chance now.

In Paris everyone believed the French army would be in Berlin in fifteen days. The excitement and emotion knew no bounds. Unfortunately, the French were ill-prepared for war. When the emperor arrived in Metz he found confusion and chaos, lack of supplies, disorder and quarrelling. The mobilisation had been badly mishandled and as a result he had only 250,000 men against 500,000 Prussians, supported by another 160,000 soldiers in reserve. The original plan to launch an attack into German territory had to be abandoned.

There were wild celebrations in Paris when a victory was announced. The announcement was an unbelievable mistake, and after this there was nothing but bad news from the front. There were defeats at Wissembourg on 4 August and at Froeschwiller two days later. MacMahon was forced to retreat from Alsace, and in Lorraine Bazaine allowed himself to be surrounded and trapped in Metz.

Wallace tried to keep the bad news from Lord Hertford as he lay dying. The latter had opposed the war from the beginning, sensing that it could only mean disaster for France. His fear for his friend Napoleon III and his uncertainty as to what would happen preyed on his mind and aggravated his condition. On 24 August it was so alarming that Wallace sent word to Edward Blount that the end was near. Blount was an English banker concerned with financing the French railways. He was one of the few Englishmen living in Paris who could claim to be a friend of Lord Hertford.

Edward Blount and Colonel Claremont, the Military Attaché at the Embassy, immediately set out for Bagatelle. The two men had a frightening drive across the Bois de Boulogne where cattle which had been rounded up to provide food for Paris in case of a siege had been left untended. Blount never forgot the drive and he described it in his memoirs:

We drove at considerable risk through the Bois which was full of cattle of every description, nearly starved and maddened by hunger. The park animals, left to take care of themselves, had devoured every species of green stuff, the leaves of the trees, and even the ivy on the walls of the fortification, and thus early in the campaign had become a public danger.

On reaching Bagatelle we found Mr Richard Wallace, who said that his lordship was despaired of. I went directly to the room where Lord Hertford was lying and took his hand. The only persons present were a physician and an elderly lady. He did not know me and died without uttering a word while I was holding his hand.

Wallace, as he himself was to confirm later, was not in the room when Lord Hertford died. The 'elderly lady' mentioned by Blount was certainly Madame Oger.

The heir to the marquessate and all the entailed property was Francis George Hugh Seymour, a second cousin of the late marquess, who had been equerry to the Prince Consort and now held the court appointment of Groom of the Robes. He was fifty-eight and became the 5th Marquess of Hertford. He was at Hampton Court when he received the telegram telling him that Lord Hertford had died in Paris. He went immediately to see Mr Frederick Capron, Lord Hertford's solicitor, and they decided to start at once for Paris.

On their arrival they went first to the British Embassy where Lord Lyons, the ambassador, told them that he believed no will had been found and that the new marquess was therefore heir to everything. From the Embassy they set out for Bagatelle, where they found Richard Wallace and Madame Oger. According to notes written much later in a diary kept by the new marquess and his wife, Emily Mary, both 'professed great indignation at having been passed over. Mr Wallace declared he had nursed him through his long illness like an *infirmier*, and that he had left him nothing; all he had was a small house which Lord Hertford had given him.'

Mr Capron, however, knew that Lord Hertford had made a will and had an idea where it might be found. He pointed to a small table with a drawer which was locked. When the key was found and the drawer opened the will, as he expected, was inside. Wallace was completely surprised by the discovery because only the year before Lord Hertford had sent him to London to fetch the table which had been in the house in Berkeley Square. He had brought it back not guessing what it contained and puzzled that Lord Hertford should want this small table of no particular interest. First it was kept at the rue Laffitte and then later Lord Hertford asked for it to be sent to Bagatelle.

There was an even bigger surprise for Wallace when the will was read and it was discovered that by the codicil made in 1850 the collections and everything that was not entailed had been left to him, Richard, son of Agnes Jackson. It was not such a surprise to the new marquess, according to his wife, who says, again in the diary written more than a year after Lord Hertford's death:

This was of course a blow, tho' not an unexpected one for Lord Hertford had never held out any hopes of the Family inheriting more than the entailed property. What made it galling was the certain amount of deception practised – it was difficult to believe that Mr Wallace and Mme Oget [*sic*] knew nothing of the provisions of the will! The deceased had been insensible for days, and they had everything in their power and in the subsequent trial, Mr Wallace confessed that he knew in which Drawer the Will was kept and the pretended mortification and disappointment were probably feigned.

Lady Hertford in making this last grave charge seems to be giving way to her own feelings of disappointment. As we shall see later, Wallace made no such confession in court during the course of the legal proceedings which were to arise from the will.

As the head of the family the new Lord Hertford had to turn his mind to arrangements for the funeral, which in the midst of the excitement of the war had to be arranged as rapidly as possible. It took place three days later on Saturday, 27 August. There was a service at the English church in the rue d'Aguesseau, opposite the British Embassy, and afterwards Lord Hertford was buried in the family vault at the cemetery of Père Lachaise, beside his mother, Lord Henry Seymour and his sister, the Marquise de Chevigné.

The last journey of Richard Seymour-Conway, 4th Marquess of Hertford, was a long one. After crossing the Bois de Boulogne the funeral procession had great difficulty in getting through the streets of Paris because of the crowds and the barricades which were being hurriedly constructed in preparation for the city's defence. Because of several forced detours the procession was late arriving at the church. Edward Blount had sent his coachmen to round up the British colony, but those of the wealthier English who might have known Lord Hertford had already left Paris and there were very few mourners. Lord Lyons, despite the crisis, came across from the Embassy to attend the service. Apart from the three men from Bagatelle – the new marquess, Richard Wallace and the solicitor – only Edward Blount and Colonel Claremont went to the cemetery.

In Paris, occupied exclusively with the war and the threat of a Prussian advance, the funeral passed unnoticed and as soon as the formalities were concluded, the new marquess went back to England. As Lady Hertford wrote in the diary: 'Franco [her name for her husband] having seen the last duties paid to his Cousin, hurried out of Paris, a longer stay there would have been useless, irksome and dangerous.'

On 2 September she wrote joyfully to her sister with many exclamation marks from the Queen's Hotel, Birmingham, to tell her that her 'dearest man' was safely back and that they were off to inspect Ragley, the Hertford family seat in Warwickshire, which was now theirs.

He is looking very well, thank God! but really all he has told me in his own simple way, is like a sensational novel! and I own I feel proud of him, for he has evidently behaved in such a dignified Christian manner and *he* is worth all the millions in the world!! . . . As far as I can make out we have 3 large empty houses, and *no* nothing [*sic*].

News of Lord Hertford's will spread rapidly and caused a sensation in both Paris and London. The day after the funeral Felix Whitehurst, a member of the English colony in Paris, wrote in his diary:

Lord Hertford died here on Wednesday. He has a house full of works of art in the rue Laffitte – works beyond value. He also owned Bagatelle, a beautiful villa near the race-course in the Bois, which he bought from the Orléans family on 9 October 1835 for £12,524. A few days ago it would have been worth twice as much; but who would buy it now? All his personal property, £50,000 a year, his Irish estates and all the works of art in Paris, are left to a Mr Wallace, a very attentive companion, to whom Lord Hertford had never said 'Thank you' for any service. It was remarked at the Embassy, 'Well he has said "thank you" out loud in his will.' Truly better late than never.

But the members of the Seymour family were not of this opinion and were not prepared to accept the will without a fight. They thought it scandalous that the fortune should pass to anyone but a Seymour. They searched frantically for a later will at Manchester Square as well as at Coutts' bank and 'Hopkinson's' but with no result. Sir George Hamilton Seymour, who under the will as written in 1838 would have inherited the Irish estates, Lord Henry Seymour being dead and having no heirs, rushed to his lawyers, who examined the wording of the codicil that deprived him of the Irish estates and left everything to Wallace. They came to the conclusion that its meaning was not clear and that it could be contested in a court of law. They therefore advised him to take possession of the Irish estates, which he promptly did.

The bitterness felt by all those connected with the Seymour family was well expressed by the Hon. Frederick Dudley Ryder, a son of the Earl of Harrowby, who was one of the executors of the will and to whom, as such, Lord Hertford had left £10,000. Nevertheless, in a letter dated 2 September 1870, he wrote:

It is of no use commenting on the horribly iniquitous alienation of the family property, and of the stripping the houses of all their pictures and furniture. If Mr Wallace has any feeling, he ought to remember this, but, of course, he must first establish his legal rights to enable him to do so. . . .

After having given vent to his feelings in this way he was forced grudgingly to admit later in the letter that the £10,000 he had been left in the will 'is a great easement to me'.

Even Lord Hertford's friend Edward Blount could not believe that this was what he really had intended. In his memoirs he says

Lord Hertford told him he meant to make another will, and much later he says he told Wallace of two people Lord Hertford had intended to mention in his will. Wallace, he says, at once sent the two people £60,000.

Curiously enough, the French also were disappointed. They had expected that Lord Hertford would at least leave something to the Prince Imperial. After all, in 1841 another English collector, Frank Hall Standish, had left his pictures to Louis-Philippe instead of to the National Gallery in London. The real reason, which the French did not know or chose to ignore, was that Lord Melbourne refused to support his claim to a baronetcy. One of Lord Hertford's finest Lancrets and a Velasquez had come from the Standish collection. Mawson had bought them for him at Christie's at the Louis-Philippe sale in 1853.

The obituary notice of Lord Hertford published in *The Times* on the same day as the funeral was not kind. The Conservative Establishment had never forgiven him for choosing to live in Paris: 'If he did not inherit his father's vices, at least he inherited some of his eccentricities, and his faults and virtues were both appreciated at their right value by the society of the gay metropolis which became his adopted home. ...''

There was no mention of Richard Wallace, who in a very short time, when the Prussians besieged Paris, found himself trapped within its walls and was therefore unable to go to England to defend his rights against the outraged Seymour family.

The new marquess went to Balmoral for his last turn of 'waiting' and then resigned his court appointments in view of his succession to the family estates. These, according to his wife, 'did not bring an increase of peace and happiness to Franco's mind'. They had found Ragley in better order than they had expected, but much money was needed for repairs, in particular to the roof. Because of this they feared they would be unable to keep Sudbourne, the other Hertford house in Suffolk.

Lord Hertford seems to have wanted to behave correctly in his relations with Wallace, but his wife grew impatient and bitter because of the delays 'in consequence of Franco's chivalrous objection to doing anything which could appear like taking advantage of Mr Wallace's inability to transact business, he being shut up in Paris'. Capron, the solicitor, was now acting for Wallace and she complained that he was hostile and that they were refused access to deeds and papers locked up in the muniment room at Manchester Square. Franco, she said, was 'looked upon by Mr Wallace in the light of an interloper, who had inherited Property and Honours, which properly belonged to himself'.

Chapter Thirteen

At the age of fifty-two Richard Wallace became a multi-millionaire overnight, but he was given no time to sit back and enjoy the sensation. The luxury-loving Second Empire was doomed and disintegrated quickly around him. In one week the French army was defeated at Sedan, Napoleon III was taken prisoner and the Prussians were advancing on Paris. When the news reached Paris rioting started in the streets and the Paris mob in all its ferocity headed for the Tuileries. For the fourth time in eighty years the people of Paris forced their way into the royal palace – this time it was not to survive – and the Republic was declared. The monarchy was dead. The Empress Eugénie, who was regent, escaped only at the last minute through the galleries of the Louvre, empty because it was a Sunday, to a back door which gave on to the place Saint-Germain-l'Auxerrois. Unrecognised, she had driven away in a *fiacre* with only one lady-in-waiting just as the Imperial standard was being hauled down by the rioters. She was friendless and had nowhere to go. In desperation she knocked on the door of Dr Thomas Evans, her middle-aged American dentist, and pleaded with him for help. With great coolness and courage he was able to smuggle her out of Paris and across the Channel to England.

In this one week Wallace's life changed completely. Suddenly the indolent Paris he knew was turned into an armed camp. He seems never to have contemplated fleeing to England even though he must have realised that the encirclement of the city was only a matter of days. His son was somewhere with the beaten and dispirited French forces, and there was the Collection. He must have been conscious that Lord Hertford had counted on him to keep it together. He could not abandon it. So he put out of his mind all thoughts of the houses and estates he now owned in England and Ireland. For him there was no doubt that his place was in Paris.

Frantic preparations were being made to withstand the expected siege. Troops were camping in the Champs-Elysées and the Tuileries gardens. All the theatres were closed by order and work had been stopped on the nearly finished new Opéra, which now was to be used as an emergency food-store. Despite the architect Garnier's frenzied warnings that the floor would give way, potatoes, wheat, flour, horsemeat and sausages were carted by the ton into his splendid domed and colonnaded building.

Wallace had to think quickly what he could do to save the Collection when the attack came. Most of the treasures of the Louvre had already been sent for safety to Brest. The exception was the *Venus de Milo* which the Préfet of Paris had placed in a secret cellar at the Préfecture. Wallace's first concern was for the contents of Bagatelle which stood in an exposed position west of Paris directly in the path of an army attacking the city from that side. He must also have heard the story of what happened to the unfortunate Monsieur Flan and his valuable library at Neuilly, then a village between Paris and Bagatelle. Outside Paris the forts and defences were being hurriedly strengthened and M. Flan had suddenly been told by military engineers that his house would have to be demolished because it blocked a field of fire vital for defence purposes. When he asked for time to move his rare and beautiful books he was told that the house must be blown up that very night. He was forced to go to a nearby hotel where he was found dead of a broken heart the next morning.

With this terrible story in mind Wallace wasted no time. He decided immediately to bring everything he could move from Bagatelle back to Paris and assemble it in the rue Laffitte house where he would protect it as best he could. He himself was living in Mie-Mie's old house in the rue Taitbout, close at hand in case of need. At the rue Laffitte all the pictures were taken down from the walls, laid flat on the floor and covered with thick planks of wood. Wallace also foresaw the risk of Paris being bombarded and ordered loads of earth which were carried up to the roof and spread over it to deaden the effect of a falling shell. In fact, when Paris was bombarded by the Prussians later the rue Laffitte was never in danger because no shells fell on the right bank. The real danger came later during the Commune when there was more shelling and fighting from street to street on the boulevard.

Despite the steady, relentless advance of the Prussians Paris was crowded. Some foreigners left, but no attempt was made to urge useless people to leave the city. The weather was hot and sunny and since there were no water-carts or street cleaners Paris began to smell. For foreigners life was not without its risks when the Parisians, as proof of their patriotism, gave way to a mad outburst of spy mania. Any foreigner with the slightest accent was denounced as a Prussian and one Englishman even went so far as to put an advertisement in the newspapers stating that he wished people to know that he had been born in Chelsea. Wallace never had any trouble: his accent must have satisfied the critical French ears.

On 15 September, only ten days after the empress had fled from the Tuileries, a train which had left Paris from the Gare du Nord was stopped by a Prussian advance party at Senlis. Two days later the encirclement of the city had begun and on 18 September a force commanded by Crown Prince Frederick crossed the Seine south of Paris and cut the railway line to Orléans. The next day the siege of Paris began and Lord Lyons and the Embassy staff left hurriedly with the Papal Nuncio, who blessed both sides as he crossed the lines. However, the American Minister, Mr E. K. Washburne, stayed behind.

As the siege dragged on week after week many people, English and French alike, were to thank God that Richard Wallace had decided to stay. The suffering and poverty he saw around him revealed an unknown side of his character: a generosity and willingness to help those in need which has seldom been equalled and which, it must be said, were never any part of Lord Hertford's make-up. He was now able to draw on as his own the money that Lord Hertford had left him, and as Lord Hertford had liked to pay cash whenever possible for his purchases there must have been a very large sum of liquid money available at his bank. After the catastrophe at Sedan Wallace immediately gave £12,000 for the equipment of a field hospital to be attached to the army corps in which his son was serving. Captain Wallace had escaped the battle only because General Vinoy's corps made such slow progress that it had not reached Sedan in time. Not forgetting his own countrymen, Wallace also gave money for another hospital for the sick and poor English people in Paris.

Before his hurried departure Lord Lyons had handed over the British Embassy to Edward Blount, the English banker, giving him power to act as temporary consul. It was to him and to Wallace that the English in Paris turned for help during the long, hard days of a winter siege. A British Charitable Fund was organised to distribute relief to those most in need and Wallace became its chairman.

After Versailles had surrendered to the Uhlans without a shot being fired, the encirclement of Paris was complete. Bismarck installed himself in the Rothschild château at Ferrières, where he was joined later by King Wilhelm of Prussia. They spent their days shooting Baron Rothschild's pheasants and their nights emptying his cellar. As his terms for peace Bismarck demanded Alsace and part of Lorraine.

After a balloon called the *Neptune* had been sent up on 23 September and landed safely at Evreux, a regular balloon post was officially organised to link the besieged city with the outside world. The balloons were made in the empty railway stations and were launched from the hill of Montmartre, near where Sacré Cœur stands today. On 7 October Gambetta made his famous escape in one to organise resistance in the provinces.

However, it seems that foreigners could get through the enemy lines and Wallace contributed generously to a fund which was organised to help British people to escape. Felix Whitehurst, writing in his diary on 19 November, says Wallace arranged for eight ladies to leave Paris and gave orders to the coachman to sell the carriage and horses when he got through the lines and divide the money among the ladies. He calls Wallace 'the most liberal of fellows' for the way he 'keeps giving money to the British exodus fund'.

By now food was beginning to be scarce and what could be bought was outrageously expensive. 'They have begun on the dogs, cats and rats,' wrote Minister Washburne in his diary on 16 November. Six thousand horses belonging to the Paris cab company were eaten during the siege, and when this source of supply ran out they started killing the animals in the zoo at the

Jardin des Plantes. Eventually all the animals, with the exception of the lions, tigers and monkeys, were handed over to the butchers. At the end of December even the two famous young elephants, Castor and Pollux, were killed with much unnecessary suffering after several unsuccessful attempts to shoot them. Only the hippopotamus was spared because no butcher would pay the 80,000 francs asked for the giant beast, not even the wealthy M. Roos, owner of the Boucherie Anglaise, who bought most of the larger animals from the Jardin des Plantes.

As is always the case, it was the poor who suffered most. The price of what little food could be found was far beyond their means and without Wallace's regular donations to English charities many would have starved. According to Whitehurst, these amounted to £200 a month by November.

We are also indebted to Whitehurst for news of what happened to Bagatelle. Wallace had been right to evacuate it when he did. Although it was not demolished, it was commandeered by the military and hurriedly fortified because it commanded a completely undefended stretch of the Seine. In November Whitehurst managed to get across the Bois de Boulogne, and saw that holes for rifles had been pierced in the walls of all its buildings and a battery had taken up position on the terrace outside the drawing-room windows. He was sure Lord Hertford 'must have turned in his grave'.

The bombardment of Paris began on 27 December and by January shells were falling on the left bank at the rate of more than three hundred a day. None reached the right bank. The leading nations, with the exception of the British government, made diplomatic protests to the Prussians. This lapse on the part of the British, as Blount put it, 'produced a painful effect'. Fortunately, there were relatively few casualties and little damage. Sandbags were put round the Chevaux de Marly and the Arc de Triomphe. The shelling had the temporary effect of uniting the Parisians, but it was not long before people became indifferent. The cold weather of January increased the hardship. The gas was being used for the balloons, supplies of oil were very low and the stocks of wood were soon used up. People living in suburbs cut down the trees and at night they raided the centre of the city, tearing down fences and trellises. Once again it was the poor who suffered the most from the bitterly cold weather because they had already pawned or sold their warm clothing to buy food. According to Whitehurst, Wallace and his helpers at the British Charitable Fund spent three hours every day distributing relief. Twelve hundred people were being cared for by the fund, each of whom went once every two weeks and was given an allowance of food and money.

Whitehurst, whose admiration for Wallace appears over and over again in his diary, was full of praise for the efficient way in which the fund was run. 'This committee works with a will and the business is managed in a way which would give a good lesson to some of our municipal authorities here.' The years of service with the meticulous Lord Hertford had taught Wallace to be efficient. He was used to handling money and was doubtless an excellent manager. Each month Whitehurst recorded in his diary a new contribution. In December he calculated that Wallace had donated £20,000, for which he was given 'an address' which provoked the comment that it was 'good to hear a word in our favour' when 'we English are so detested'.

In the new year the gifts continued. After noting on 15 January a donation of £4,000 to start a subscription for victims of the shelling, Whitehurst calculated that Wallace had now given more than £30,000 to war victims. In French as well as English eyes he was the great philanthropist of the siege. When, also in January, he gave £1,200 to buy 300,000 soup tickets, the newspaper *Electeur Libre* called him the 'bienfaiteur de Paris' and it was proposed that a street should be named after him. Whitehurst was not impressed by this gesture to immortalise his hero. 'I cannot say I think it is a great compliment,' was his bitter comment. The British government remained silent about the bombardment. But Wallace was a hero to the Parisians and when the glasshouses at the Jardin Plantes were destroyed and when the glasshouses gave him the two surviving camellias. Even the Jockey Club opened its doors to him and elected him a member.

The city was on the brink of starvation, although the wine had never run out. An attempt to break out and capture the Prussian headquarters at Versailles had ended in defeat and disaster at Buzenval. It was impossible to hold out any longer. General Trochu was relieved of his command and, despite the opposition of the Leftists and the National Guard, Jules Favre was sent to Versailles to negotiate an armistice. On the eve of the capitulation a final tribute was paid to Wallace before the siege ended. What should have been the last balloon to leave besieged Paris was named after him. The balloon *Richard Wallace* was launched on 27 January at 3.30 in the morning. The temperature that dark morning was minus seven degrees. The pilot, Jean-Emile Lacaze, was trying to reach Bordeaux and carried, as well as the ordinary mail, a letter from Favre for Gambetta informing him of the armistice terms. The balloon never reached its destination and was last seen, high in the sky, heading out to sea off Arcachon. It was not discovered whether the pilot had died of cold or whether the valve that released the gas to allow the balloon to come down had perhaps frozen up or ceased to work. The balloon must have come down in the sea because for several weeks afterwards letters carried by the *Richard Wallace* were washed up on the shore. The armistice was signed on 28 January and another balloon, actually the last, with the resounding name of *Général Cambronne* was launched as a last spark of defiance. The pilot was given another letter for Gambetta with details of the armistice, but in the end Gambetta learned of the capitulation of Paris not by the balloon but by telegram direct from Favre on 29 January.

Of the sixty-five balloons which were sent up from Paris during the siege only five fell into enemy hands. Apart from the *Richard Wallace* only one other balloon was lost at sea. It was the thirty-fourth, called *Prince*, and it was last seen from the Lizard lighthouse heading out into the Atlantic. Six landed in Belgium, four in Holland, two in Germany and one in Norway. In addition to their pilots they carried ninety-nine passengers, 407 pigeons and more than 10,000 kilos of mail. The pilots of these balloons were mostly volunteers from the army and navy and, it is interesting to remember, were the first aviators in uniform. A plaque at the Gare du Nord commemorates the death of Lacaze, the pilot of the *Richard Wallace*. The story of his flight was set to music and as 'Le Marin du Wallace' it became a popular song at the music halls after the siege.

In the midst of all the suffering and misery of the siege one person found happiness – Mademoiselle Amélie Julie Charlotte Castelnau. Wallace, at long last, married the mother of his son who was now a thirty-year-old captain in the French army. If Lord Hertford's opposition had been the reason for their not getting married before, his death had removed this obstacle. Even then their union did not take place without a hitch. They were married at a consular ceremony by Edward Blount, but when the Embassy staff returned to Paris it was discovered that the temporary powers that had been given him did not include officiating at marriages. The marriage was declared not to be legal under British law and the record was torn out of the register. Wallace and Amélie Castelnau were therefore married again, this time under French law, at the Mairie in the rue Drouot on 15 February 1871. She had waited so long, and now she wanted to be absolutely sure that she was married to Richard Wallace at last. He described himself as a landowner, born in London 26 July 1818, living at 3 rue Taitbout. Wallace was not the only British subject to be married by Blount during his period at the Embassy. Letters were hurriedly sent to the other couples to inform them that they were not legally married.

The end of the siege meant food above all things to the Parisians. In London the Lord Mayor set up a relief fund and Gladstone's government requisitioned ships to carry army stores to France. This prompt response from London did much to restore England's popularity. The misery in Paris was extreme and Wallace was universally praised for his help which continued until, after a chaotic start, the supplies could be distributed smoothly. It is said, and there is no reason to doubt it, that he gave two and half million francs to help those in need, mostly English, during the siege.

One of the armistice conditions stipulated by Bismarck was that the French must quickly elect a government that could legally accept or reject the peace terms, and on 8 February France went to the polls to elect a National Assembly. So great was Wallace's popularity in Paris that there was a movement to elect him to the Assembly. Garibaldi, who had come to France in October to fight for the new Republic, was also a candidate. Although Italian, he was eligible because he had been born in Nice. In Paris he was the hero of the Republicans. Presumably it was the mistaken belief that Wallace was another French-born foreigner that had led to his name being put forward. In fact, he was disqualified from being a candidate because he had been born in England.

The results were a bitter disillusionment. Republican Paris, with her traditional contempt for the provinces, was firmly convinced that she alone had borne the full brunt of the war. Of the 768 seats in the new Assembly the vast majority elected were conservatives who were in favour of accepting the peace terms. More than half were monarchists. Paris, as the Department of the Seine, had only forty-three seats, and to her it was a defeat second only to the capitulation. The only crumb of comfort was that Garibaldi had been elected.

The Assembly met in Bordeaux at the Grand Theatre on 12 February and elected the seventy-three-year-old Thiers to head the government. On the second day when the venerable Garibaldi, in his red shirt, rose to speak there was uproar. The Assembly did not want to listen to the foreign hero of the Paris Reds. They booed him until he gave up and walked out. That same night he left for Italy, never to return to France. When the peace treaty was ratified Gambetta, the Alsace–Lorraine deputies and six left-wing Paris deputies resigned, but the session dragged on until 10 March, when it adjourned to reconvene ten days later at Versailles.

In Paris the situation was explosive. Revolution was in the air, but when it came it was not started by the politicians of the Red clubs but by the National Guard who had been idle and discontented since the capitulation. On 18 March Thiers tried to recover the National Guard cannons from Montmartre but bungled the operation and two generals were lynched. By nightfall the National Guard controlled the east of Paris and the red flag was flying at the Place de la Bastille. Thiers and the government fled to Versailles, leaving Paris to the Commune.

Once again Wallace found himself behind the barricades in a besieged Paris, but this time it was Frenchmen fighting Frenchmen. Spy mania was even worse than before. Renoir was arrested when he was painting by the Seine, suspected of being a Versailles spy making sketches of the defences. An angry crowd gathered and he narrowly escaped being thrown into the river. Paris was again bombarded, but this time it was not the Red strongholds but the friends of the government in the bourgeois quarters to the west, Passy, Trocadéro, Champs-Elysées, that were hit by the Versailles shells. The British Embassy was hit six times. There was nothing Wallace could do but wait and watch. The house in the rue Laffitte was closely shuttered and still had earth on its roof to protect it from shelling. But now there was the additional danger of looting.

At the Hôtel de Ville, despite the shelling, the Commune was in festive mood. There were public concerts in the Tuileries gardens and the palace was opened for the public to see the splendour of the royal apartments. In May in the place Vendôme, renamed place Internationale, Napoleon's column, which was considered a symbol of 'brute force, false glory and militarism', was pulled down. Gustave Courbet had been urging that the column should be demolished ever since the early days of the siege. He said it offended his artistic sense and finally he got his way with the Commune, who decreed its destruction on 12 April. The whole affair was organised as a great spectacle on 16 May. Three bands and a large force of the National Guard were lined up in the *place* and entry was by invitation. At the first attempt the ropes broke, and it was only after a long delay that the column yielded and came crashing down, to tremendous cheers and cries of 'Vive la Commune'.

John Murray Scott, Wallace's young secretary, was in the crowd when the column was pulled down and that night he went back to the place Vendôme to look at it. Dumont's statue of Napoleon, as Caesar holding Victory in his hand, which had been on top of the column was lying on the ground. Murray Scott noticed that the little statue representing Victory had broken off and he persuaded the National Guard watching over the column to sell it to him for fifty francs. He got a wheelbarrow and took it home to Wallace.[1] But these heady days were coming to an end.

[1] Wallace did not keep it long, although he took it to London. On 16 May 1873, the second anniversary of the demolition, he gave it back to Murray Scott who kept it all his life, leaving it on his death to his sister Mary. In 1943 it was sold at Christie's for £40 to Louis Clarke, of the Fitzwilliam Museum, Cambridge, who in 1952 presented it to Versailles. The Victory statuette was not by Dumont, but came from an earlier statue of Napoleon by Chaudet which had been on the Vendôme column.

On a bright, sunny Sunday five days later, the Versailles troops entered unnoticed at Auteuil and there began the terrible week of bloodshed and destruction known in French history as 'La semaine sanglante'.

Street by street, the Versailles troops fought their way into the centre of Paris. There was shooting at every street corner. There were acts of mad heroism and appalling savagery. Every barricade held out to the last man or woman. The barricade at the place Blanche was manned entirely by women. As the Communards retreated they set fire to the city. The Tuileries was set on fire on Tuesday, 24 May, and by the following night the centre of Paris was burning – the Palais Royal, the wing of the Louvre on the rue de Rivoli, the Cours des Comptes, the Palais de Justice, the Préfecture, the Conseil d'Etat. Notre Dame was spared at the last minute. Finally the Hôtel de Ville was set on fire the next day. The smoke blotted out the sun, but in the streets the battle continued until only the east of Paris still held out. The next day, Friday, rain put out many of the fires and saved the Louvre. The Tuileries continued to burn for three days and three nights. On Saturday, 28 May, the final battle was fought among the tombs in the Père Lachaise cemetery where Lord Hertford had been buried nine months before. When the last Communard cannon had been silenced the fighting continued hand to hand until the last of the defenders was caught and killed near Balzac's tomb. By Sunday, which was Whit Sunday, it was finished.

Powerless, Wallace lived through it all in a state of growing disillusionment and horror. He saw innocent men, women and even children shot down in the streets; three hundred dead bodies piled on top of one another in the place de la Madeleine; and the city in flames. How many people were killed in the bloody week of repression and in the summary executions that followed has never been established, but it was certainly more than 20,000. Paris had surpassed itself. In the Revolution between 2,500 and 3,000 people had been sent to the guillotine during the Terror, and that was spread over more than a year.

Chapter Fourteen

In June 1871 peace and order returned only slowly to a shocked and stunned Paris, bloodstained and still smelling of smoke. The *Venus de Milo* was brought out of her dark hiding-place. She had escaped being burned when the Préfecture was set on fire only because a burst pipe had miraculously kept her drenched in water. The Third Republic put the column back in the place Vendôme, and Courbet was given a prison sentence of six months and ordered to pay 250,000 francs towards the cost of its re-erection. To avoid paying he fled to Switzerland, where he remained until his death six years later.

For Richard Wallace there were to be honours and official recognition for his gifts and generosity to the people of Paris during the siege. He received the Legion of Honour, an avenue was named after him and the XI Arrondissement of Paris presented him with a gold medal. In August Queen Victoria created him a baronet. Wallace was now the best-known and the greatest philanthropist of his day.

With the peace, Wallace was able to start buying works of art again. He seized a unique opportunity of making a major addition to Lord Hertford's collection by buying the whole of the Comte de Nieuwerkerke's collections of European arms and armour as well as his collection of medieval and Renaissance works of art. The Comte de Nieuwerkerke, who had been Surintendant des Beaux Arts under Napoleon III, was famous as the lover of Princesse Mathilde, the emperor's cousin. Before the collapse of the Second Empire he had broken with her and at the first sound of gunfire had fled to Italy. There had been many anxious to buy his collections, but Wallace forestalled them all by putting down without a moment's hesitation the 400,000 francs Nieuwerkerke was asking.

Almost immediately after this coup he made another important purchase of European armour, the pick of Sir Samuel Meyrick's collection, from the Paris dealer Frédéric Spitzer. It is unlikely that he had any specialised knowledge of armour, but through being on the spot at the right time Wallace secured two collections of fine quality, particularly strong in sixteenth-century armour, by the foremost craftsmen in Europe. They were a splendid addition to the collection of oriental arms and armour which Lord Hertford had sent to the Musée Rétrospectif.

These two purchases, made almost immediately after the Commune, are interesting because they show the direction in which Wallace's personal tastes lay. It is doubtful if Lord Hertford would ever have bought a complete collection from anyone. It will be remembered that the collection which Wallace had made on his own initiative, but which he had been forced to sell, contained Renaissance bronzes and jewellery, ivories and Limoges enamels as well as eighteenth-century French objects. Now, when for the first time he started collecting for himself again, it was to the Middle Ages and the Renaissance that he turned rather than to the eighteenth-century art preferred by Lord Hertford. It was at this time also that he started to form the collection of sixteenth-century Italian majolica now in Hertford House. The collection he had inherited was almost entirely seventeenth and eighteenth century in character, but by these purchases Wallace extended its range and representative balance.

However, it is probable that he did buy at this time the one Ingres in the Collection. It is the pencil drawing *Hope and Charity* after Raphael, which Wallace is believed to have bought in 1871 at a sale of drawings belonging to Luigi Calamatta, an Italian engraver who had settled in Paris and become a follower of Ingres.

During the long, anxious weeks of the siege Wallace had been turning over in his mind what he ought to do with the Collection if it survived the war unharmed. He had not forgotten how Lord Hertford had been forced to leave everything behind when they had fled to England in 1848. To think of doing that again was impossible. Then had come the Commune. Shocked and disgusted by what he had seen he had made up his mind to go to live in England, and to take with him the most valuable objects in the Paris Collection. If by a miracle the Collection were to survive this uprising, he could not risk it being lost in the next. And so, when he opened up the house in the rue Laffitte, he began to make his plans to move nearly half the Collection to London.

Furthermore, he had inherited considerable property in England and Ireland which he had been prevented from visiting until now. It was demanding his attention. Sir Hamilton Seymour was claiming the estates in County Antrim and Wallace's first step was to instruct his lawyers to bring the case before the Irish courts. From besieged Paris he had already written to his tenants telling them not to pay rents to Sir Hamilton and he was determined to prove his right to the ownership of the Hertford Irish estates. In England there were still a number of questions to be settled with the new marquess concerning pictures and plate. There was also some property near Ragley which, according to Lady Hertford, Wallace at one time was claiming. Though much was settled in July, she recorded 'there still remain many minor difficulties and annoyances'. Wallace must have passed through London in July on his way to Ireland and there had been a meeting on these questions.

Wallace's case against Sir Hamilton Seymour opened at the County of Antrim Assizes on 31 July 1871 before Judge O'Brien and jury. The Attorney-General, Isaac Butt, Q.C., led for Richard Wallace, the plaintiff, and Dr Ball, Q.C., M.P., for Sir George Hamilton Seymour, the defendant.

In his opening speech the Attorney-General stated that the action was one of ejectment to recover the possession of forty-four acres, two roods and thirty perches of land in the County of Antrim but, he pointed out, the result concerned not only this piece of land but would determine the future ownership of what had been known as the Hertford Estates in this county.

Wallace was called as the first witness. In answer to questions from his counsel he told in simple terms the story of his life with the late marquess from the day his mother had brought him to Paris from London until the day Lord Hertford died at Bagatelle. He confirmed that he was in the house when Lord Hertford died, but not in the room.

'I always went with the marquess and his mother wherever they went,' he said, adding that from 1848 until 1855 he had stayed in Boulogne with Lord Hertford's mother.

Asked if he had ever been brought up to any profession he said he had not. He had once wanted to enter the navy, but Lord Hertford had objected. 'He said I did not want a profession.'

He told how when he started to work with Lord Hertford he was at first paid £500 a year and then £1,000 – 'I had everything I wanted, and carriages and horses' – and admitted that Lord Hertford had made payments of 330,580 francs in September 1854 and a further 271,000 francs in November 1856 to settle his debts.

Throughout the whole of his evidence he stressed the kindness and generosity that Lord Hertford had always shown to him. But never once did he give any hint that Lord Hertford was his father.

In conclusion, he told the story of the finding of the will which he said had been in England until 1869, when he had been sent by Lord Hertford to fetch the table in which it was found. The drawer had been opened by the solicitor. When asked to confirm Lord Hertford's handwriting he said it was 'the first time I saw the will'.

There was no cross-examination.

Dr Ball, opening the case for Sir Hamilton Seymour, said firstly it was a question of law whether a clear and specific devise can be revoked by a codicil containing doubtful words; and, secondly, the defendant was in possession.

The Attorney-General intervened to say that there was no one in possession. The tenants were refusing to pay rents until they knew who was the right person to pay.

No witnesses were called for the defence.

The judge said the claimant had not made out his case clearly and directed the jury to bring in a verdict for the defendant, but added for the enlightenment of all present: 'Don't imagine this case is decided – it has only gone the first step.'

How right he was, since Wallace immediately took steps to appeal against the judgement.

The case had attracted a great deal of attention in the county and although Wallace had lost he had made a big impression on the people of Antrim. Everyone had come to see the man whose philanthropy during the siege of Paris had made him famous and who was claiming to be their rightful landlord. His future tenants were impressed by his open and dignified manner. Even the Press commented favourably on his frankness in the witness-box. This man was different from the landlords they had heard of but hardly ever seen, and the lawsuit was the beginning of Wallace's long and happy association with Antrim. Later he sat as M.P. for the county in the House of Commons.

The appeal against the judgement at Antrim Assizes was heard in Dublin before the Court of Common Pleas on 4 December 1871. Again the decision was against Wallace and the position remained unchanged. But Wallace had not given up. On 14 December *The Times* announced that he intended to take his case to the Court of Exchequer Chamber and warned his tenants not to pay rent to Sir Hamilton Seymour before the end of the litigation as they ran the risk of having to pay twice. There the case was argued again in February 1872 before seven judges. This time four out of the seven judges decided in favour of Wallace. One of the four was Judge O'Brien, who had first heard the case at Antrim Assizes. Now it was Sir Hamilton Seymour's turn to talk of an appeal and he spoke of taking the case to the House of Lords. But after a long silence *The Times* announced on 26 July 1872 that there had been a settlement. Sir Hamilton had decided to accept the compromise offered and renounced all claim to the Irish estates in return for a payment of £400,000, one half to be paid immediately, and the other half in two years. During these two years he was to receive an additional £8,000 a year. If Lord Hertford had only asked his lawyers to draft the codicil it would never have been disputed and Wallace would not have had to pay this vast sum.

While his lawyers in Dublin were continuing his fight for the Irish estates in two different appeal courts, Wallace reached an agreement in London with the new Lord Hertford which enabled him to take possession of the house in Manchester Square. Although there was no doubt that all the pictures, furniture and other objects that the late marquess had bought in England and which were stored there belonged to him, the house itself and its furniture were not his. It was part of the entailed property and under the will the remainder of the lease had passed to the new Lord Hertford. In fact, the lease had nearly expired and Lord Hertford was willing to relinquish the remaining few months in consideration for which he would not be responsible for dilapidations. In any case, according to Lady Hertford, he did not want the house. 'We had no wish to live in the House,' she wrote in her diary, 'which was dirty, and though large as to public rooms, could not have contained our family.' They bought themselves a house not far away, at 13 Connaught Place. In March the following year, when the lease of the Manchester Square house expired, Wallace renewed it in his own name and became its owner. He knew it well because, although the late marquess had never lived there and had not visited it for twenty years, he himself had stayed there on many occasions when he had come to London on business for Lord Hertford. He had a room in the house, which in the inventory of furniture prepared for the new Lord Hertford was referred to as 'Mr Wallace's room'; its furniture included a large mahogany fourposter bed and a library table.

Having acquired the lease of the Manchester Square house, Wallace could now go forward with his plans to move the Collection there from Paris. It was an important moment for him because he himself was also planning to move to London. Now that he was Sir Richard Wallace, Bt, with ample means, he had made up his mind to become an English gentleman and to make England his home. Furthermore, he intended to do everything in his power to improve the reputation of the late marquess, who had been so criticised in England. He saw it as the filial duty of the never-admitted son and he would do it in memory of Lord Hertford. For this reason one of his first acts after he had obtained possession of the house was to change its name from Manchester House to Hertford House. This infuriated Lord and Lady Hertford who were intending to call the house they had just bought in Connaught Place Hertford House. So deeply did they feel about Wallace using the Hertford name and his intention, in their view, to usurp the rights of the Hertford family that Lord Hertford, who as a former equerry to the Prince Consort knew everyone at Windsor, wrote an extraordinary letter to his friend Sir Henry Ponsonby, Queen Victoria's private secretary. In it he not only complained of Wallace's behaviour but added that the late marquess had assured him that he was not Wallace's father and repeated the old story, widely believed at one time, that Mie-Mie was Wallace's mother, but then went on to throw doubt on that in order to show that Wallace had no claim to any connection with his family. It is worth quoting this letter in full:

Private and Confidential

Septr. 2/71
Penrhyn Castle, Bangor, N.W.

My dear Henry Ponsonby,

Far be it from me to impugn or find fault with honors conferred upon any individual by our gracious Queen, & therefore I hope my writing on the subject of Sir Richard Wallace having received a Baronetcy will not be misunderstood; but my Family do feel that his description being 'of *Hertford* House Manchester Square' gives him a connection with the family Title which would better have been avoided. To begin with that House has been for many years known as 'Manchester' not 'Hertford' House and was entailed on me, not left to him by Lord Hertford & I have only given it up to him as a Warehouse for his Pictures until Lady day next when my Lease of it expires. It is true that he has renewed the Lease from Ld Portman in his own name, so it will be his from that time. I have just bought a House in Connaught Place which I should have liked to call Hertford House, but now can hardly do so without confusion. However this is a small matter, but I have reason to believe from Wallace having refused to allow me to buy any of the Family Plate, China, Linen &c. at a valuation which had the Arms or Coronet upon them that he is only preparing to adopt them as if he were one of the Family & to this I do object most strongly, having the late Lord's most solemn assurance that he was not Mr Wallace's Father. The relationship therefore can only be thro' Lord H's Mother, but there are *now* reasons to doubt the existence of even this connection, & after all he could only be the illegitimate son of Lady Hertford, née Fagiani by some unknown man & can have no possible claim to the name or Arms of Conway or Seymour. It is on this point that you may still be able to do me a service. If you hear of his applying for permission to use either the one or the other will you have the kindness to give me notice. I conclude the Queen's sanction must be obtained & you would therefore know it, tho' it may perhaps be done only thro' the College of Arms. If so, please advise me how to act. We have already one illegitimate Baronet using the family name & Arms & we do not want another. Especially as there are all sorts of claims & questions still unsettled between Wallace & myself besides the Irish Estates. He claims for instance a considerable property in the heart of my Warwicksh. Estate. He retains some valuable Family Pictures which were marked as entailed & there are many Articles not forthcoming from Manchester House, acknowledged by him to belong to me which have to be settled. Valuable Papers & Patents to be given up &c.

I leave it to Sir Hamilton Seymour to say what he feels about honors being given to his opponent before the Irish Estate question is settled, but I know that I myself shall not get a shilling of Rent paid me on the Antrim property still belonging to me if further concessions are made to Sir Richard as one of the Family.

Believe me

Your's always sincerely

HERTFORD

Unfortunately, he gives no details in support of his extraordinary claim that Lord Hertford told him Wallace was not his son. When and how this unlikely reference by Lord Hertford to Wallace's parentage can have taken place we do not know, but the fact that he mentions it would seem to indicate that it was becoming widely accepted that Wallace was Lord Hertford's son since he had inherited his fortune and come to live in England.

In the end, despite his bitterness, he did call his new house Hertford House, so that for years there were two Hertford Houses in the same part of London. In fact, Wallace had the better claim to the name because it had been called Hertford House at various times before the death of the 4th marquess. The reason it was usually known as Manchester House was that the 4th Duke of Manchester had built the original house there in 1776 at a time when there was particularly good duck shooting in the surrounding grounds.

Lady Hertford seems to have been right when she said that the house was dirty. Charles Yriarte, who went with Wallace to see the house, said it was like 'the Palace of the Sleeping Beauty'. Lord Hertford's pictures, which hung in the silent and empty drawing-rooms, were covered with cobwebs and dust. Yriarte says that Wallace sent for pails of soap and water, and had them washed. The house was smaller then than it is today and Wallace saw that, if he and Lady Wallace were going to live there and if it was to house part of the Paris Collection, considerable additions and alterations would have to be made. In the end, the alterations he decided upon resulted in the house being virtually rebuilt as well as enlarged.

In the garden, which then existed behind the house, he planned to build on one side a tiled smoking-room (now Gallery IV) and on the other side, and at the bottom, stables and coach-houses. Above these he would build a large picture gallery (now XVI) and side galleries to provide the extra space needed for the Collection. Nor was that all. A storey was to be added to each of the wings of the old house, which would completely change the whole appearance of the north and south sides, and the whole exterior of the house was to be faced with the red brick we see today. Furthermore, the windows at the front and back were to be altered, a new portico and a new conservatory were to be built, while what was left of the garden was to be converted into an interior courtyard for sculpture and statuary. Finally, he decided to rebuild the main staircase. He would bring over from Paris the unique forged-iron and bronze Louis XV balustrade, which Lord Hertford had bought as scrap iron, and adapt it to stand on either side of the new staircase.

All this work was to take several years and a little-known architect named Thomas B. Ambler was put in charge. Wallace must have had good reason for his choice because Ambler was in charge of other work for him later in Ireland and at Sudbourne in Suffolk. 105 Piccadilly, the house the late marquess had left without a staircase, was made ready for Wallace and his wife to live in while the extensive alterations to Hertford House were taking place.

To complete the image of the English gentleman Wallace, now that he was a baronet, applied for a coat of arms and a crest based on those of the Wallaces of Craigie, from whom he claimed descent through the family of his mother, Agnes Jackson.

That he had decided to settle in England even before his claim to the Irish estates had been settled in the courts is clear from the memorandum, dated 5 August 1871, which Gladstone submitted to the queen recommending Wallace 'for the honour of a Baronetcy in recognition of his splendid munificence during the trying period of the Siege in Paris'. It goes on to state that he has 'taken measures for fixing his domicile in England' and whether he wins or loses the 'great Antrim Property, he will stand in a high class of wealth and influence'. The memorandum ends mysteriously by asking if the queen will allow Lord Granville, who was to see the queen that day, to refer to the subject as 'there are other circumstances in the case which Mr Gladstone has considered and which ought to be within your Majesty's view'. Could he have been referring to the fact that Wallace had only been married for six months although he had a grown-up son in the French army who was a French citizen? Whatever the circumstances were, the queen does not seem to have objected and the baronetcy was granted and announced.

As for the son, Edmond Richard Wallace, he was also swept up in the movement to be English. He retired from the French army, with a Legion of Honour for distinguished services, and became a British subject in July the following year by Royal Assent.

Although he was busy preparing to leave Paris Wallace was still making gifts to French charities and many kind and generous acts come to light during this period. For example, he had bought the shooting rights in the woods at Compiègne, which had been Napoleon III's favourite royal residence, and given instructions that the pheasants should be shot and distributed among the hospitals.

We learn also, for the first time, that one of Wallace's first acts after he became rich had been to ensure that his old love, La Présidente, should never be short of money. On 9 November 1871 Edmond de Goncourt wrote in his *Journal* that Flaubert had told him that, two days before Paris was surrounded, Wallace sent to Madame Sabatier an 'undreamed of fortune', having promised her that if ever he became rich he would not forget her. He kept his promise and she lived until she was sixty-eight, dying on the last day of 1889.

Finally, as a parting gift Wallace decided to present fifty drinking-fountains to the city of Paris. Many of these are still standing and are still called 'les Wallaces'. They were designed by the sculptor Charles Auguste Lebourg, who also executed busts of Lord Hertford and Lady Wallace which are still in the Collection. Originally there were to be two types of fountain; the familiar free-standing 'Wallace' with drinking-cups and a trough for dogs and animals at the base, and another design which could be fixed to walls. No examples of this second model, which included the letters R.W. in its design, were ever erected because the city authorities said they were unable to find any suitable places to put them. Each fountain of the first design cost at the time 1,000 francs to cast.

John Murray Scott, who by this time had made himself indispensable, also moved to London with Sir Richard and Lady Wallace. After Wallace's death he was to play a major role in the future of the Collection.

Chapter Fifteen

WHEN RICHARD WALLACE MADE UP HIS MIND in 1871 to go to live in England and take with him the finest objects in the collection he had inherited in France it was not with any intention of making them available for the public to see. His main concern was for their safety. However, his plans for the alterations to Hertford House meant that for at least four years it would be impossible to house them there. A new home had to be found for them, as well as for the present contents of that house. He wished to do everything possible for the memory of Lord Hertford and this was probably the motive behind his eventual decision to put the collections on public exhibition. It was probably Philip Cunliffe-Owen who suggested that Wallace should lend the collections at Hertford House to the South Kensington Museum, the forerunner of today's Victoria and Albert Museum, which under the energetic direction of Sir Henry Cole was specialising in the decorative arts and art education.

Following the Great Exhibition in Hyde Park in 1851, there had been a great movement in England to establish 'museums, by which all classes might be induced to investigate those common principles of taste which may be traced in the works of excellence of all ages'. Land had been acquired at South Kensington and the first South Kensington Museum had been built in 1855. It was a prefabricated iron and glass construction, of the kind that had been used for the Crystal Palace, and was popularly known as 'Brompton Boilers'. It had been designed by an army engineer, Major-General H. Scott, who also designed the Royal Albert Hall. In 1867 this building had been taken down and re-erected at Bethnal Green as a branch museum to serve the population of East London and in its place a new museum had been built at South Kensington.

Cunliffe-Owen was Sir Henry Cole's assistant at South Kensington and must have known Wallace. They had probably met in Paris in 1867 when he had been responsible for the British Section of the Exposition Internationale. We know that Wallace was already lending objects to the South Kensington Museum before the end of 1871 because in the nineteenth Report of the Science and Art Department published in 1872 the Keeper of Art Collections lists in his report among the loans to the Art Department during 1871: 'Wallace, Sir Richard, Bart. Gold and enamelled Jewels, etc.'

Wallace must have agreed to lend the collections early in the new year and arrangements were being made for all the pictures, furniture and porcelain at Hertford House to go to the South Kensington Museum when either Cole or Cunliffe-Owen came forward with a bold new suggestion.

The re-erection of the Brompton Boilers at Bethnal Green had been completed and plans were being discussed for the opening of this new museum, the first ever to be built in a densely populated working-class district. It was an experiment, and the Science and Art Department, eager that it should be a success, considered that the choice of exhibits for the opening was of the utmost importance. What could be better than 'the Hertford Collection'? But would Sir Richard Wallace agree to lend his valuable collection for this experiment? Someone must have approached Wallace with this new suggestion sometime in February 1872 because Henry Cole wrote in his diary on 22 February that when he had been asked by the Marquess of Ripon, the Chairman of the Lords of the Committee of Council on Education, what would be sent to Bethnal Green he had answered, 'Lord Westminster's pictures and perhaps Sir Richard Wallace's.'

Before giving his consent Wallace asked to see the Bethnal Green Museum in order to have an idea of what the galleries looked like and what would be the risks if he sent his treasures to this poor district. On 12 March he went to Bethnal Green with Lady Wallace and met Cole at the museum. The building was much the same then as it is today and Wallace must have been impressed by the space and light this iron and glass structure provided. He inquired about weather and the temperature, obviously thinking about the marquetry of his furniture, and finally agreed.

When Cole got home he wrote in his diary that night: 'He [Wallace] said "It is understood that my pictures, China and furniture come and that you will take the same care of them as at the South Kensington Museum." Discussed fog: temperature.'

The next day Wallace wrote to Cole confirming his agreement and repeating the condition that the same security measures as at South Kensington would be taken to protect his collections.

Two days later there was a meeting of the Lords of the Committee of Council on Education at which Cole submitted Wallace's letter of agreement to lend his Collection to the Bethnal Green Museum, and the text of the letter accepting this offer, to be signed by Lord Ripon, was approved. The letter, dated 15 March, read as follows:

Sir,

The Lords of the Committee of Council on Education have read your letter of 13 March, stating that you are willing, for a period of twelve months, to place at their Lordships' disposal in the South Kensington Museum for exhibition to the public your collections of pictures, furniture, porcelain, and other Art objects; that you are aware that a museum is about to be established at Bethnal Green as a branch of the South Kensington Museum, that it would give you additional pleasure to see any or all of your collections exhibited in that populous neighbourhood of working people which has hitherto not had the advantage of any National Museum, and your assurance that all the security which the South Kensington Museum affords will, at least, be guaranteed by necessary arrangements at Bethnal Green, and even increased precautions taken against risks.

I have the pleasure to convey to you the expression of their Lordships' thanks for your liberal offer, and especially for your interest in the working classes of the east of London. On behalf of the Lords of the Committee of Council on Education, I beg to assure you that the rules, of which a copy is enclosed, and the measures necessary for the protection of your fine collections, will be administered so as to give all the security which is in the power of their Lordships to afford.

I am, &c.,
RIPON

The preparation of the catalogue of Sir Richard Wallace's collection of pictures was discussed at a meeting of the Science and Art Department on 22 March when it was agreed to pay sixpence for the descriptions of each object to C. C. Black, who was to prepare the catalogue and labels. Mr Black's catalogue was to run into five editions. It had 125 pages, the first sixty-nine devoted to pictures. Two thousand and thirty separate items were numbered and it sold for sixpence.

Wallace went back to Bethnal Green on 27 March where he had a second meeting with Cole to discuss the practical details of transporting his Collection from Hertford House to Bethnal Green. But he was turning over in his mind something much bigger and once again it was connected with his duty to the memory of Lord Hertford. Having seen the possibilities of the Bethnal Green Museum (and Cole may have hinted as well that they were hoping that the queen would consent to open the museum), ought he not to lend also that part of Lord Hertford's collection in Paris that he was proposing to bring to England, instead of shutting it up in store, as he planned, while waiting for the work at Hertford House to be finished? What better opportunity could there ever be of proving the taste and genuine love of beauty and perfection of his benefactor whom nobody in England seemed to have understood? In this way he could establish Lord Hertford's reputation as the greatest collector of all time. He saw it as his clear duty. He decided to speak to Cunliffe-Owen.

On 30 March, before returning to Paris, he sent for Cunliffe-Owen and told him what he proposed. He told him he wanted to make one exhibition showing Lord Hertford's Collection as a whole and offered to pay all the expenses of bringing to London that part of the Collection that was in Paris. He made no secret of the fact that his reason was that he felt that he owed it to Lord Hertford and that such an opportunity might never occur again.

The next day the delighted Cunliffe-Owen wrote to Cole as follows:

Private

Sir Richard sent for me on Saturday afternoon and began to talk over the advantages there could be in making one exhibition (in addition to those in London) of his Paris Pictures, Furniture, Bronzes and China – having heard that the Queen, Lords Westminster and Eldon were lending art objects, this proposal might be inconvenient but it had struck him that it was due to Lord Hertford and that such an opportunity would never exist again. He made only one condition that every expense of removal from Paris to London, should be paid by him – I answered him, how much gratified you would be with this noble and generous offer and that I felt quite competent to say so. But that I would write to you and beg of you to give an assurance of the same – he is in Paris 2 Rue Laffitte – would you telegraph to him your thanks and readiness to receive – Mr Redgrave, MacLoed and Thompson are of course enchanted and I have written to Sir Richard expressing the general satisfaction felt at this generous offer – Sir Richard particularly wishes that Lord Hertford's collection should be shown as a *whole*. Afterwards when he has placed them in his own galleries he will wish to enjoy them. The first van goes tomorrow the men go tonight and every precaution is being taken to provide for the safe removal. . . .

Cunliffe-Owen was not wasting any time. He knew that the opening of the Bethnal Green Museum was being planned for the summer and that they would have to move quickly. Fortunately, he had experience of moving fragile works of art across the Channel. He had done it for the British Section of the 1867 exhibition in Paris. The Science and Art Department had an expert and efficient staff, as well as special vans of their own design for moving valuable pictures and works of art safely. He also had worked closely with the South-eastern Railway and he knew he could count on them again. How quickly he and his staff worked we can tell from a volume called 'Van Book, 1872' which has fortunately been preserved at Bethnal Green. It was the duty of someone at the museum to record in this book every delivery to the museum, and on 19 April the arrival of the first railway-van from Paris at 9 p.m. is recorded. It contained eight cases of furniture marked R.W. 'from Sir Richard Wallace, Paris. Objects on loan to Museum'. The next day another railway-van arrived from Paris containing six cases of furniture. And so it went on with arrivals almost daily from Paris or from Hertford House.

In the month of April fifty-one cases of furniture from Paris arrived in six railway-vans and two vanloads of pictures, bronzes and marble busts were delivered from Hertford House. In one of these, according to the Van Book, was a 'large gilt frame of wood carved labelled "Domenichino"'. This was clearly the famous frame that had caught Lord Hertford's eye at the Stowe sale, and which he had mentioned in a letter to Mawson from Boulogne in September 1848.

The deliveries continued all through the month of May – eleven vanloads from Paris, five from Hertford House and seven, mostly pictures and porcelain, from 105 Piccadilly.

One picture from Paris was marked with a cross and it was not unpacked but put on one side until Wallace came to fetch it. It was probably Terborch's *Peace of Munster* which he later presented to the National Gallery.

On 3 June one oil painting, a landscape, was delivered from Hertford House, and on 11 June the last delivery is recorded – 117 miniatures which Wallace brought himself from Hertford House in his own carriage.

In all 736 pictures, 227 miniatures, 446 pieces of furniture, sculpture and decorative bronzes, 240 porcelain objects – mostly Sèvres – 141 pieces of majolica and 200 items of jewellery and snuff-boxes were delivered safely to Bethnal Green. There was another part of the Paris collection – notably the armour – which was not sent to be exhibited and which was put into store at the Pantechnicon, the large furniture depository in Motcombe Street.

The opening ceremony had been fixed for Monday, 24 June. Queen Victoria could not be persuaded to go to Bethnal Green, and it was the Prince of Wales who was delegated to open the museum on her behalf. He was to be accompanied by the Princess of Wales. Wallace had arranged, with furniture and pictures, two retiring rooms for the use of the prince and princess. For the prince's room he chose pictures by Fragonard. During the ceremony, while seated on the dais, the royal couple used two of the set of eight Venetian state chairs which Lord Hertford had bought at the Stowe sale in 1848. They had been freshly gilded and upholstered and matching footstools had been made specially for the occasion.

It is difficult to realise today that at that time the East End was almost unknown territory. Until the opening of the Bethnal Green Museum, in itself a daring admission that the poor had a right to museums, royalty had never penetrated east beyond the City of London, and no royal carriage procession had ever before driven through these shabby and crowded streets. There was therefore a certain amount of anxiety as to how the Prince and Princess of Wales would be received on that opening day.

Henry Cole recorded in his diary that he left his house at about 9.15. The prince and princess were due to arrive at 'a quarter-past twelve o'clock'. It was to be an occasion of the greatest ceremony – levée dress and a collar day. The carriage procession of the Prince and Princess of Wales, consisting of five carriages accompanied by a Captain's Escort of the 1st Regiment of Life Guards, left Marlborough House at 11.30 and drove via the Mall, the Embankment, Queen Victoria Street, Threadneedle Street, Bishopsgate and Bethnal Green Road.

The Marquess of Ripon received their Royal Highnesses at the entrance to the museum, where there was a guard of honour. As the royal procession entered the building a flourish of trumpets was given by the state trumpeters after which 'God Save the Queen' was played by the band of the Honourable Artillery Company stationed in the East Gallery above the dais.

The ceremony opened on a religious note. The Bishop of London offered a prayer and in the West Gallery a choir of children from the local schools, conducted by Dr Stainer, sang the Hundredth Psalm – 'All people that on earth do dwell'.

Lord Ripon, as Lord President, then read an address to His Royal Highness to which the Prince of Wales replied and declared the museum to be open, after which the choir sang all three verses of 'God Save the Queen'.

All this time Wallace, with Lady Wallace and their son Edmond, had been nervously waiting for the moment when he was to conduct the prince and princess round the Collection. Henry Cole wrote in his diary afterwards that Wallace was 'at first put out because he was not in Court Suit'. Now his big moment had come. As the printed ceremonial of the occasion said, 'Sir Richard Wallace will have the honour of receiving Their Royal Highnesses at the North Gallery Staircase and conducting them round his Collections of Fine Art objects.'

Wallace seems to have recovered from his embarrassment at not being in court dress and everything seems to have gone very well. The prince and princess spent an hour going round the collection, with Wallace, as *The Times* said later, 'pointing out to them the gems of a collection of gems'. The Princess of Wales said she was 'jealous' of Sir Richard Wallace and the prince told Henry Cole that he was very pleased, but he may have been thinking more of his reception from the crowds in the streets than of the Collection.

After another flourish of trumpets the royal carriage procession left the museum to the strains of 'God Bless the Prince of Wales'. It took a partly different route back via Cambridge Heath Road, Hackney Road, Shoreditch High Street and Bishopsgate.

In another part of the museum there was what was described as 'the Animal Products and Food Collections from the South Kensington Museum', also on exhibition, all in glass cases and neatly labelled. But this part of the museum was not visited by the Prince of Wales. Only the Fine Art Galleries were to receive the royal visit.

As soon as the royal party had left the museum staff started clearing the ground floor in preparation for the public opening the next morning. The fittings and dais erected for the state opening were removed and the large central hall was arranged with furniture, sculpture and watercolour pictures. It meant working late into the night so that the entire museum was ready to be opened to the public at ten o'clock the next morning. On Mondays, Tuesdays and Saturdays admission was free and the museum was open from 10 a.m. to 10 p.m. Sixpence was charged for admission on Wednesdays, Thursdays and Fridays when the museum was open only until 6 p.m.

The first day attracted a record crowd. 'More than 25,000 persons – dirty and pleased and orderly, ...' wrote Henry Cole in his diary when he got home after driving out after dinner to see how the first free day had gone.

Victorian reviewers and art critics seem today to have been absurdly obsessed by the contrast between the richness and perfection of the objects in the Collection and the grim, poverty-stricken community which lived in the streets surrounding the museum.

By a strange hyperbole of contrast [wrote Sidney Colvin in the *Fortnightly Review*] one rich man has poured out for show, in the heart of a world like this, the concentrated arts and luxuries of worlds how opposite.

The children of Bethnal Green life tumble in the gutter outside; inside, the satin children of Watteau tumble in much the same attitudes upon a sward that fancy has spread more soft than sleep. . . .

Henry James went out to Bethnal Green to visit the Collection and wrote: 'The journey to Bethnal Green is a long one, and leads you through an endless labyrinth of ever murkier and dingier alleys and slums.'

He did not risk going on a free day but preferred to pay his sixpence which, he says, 'had excluded the local population so that we are obliged to repeat from hearsay a graceful legend that the masses, when admitted, exhibit, as one man, a discrimination of which Mr Ruskin himself might be proud, and observe and admire on the very soundest principles'.

To celebrate the opening, Wallace gave a dinner to the staff of the museum of 10 July. Cole was there and says he went afterwards with Wallace to a Foreign Office reception. The Bethnal Green Museum was an undreamed-of success from the very first day it opened. Originally Wallace had agreed to lend his Collection for only one year. In fact, it was to remain there until April 1875 and was visited by five million people.

But the greatest success of all was Richard Wallace. He was a hero whom everyone wanted to meet. He became a legend to which he responded with the inexhaustible, unfailing Wallace charm. This is what the *Graphic* had to say about him on 29 June 1872:

Sir Richard Wallace is the very type and model of what a rich man ought to be, and we hope some other of our millionaires will profit by his example. There are a good many men in England who cannot possibly spend their annual incomes (unless they are fools enough to go on the turf), while regulations which no Act of Parliament can repeal prevent them from carrying any of their money into the next world. The obvious alternative is to spend it here in doing good, and the charity of which Sir Richard Wallace has just set such a noble example is of a sort which never degrades the recipient.

The extraordinary thing is that, despite all the arrangements for Bethnal Green and the problems connected with the move from Paris, Wallace found time to keep his eye on the art market and buy a large number of pictures. In the year 1872 he bought thirty-nine pictures – more than twice as many as he bought during the remaining eighteen years of his life. Moreover, thirty of these thirty-nine were bought in time to be included in the Bethnal Green exhibition.

Richard Wallace was now a famous man in both England and France. His unfailing charm, liberality and gentlemanly manners were noted and admired by all who had contact with him. We do not know what impression Lady Wallace made on London society when she was suddenly brought into the limelight with him. She refused to speak a word of English, and she was shy and retiring. She seems to have remained discreetly in the background, leaving everything to her husband, of whose every action she approved. This was her chosen role, which she maintained throughout the whole of her life in England. Later, not unnaturally, she was to earn the reputation of being difficult. The fact is that her lack of confidence and her inability to speak the language made it impossible for her to enjoy English society, and at times she tended to show it.

In this year of fame and social success in London Wallace lacked one thing to complete his image of himself as an English gentleman – a house and estate, with shooting, in the country. Ever since the death of the 4th marquess he had been hoping to acquire Sudbourne Hall in Suffolk, the second Hertford country estate, which under the will had passed to the 5th marquess as entailed property. Finally, in the summer of 1872, Lord Hertford decided that the expense of keeping Ragley, the Hertford seat in Warwickshire, was too heavy a burden, particularly when all the cottages on the estate were sadly in need of repairs. So he agreed to sell Sudbourne to Wallace.

'As to Sudbourne,' Lady Hertford recalls, 'Mr Wallace had from the first, expressed the greatest anxiety to possess it, and offered to give a higher price than anyone else. The place was put into the market, and in the summer of 1872 Mr Wallace became the purchaser.'

The 'higher price than anyone else' was £200,000. If this is added to the more than £400,000 paid to Sir Hamilton Seymour it seems clear that it was Wallace's intention to recompense the disappointed members of the Seymour family as much as was in his power. 'Thank God it is all settled,' Lord Hertford is said to have exclaimed in relief when he heard that the purchase had been concluded. The expense of the estate was well beyond his means.

Sudbourne Hall no longer exists. It was about a mile from Orford in Suffolk. Lord Clark, whose father bought it later from Sir John Murray Scott and made big changes both inside and outside the house, remembers it from his childhood as 'a large, square house with a frigid neo-classical interior'. He is surprised that Wallace wanted the house. 'I should not have supposed that so great an exponent of self-indulgence as Sir Richard could have found much to attract him in this featureless house, set in the cold East Anglian countryside, but he seems to have liked it.'

Bagatelle was also demanding Wallace's attention. After its occupation by the army it had been restored to him in a deplorable condition. So great was the damage that there was no question of making minor repairs here and there. Half measures were not to his taste and, although he was engaged in extensive alterations at Hertford House, he decided to modernise and, to a large extent, rebuild Bagatelle to make it into a more spacious and comfortable permanent residence. Once more the roof was raised – Lord Hertford had done it in 1860 – to give higher ceilings and larger bedroom windows – and the dome was altered. In order to lengthen the courtyard in front of the house he pulled down the pretty little 'pavillon des pages' which had stood at the entrance, and on either side of the new courtyard he built two long terraces at the same level as the ground floor of the house. Beneath the terrace on the north side he arranged kitchens and rooms for servants. On the other side of the courtyard he built what is known as 'le Trianon' which was to have been a house for his son, who, however, never lived there. An underground passage was made to lead from outside the entrance of the courtyard, beneath the Trianon, to the basement of Bagatelle. This was for the use of the servants so that no servant need ever be seen approaching or leaving the house – an almost royal attitude.

Wallace was very proud of his alterations at Bagatelle, which he considered in keeping with the spirit of the eighteenth century. But the French have always considered that Wallace's extensive alterations finally destroyed the charm and harmony of Bélanger's little masterpiece and changed what was meant to be a discreet retreat in which to pass a few gay hours into an austere, bourgeois residence.

Although officially he had left to go to live in London, Wallace was still very much in the news in Paris.

It appears that he was trying to distribute 100,000 francs that Lord Hertford had left for a home for stray cats and dogs.[1] Such a bequest, so foreign to French conceptions, provoked some comment in the Press. In *Le Monde Illustré* of 30 March 1872 Pierre le Hestre, a columnist of the time, after admitting Wallace's generous gifts to the French and hesitating to criticise 'une fantaisie aussi louable', quotes a letter found on the body of an unfortunate man who drowned himself out of misery and despair. Whatever pity he may be inspired to feel for 'les chiens à trois pattes, les perroquets goutteux et les chats hystériques' he considers would be misplaced, and one ought to think of the man who drowned himself.

The Wallace fountains were going up in Paris and on 7 September 1872 *Le Monde Illustré* reported that they were being spoiled by vandals almost as soon as they had been installed. The fountains on the boulevard de la Villette had had two drinking cups wrenched off and someone had even tried to remove one of the caryatids.

[1] There are several indications that Lord Hertford made a French will. Unfortunately, wills are not made public in France, and although the author has traced the descendants of the notary who acted for Lord Hertford, and they are still in practice, no such will has been discovered in their files.

Chapter Sixteen

One debt remained outstanding in Richard Wallace's mind, that of Lord Hertford's to his long-neglected tenants in Ireland. The opportunity to repay it presented itself in 1872 when Edward Verner, who had been the Member of Parliament for Lisburn since 1863, gave up the seat in favour of the family one in Armagh. The people of Lisburn had not forgotten the good impression Wallace had made on them when they saw him in the witness-box at Antrim Assizes, and although his claim to be their new landlord had not been finally settled in the courts they offered him the vacant seat at a packed public meeting. No other name was put forward. Wallace was in the middle of making arrangements to transfer his Collection from Paris to England, but he did not wish to disappoint the voters of Lisburn, so he dropped everything and went to Ireland. In Lisburn he was given a tumultuous welcome and unanimously adopted as their candidate. At the subsequent by-election he was returned unopposed. Thus, in the short space of three years, Richard Wallace had inherited the major part of the Hertford fortune, had lived through the siege of Paris and the subsequent revolution, had been made a baronet and become a Member of Parliament. It says as much for his energy as for his popularity that he was able to achieve so much in so short a time. He sat as a Conservative from 1873 to 1885, being returned unopposed in the general elections of 1874 and 1880. He was the last M.P. for Lisburn, because after 1885 it became part of the new constituency of South Antrim. Wallace opposed this during the debate on the Parliamentary Election (Redistribution) Bill. It was his last speech and in it he declared that the ancient borough of Lisburn, the most important town in the county, should give its name to the Southern Division of the County of Antrim and not be 'consigned to political oblivion'.

His appeal was not successful, nevertheless he was invited to stand again but declined for reasons of ill health. Although Wallace sat in the House of Commons for twelve years and was a regular attendant, as far as it is possible to tell from the Hansards of the time, he spoke very infrequently. Most of the time he sat silent through the debates, speaking occasionally on matters concerning Ireland.

One of the first things he did after becoming an M.P. was to fulfil Lord Hertford's promise to build a house in Lisburn. Known as Castle House, it was a two-storey red-brick building which he intended to be his residence when he was in Ireland. The obscure Thomas Ambler was again the architect and its design was obviously inspired by the newly constructed Hertford House. Today it belongs to the town of Lisburn and forms part of the technical college. Later he presented twenty-five acres of wooded land to be made into a public park, and paid for the building of a bandstand, entrance gates and lodges. It is called Wallace Park today.

One cannot help wondering what impression Wallace made upon his fellow Members at Westminster. After spending all his adult life in France, did he speak with an accent? Hansard does not help, for in those days speeches were not recorded verbatim. It is impossible, therefore, to tell if there were any gallicisms in his spoken English. As for his accent, Sir Charles Dilke, who sat in the House as the Member for Chelsea at the same time, says he had an accent. He recalls him as a 'kind, cheery, polished gentleman' but was categoric about his accent. 'He was French, not English, speaking English imperfectly.'

Dilke's view was probably exaggerated. If when he first came to England there was a slight trace of an accent, it must soon have disappeared because no other person who knew him ever mentioned faults in his English. One thing is certain, however: when he first came to England his imperial beard and moustache, turning white with age, must have looked very French to English eyes. T. P. O'Connor, who also knew him at Westminster, thought he looked like a Frenchman to the end of his days. He was always dressed with extreme care, a model of neatness in his morning coat and well-pressed trousers.

Wallace seems to have stopped buying pictures after 1872. In that year he had added thirty-nine pictures to the Collection, among them Fragonard's *A Boy as Pierrot* and the two J. F. de Troy oil sketches for the pictures commissioned by Louis XV for the dining-room of the *petits appartements* at Fontainebleau. In 1873 two paintings only can be traced as having been bought by him. Both were English subjects: one a copy of a view of Northumberland House painted by Canaletto in England in 1752 and the other the single Morland in the Collection, *A Visit to the Boarding School*. During the next year he bought nothing.

Was it because in this year that part of the Collection that he had put into store at the Pantechnicon was destroyed in a disastrous fire? The fire broke out on 13 February and the next day *The Times* announced that 'one of the many valuable collections of Sir Richard Wallace M. P. – estimated to be worth no less than £120,000 – was among the property stored there and has perished in the flames'. Four days later *The Times* said that Wallace's loss 'comprises a very valuable library, a large quantity of plate, a collection of ancient armour, two enamelled dishes insured for £2,500 each, and a few pictures though none of very great importance'. Wallace, *The Times* said, was insured for £28,000 but it is estimated that the property he had deposited there in ten huge boxes was worth 'at least five times that amount'.

At first it was believed that much would be recovered unharmed and it was arranged that a special search would be made by the Salvage Corps. The search started on 18 February, but nothing had been found by the end of the first day. On the next day a shield bearing the Hertford arms was recovered almost undamaged as well as some melted silver and several swords. When at the end of the third day nothing more was discovered the discouraged searchers began to think that they must have been looking in the wrong place and the search was stopped.

The fire had attracted a great deal of attention. The Pantechnicon covered two acres of ground bounded by Motcombe Street, Lowndes Square, Belgrave Square and Kinnerton Street. It was the biggest furniture depository fire on record and the fact that the famous Sir Richard Wallace had lost a part of his Collection added to the interest. Even Queen Victoria was interested enough to go to see the ruins on 27 February. On the same day *The Times* announced that the Salvage Corps had started a new special search in a different place for the 'Hertford collection of armour and plate belonging to Sir Richard Wallace'. Wallace had refused to give up hope of recovering some of his treasures. This new search was more successful and on 2 March *The Times* announced that the Salvage Corps had recovered from the northern extremity of the building, close to where the fire started, 'the remains of a small but valuable collection of armour'. Six enamelled dishes, some badly burned, were also recovered. One of these Limoges dishes is now in the United States in the Walters Art Gallery, Baltimore.

Wallace refused to take back any of these objects and claimed the full amount of his insurance. They included the famous sixteenth-century suit of embossed armour, known as the Crozat suit, which had been badly damaged. Now, partially restored, it is in the Metropolitan Museum in New York.

However, he did take back some damaged objects, the most important of which were the two elaborate gilt-bronze chandeliers by Caffieri which were probably made for Louis XV's eldest daughter, Madame Infante, Duchess of Parma. The chandeliers had suffered in the fire – Murray Scott is reported to have said that one of them looked like scrap iron. Now repaired and restored, they are hanging in Hertford House today. It seems that in the end there were no pictures lost in the fire and Wallace was paid £15,000 by the insurance companies.

It is true to say that Wallace, by following his own tastes in purchasing medieval and Renaissance objects, broadened the range and improved the balance of Lord Hertford's Collection. In his choice of pictures, however, he followed completely the taste of Lord Hertford. He bought paintings by his patron's favourite contemporary French artists, Robert Fleury, Decamps, Scheffer, Horace Vernet, de Mirbel, Heilbuth. Many of them had been friends of Lord Hertford and Wallace must have known them all, and both he and Lord Hertford may have bought their paintings as much out of a desire to help as from admiration of their work. But there were still no Impressionists in the Collection.

As we know, Lord Hertford never had a chance of seeing any examples of what we know today as Impressionist painting, but the same cannot be said in defence of Wallace. For it was in 1874, the year when he bought no pictures at all, that this group of painters held their famous first exhibition in the unused studio of Nadar, the photographer, at 35 boulevard des Capucines, and came to be called Impressionists after a painting by Monet at the exhibition entitled *Impression, soleil levant.*

It had been Monet's idea to exhibit as a co-operative group to get round the jury which decided who should be admitted to the Salon, and to get themselves noticed. The exhibition opened on 15 April 1874, chosen deliberately because it was two weeks before the opening of the Salon. Monet showed twelve paintings, Degas ten, Pissarro five, Renoir six, Cézanne three, and 129 other pictures were shown by twenty other painters who were friends, among them Berthe Morisot, Guillaumin and Boudin. Corot, Manet and Jongkind had refused to participate. The exhibition remained open until 15 May from 10 a.m. to 6 p.m. and, curious innovation, from 8 p.m. to 10 p.m. It did not have such a great success with the public as the Salon des Refusés in 1863. There were only 175 visitors on the opening day, but all the leading critics wrote about it in the Press and it did attract the publicity this group of painters had been seeking.

Wallace must have known about this exhibition, which was to revolutionise painting in France. Even if he did not visit it he would have heard about it from his friends and read the notices in the Press. All the critics had their reservations, but they were less hostile than the public who in most cases went only to laugh. Only about a dozen pictures were sold. The well-known singer Faure was mocked by the critic Emile Cardon in *La Presse* because he bought a Cézanne: 'We all know M. Faure has always liked to draw attention to himself. Buying Cézanne is as good a way as any other of getting yourself talked about, and make unusual publicity for yourself.'

What would he have said if Wallace had bought a Cézanne? But he never did and there was little danger, for it is almost certain that he was never even tempted. Wallace, it should be remembered, was nearly fifty-six years old at the time of the Impressionists' exhibition. He had spent all his life with Lord Hertford and it was most unlikely that suddenly he would become drawn to support a new, revolutionary group of painters all younger than himself. Pissarro at forty-four was the oldest,

Cézanne was thirty-five, Monet thirty-four and Renoir thirty-three. It is unlikely that Wallace could ever have admired the Impressionists. The gulf between them and himself was too great, but it would be unfair to call him, as Pissarro put it in a letter to his son about people who were impervious to the charm of Cézanne, one of those 'collectors who have shown by their errors that their sensibilities are defunct'.

His new life as a member of the landed gentry in Victorian England was now becoming one of Wallace's main interests. Having acquired the Sudbourn[1] estate, his first ambition had been to revive the shooting parties that had made it famous in the time of the 3rd Marquess of Hertford in the early part of the century. Ever since the 2nd marquess had stocked the estate with French partridges in 1770, Sudbourn had been famous for its partridge shooting. Croker, as we have seen, wrote to Peel from Sudbourn in 1821 describing one of these parties given by the 3rd marquess. Both the Regent and Peel had been guests at Sudbourn. In reviving these shooting parties Wallace would be the host, exactly as a Marquess of Hertford had been before him, in the house that had always belonged to the Hertfords. He would be following in the Hertford tradition and it fitted in with his desire to be the complete wealthy Englishman.

Typically, he set about it in the most lavish manner. Twenty-three gamekeepers were permanently employed to maintain the shoot, and specially designed game-cards, with coloured borders of pheasants, partridges, rabbits and hares, were printed to record the bags.

Although Wallace had only bought Sudbourn from the 5th marquess in the summer of 1872, it was made ready to entertain guests by the time the shooting season opened. One of the first guests was the 1st Earl of Cranbrook, the Conservative politician. Finding himself forced to speak French to Lady Wallace at dinner, he remarked afterwards: 'The dinner was too good, and required care and firmness. Lady Wallace speaks only French, and I took her in, to my dismay, and stumbled through some very bad language.'

[1] About this time the spelling for some reason changed and the final 'e' was dropped.

By 1874 the shooting parties had become important social occasions. At least half a dozen guns were invited to stay at Sudbourn Hall and neighbours were asked to join the visitors every day. Edmond Wallace, now retired from the French army and a British subject, and Murray Scott were usually members of the party. On occasions French friends, such as the Comte and Comtesse Louis d'Armaillé, also a collector, came over from Paris for the shooting.

On three occasions, in 1874, 1876 and 1879, Wallace had these lavish parties at Sudbourn recorded in paintings. He chose a minor French painter named Decaen who had painted the picture, now in the possession of the Prince Napoleon, of the little Prince Imperial driving out of the gates of Bagatelle with his escort of Spahis, of which Lord Hertford owned a replica. It seems likely that Decaen painted the three pictures in France from photographs. Fortunately they have survived, although Sudbourn Hall has been pulled down, and today they hang in the Town Hall at Orford, an interesting record of rich Victorians out shooting.

One of the pictures, painted in 1876, shows the setting for the lunch in the open air in the Great Wood, behind the house, after the morning's shooting. While Todd, the butler, carves a large game pie, the guns gather round the table with its white cloth set under a large tree. Wallace is seen being helped out of his overcoat by a footman. At the left of the picture Lady Wallace, who has just arrived to join the lunch party, is shown being handed out of the victoria by Edmond Wallace while the head groom holds the horses' heads. Others in the picture are believed to be the Comte and Comtesse d'Armaillé, Mr Edgar Disney, the Mayor of Orford, and the Rev. C. Pickthall, the rector of the nearby village of Chillesford. There is every indication that everybody was going to enjoy a good, solid lunch.

The third picture was probably exhibited in France at the Salon of 1880 with the title *Battue de perdreaux dans le comté de Suffolk*. Replicas of two of these pictures came on to the Paris art market some years ago. It would seem that Wallace ordered these replicas to give as handsome souvenirs to his French friends who had been invited to the shoots, perhaps the Armaillés.

When the Prince of Wales accepted his invitation to shoot at

Sudbourn Wallace must have been delighted. The future King Edward VII came on more than one occasion and Wallace must have felt himself the equal of the 3rd Marquess of Hertford who had entertained the future George IV in the same house.

Chapter Seventeen

THE NEXT SUMMER, DURING A VISIT TO PARIS, Wallace had one of his rare quarrels – and it was a bitter one – over a picture with his old friend Meissonier. The picture, which is now in New York and is known as *Friedland – 1807*, was to have been one of a series of five pictures to celebrate the important dates in the life of Napoleon. Meissonier started his studies for the picture as early as 1863 and it had been agreed that the finished picture would go to Lord Hertford, who was still alive then, for 200,000 francs.

The picture was far from being finished when the Franco–Prussian war broke out and Lord Hertford died. Meissonier, who escaped the siege of Paris, spent the war at his studio at Poissy, on the Seine eighteen miles away. On his return to Paris after the Commune, work on the picture proceeded very slowly and Wallace was asked by Georges Petit, a Paris dealer who handled Meissonier's pictures, to make a payment of 100,000 francs in advance, which he did. Nothing more was heard of the picture and when Wallace inquired about it in August 1875 he learned that it had been exhibited by Meissonier in Vienna in 1873 and that Petit had had it in his gallery. Nettled, he told Petit to tell Meissonier that he no longer wanted it. He was tired of waiting and asked for his 100,000 francs back.

Petit told Meissonier on 29 August that Wallace was not taking the picture, and as soon as he had gone Meissonier sat down and wrote a furious letter to Wallace.

'It is astonishing', he wrote, 'to wait until the very minute when you are told with certainty that the picture is ready to be delivered and then to refuse it in this way.'

His professional pride was wounded. He claimed that he alone could be the judge of when a picture was finished and nothing would make him deliver any work before he considered it worthy of his signature.

> We were both bound by an agreement. You go back on your word because, you say, you are tired of waiting. So be it. But I have the right to demand that you admit that not having seen the picture, which is now finished, for several years, it is only your impatience that makes you refuse it.
>
> The future will judge between us. My talent has time to wait if you have not.

Wallace replied to the wounded Meissonier, but unfortunately the letter has not survived. If he tried to soothe his injured pride it is clear that, in this case, the Wallace charm did not work because two days later, more furious than ever, Meissonier wrote a second and longer letter to Wallace defending himself.

Wallace must have given the impression that he was only buying the picture to help him. Angrily Meissonier says he does not believe it and refers to a favour he did Wallace thirteen or fourteen years previously which Wallace in his present situation has been able to return and he never asked him for anything. On the contrary, he thought he was doing Wallace a favour when he agreed to his proposal to buy the picture on the same terms as he had proposed to Lord Hertford some years before the war. He goes into long explanations as to why the picture had taken so long to finish – the interruption of the war, how he took it unfinished to Vienna, how he could not get it back because it had pleased the emperor. He says he only requested M. Petit to ask him for the 100,000 francs in 1872 because he needed the money for his daughter's dowry. He was clearly mainly concerned with what effect it would have on his reputation if it became known that Wallace had refused the picture and he ended his letter by again insisting that Wallace should admit his impatience.

> You have not seen the picture for several years, you do not know what it is like now and you refuse to take it because you are impatient and won't wait for it any longer. That is the real truth that you cannot refuse to admit and I am surprised that I should have to ask you to admit it.
>
> I am surprised also to have to point out that you cannot by yourself, without going back on your word, refuse this picture, well known as having been painted for you (believe me I was pleased to say so). Each of us is equally involved in this business and you could no more send

it back to me if I had not agreed, which I am very pleased to do today, than I could have sold it before this to others. I would like you to know, by the way, that I had the opportunity.

Another opportunity was not lacking because shortly afterwards Meissonier sold it to an American collector, Alexander T. Stewart of New York, for 300,000 francs, half as much again as Wallace would have paid.

Henry James saw the picture in Paris and in an article under the heading 'Parisian Sketches', published in the *New York Tribune* on 22 January 1876, he recalled the story of Wallace having refused it and its purchase by Mr Stewart. 'The thing is exceedingly clever, but it strikes me as the dearest piece of goods I have ever had the honour of contemplating.'

He went on to reveal that Mr Stewart in the end had to pay 'the prodigious sum' of 380,000 francs because he was asked to pay the duty charged by New York customs when it was sent to America and the cost of bringing it back to Paris for the exhibition at the Club des Mirlitons, which was where Henry James saw it. It was one of Meissonier's attempts at painting larger canvases and was not altogether successful. Whether this was the true reason why Wallace refused it we do not know, but Henry James had his reservations.

It seems to me it is a thing of parts rather than an interesting whole. The parts are admirable, and the more you analyse them the better they seem. The best thing, say, is a certain cuirassier, and in the cuirassier the best thing is his clothes, and in his clothes the best thing is his leather straps, and in his leather straps the best thing is the buckles.... That great general impression which, first and foremost, it is the duty of an excellent picture to give you, seems to me to be wanting here.

Mr Stewart died the next year and at the sale of his collection in New York in March 1887 Meissonier's picture was bought by Judge Henry Hilton of New York, who gave it in the same year to the Metropolitan Museum where it is today.

Meissonier finished only one other picture in the series of five he had planned. It is the *1814* which is in the Louvre.

The British hospital that Wallace had given to the British community in Paris during the siege was still functioning, with help

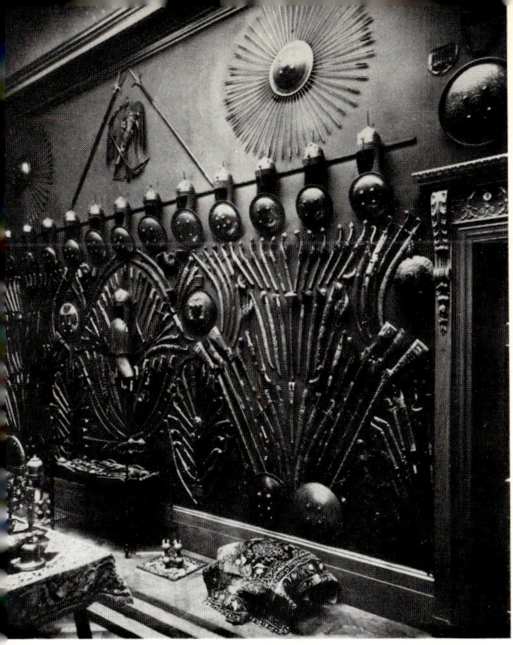

8. *Lord Hertford's collection of oriental armour as it was displayed at Hertford House when Wallace lived there.*

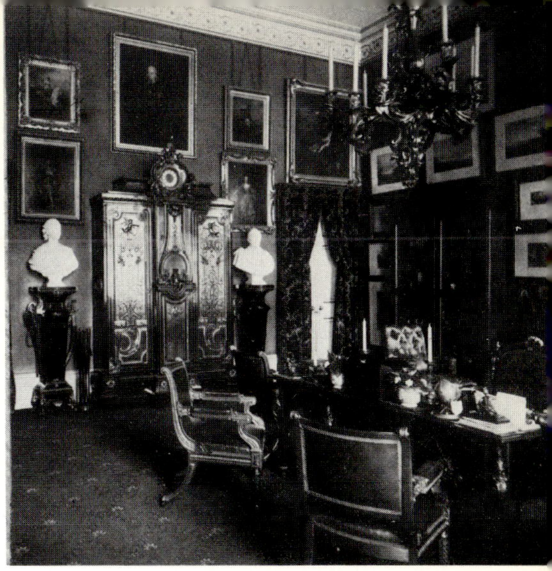

19. *Wallace's study at Hertford House (now Gallery XXI) in which were hung Lawrence's portrait of the 3rd Marquess* (Plate 6), *Boucher's portrait of Madame de Pompadour and the larger of the two Caffieri chandeliers which survived the fire at the Pantechnicon warehouse.*

o. *The inhabitants of the East End admiring the Collection at Bethnal Green Museum – a contemporary drawing.*

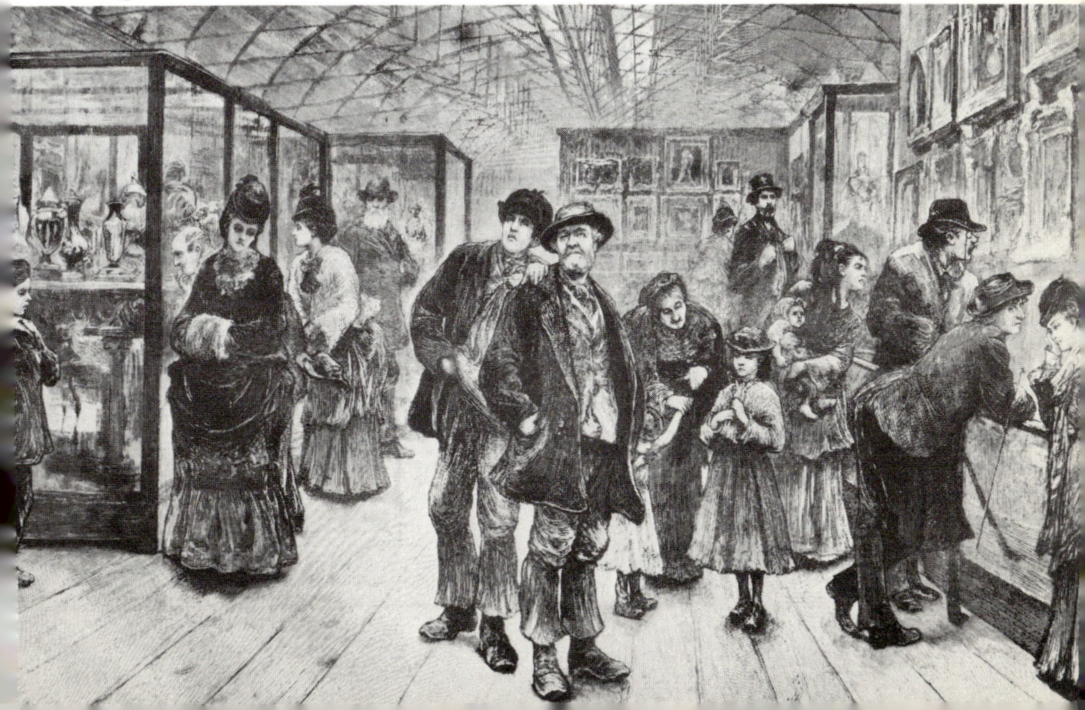

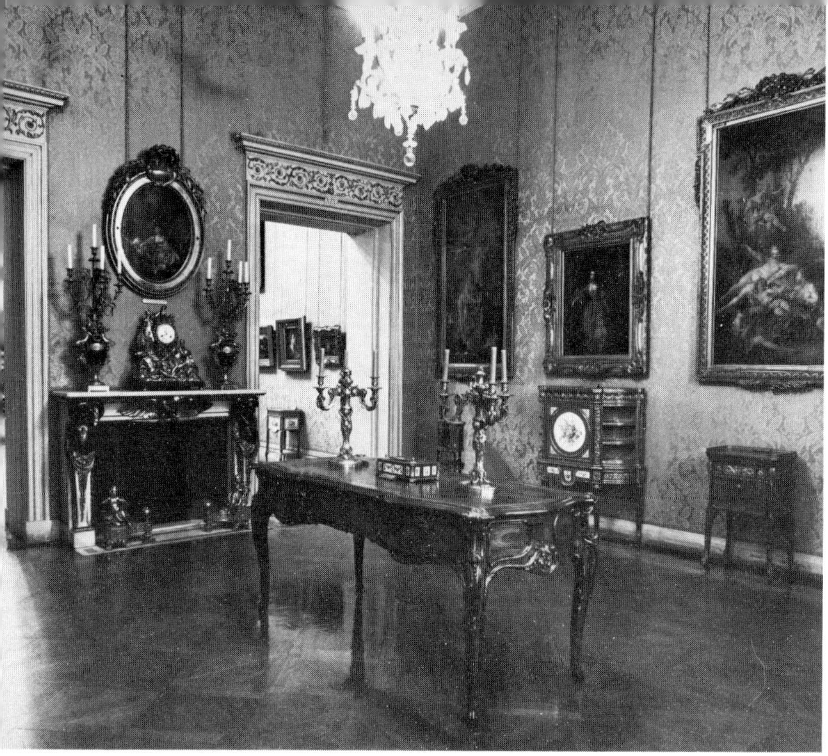

21. *Gallery XIX, which was once Lady Wallace's bedroom. On the chimney-piece is the Avignon Clock. All the pictures are by Boucher.*

22. *The Long Gallery at Hertford House in Wallace's day.* The Laughing Cavalier, *the Salvator Rosa,* Apollo and the Sybil, *and the* Rainbow landscape *by Rubens were on the end wall. The furniture included the Venetian state chairs, two of which were used by the Prince and Princess of Wales at the opening of the Bethnal Green Museum.*

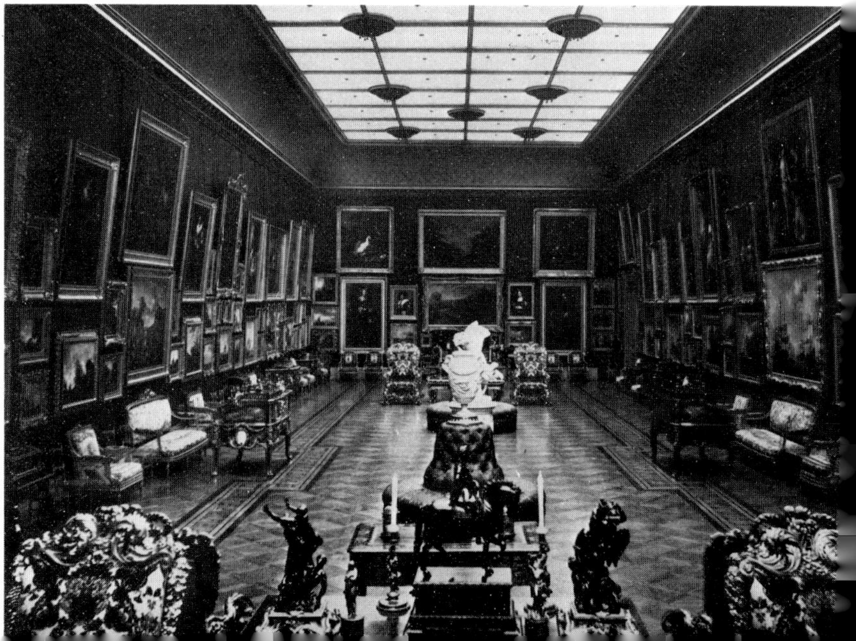

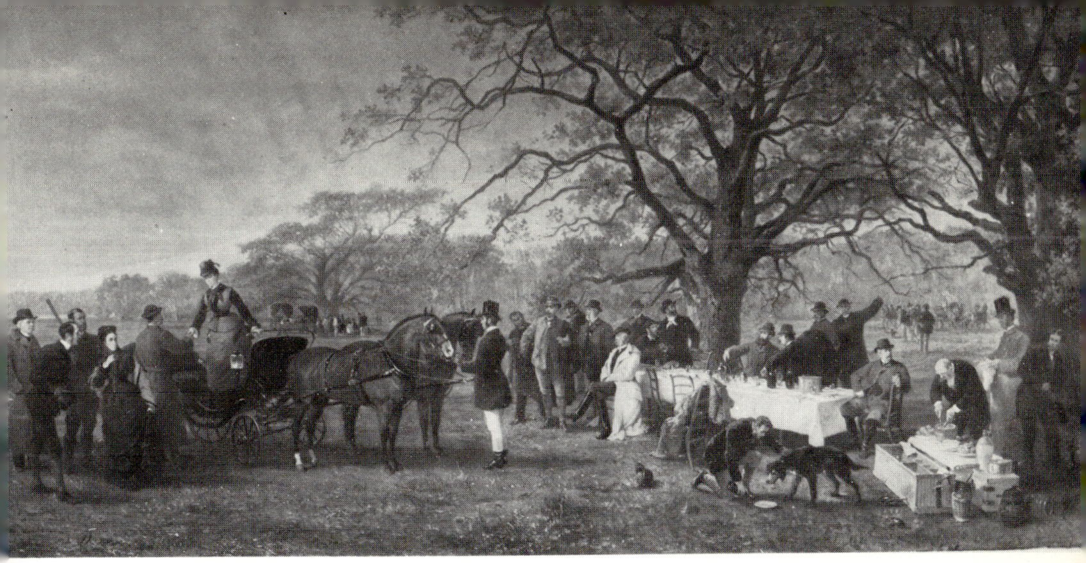

23. *The painting by Alfred Decaen of a shooting lunch at Sudbourn. Lady Wallace is being handed from her carriage by Capt. Edmond Wallace; Sir Richard is in the centre being helped into his coat by a footman.*

24. *The photograph of the shooting lunch on which Decaen based his painting. Sir Richard is standing at the right of the table.*

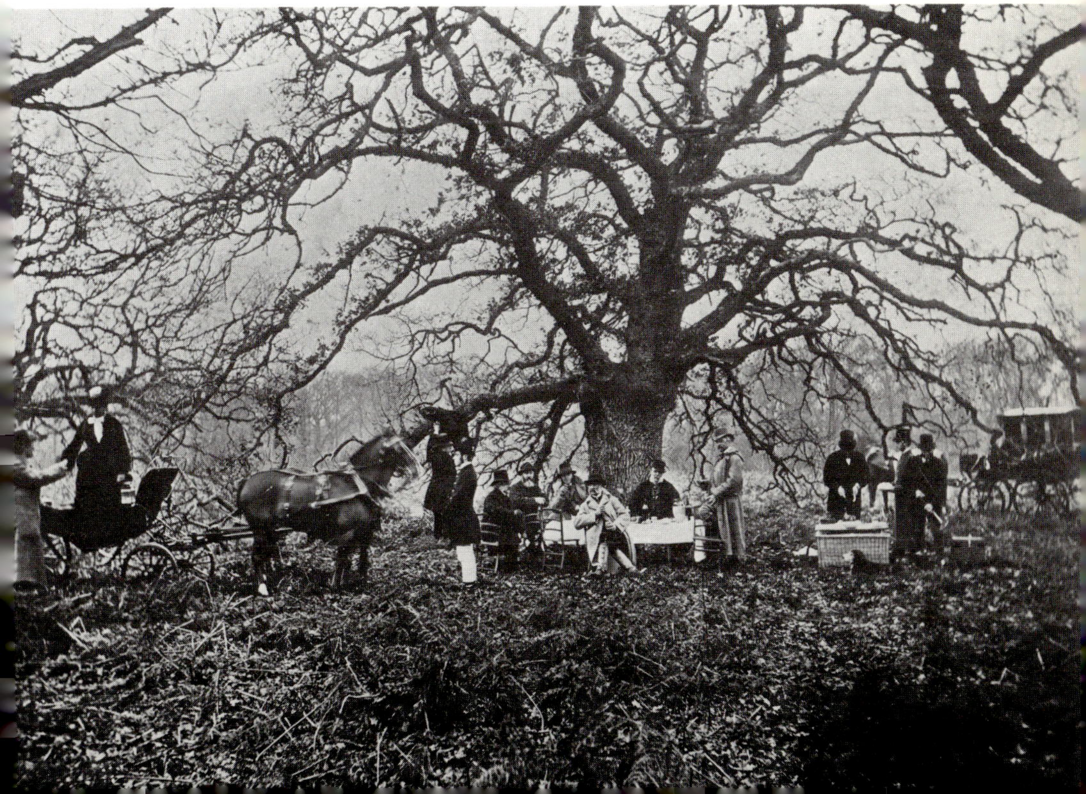

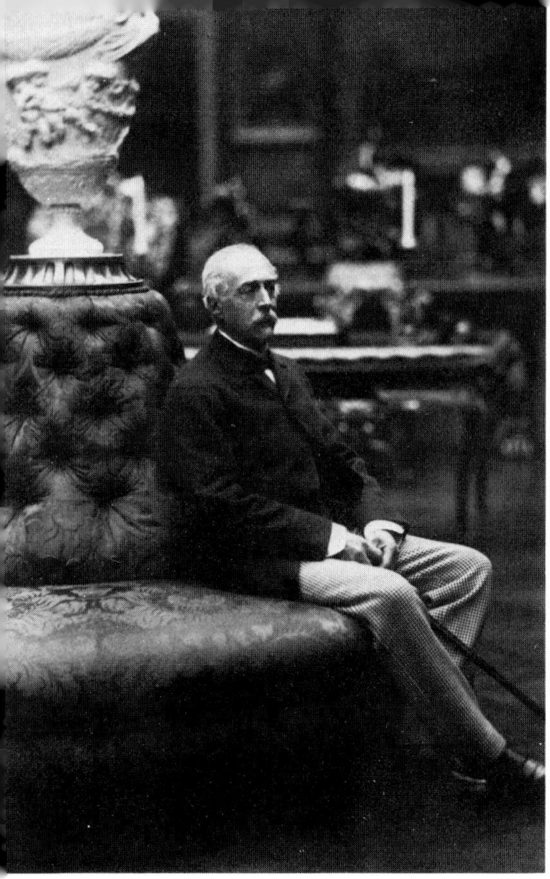

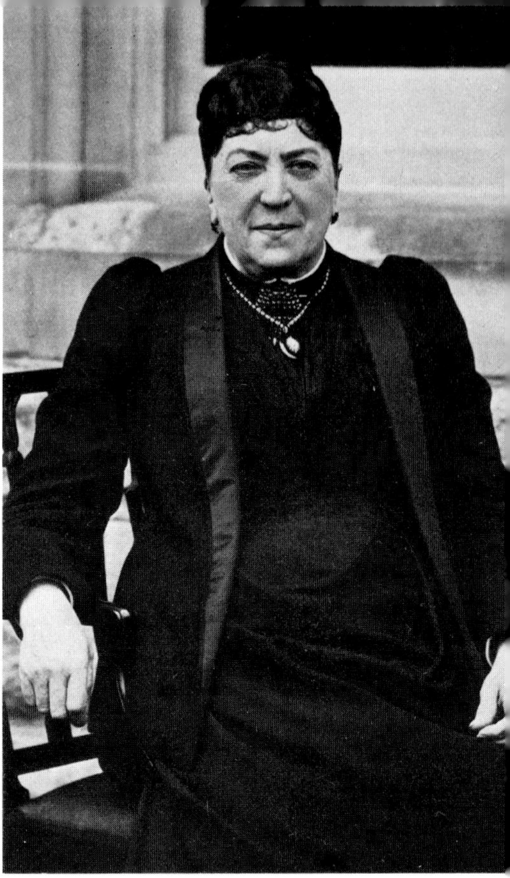

25. Sir Richard Wallace seated in the Long Gallery.

26. Lady Wallace as a widow.

27. Sir John Murray Scott.

28. Richardine Poirson, Wallace's god-daughter.

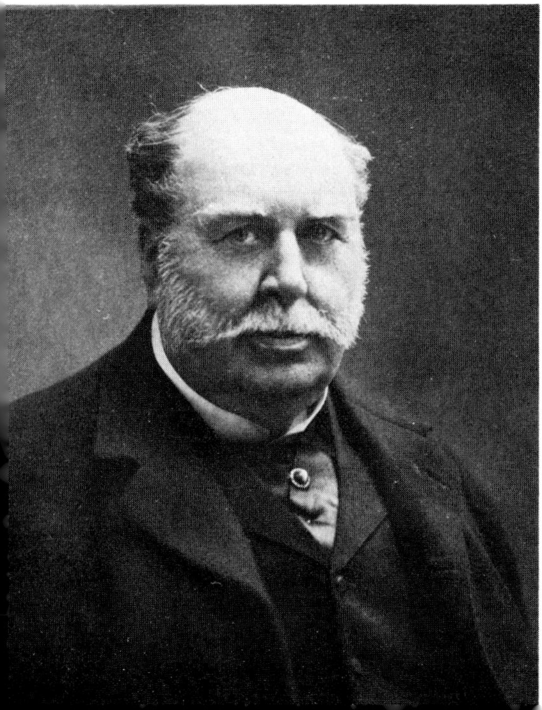

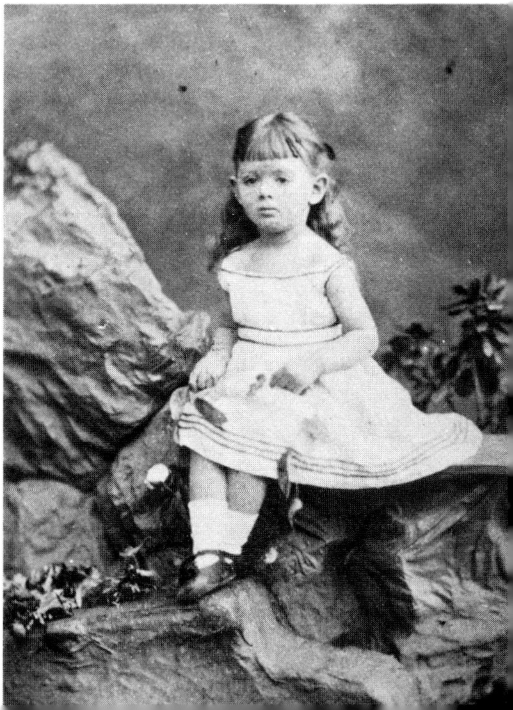

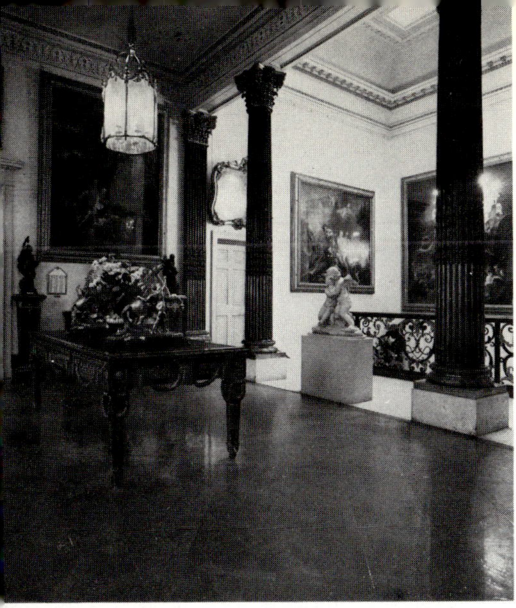

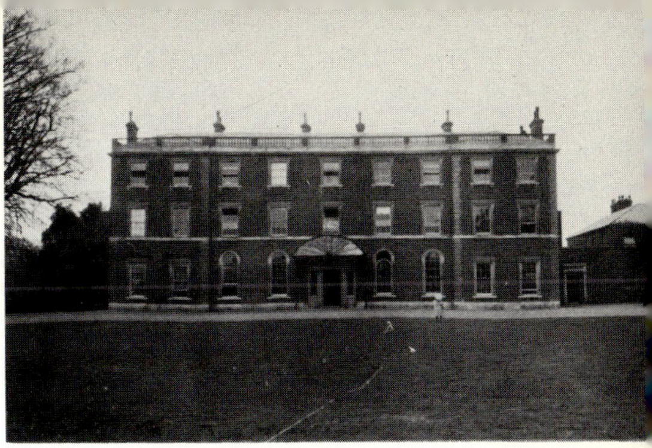

30. Sudbourn Hall as it was when Wallace lived there.

29. The landing at the top of the Grand Staircase at Hertford House, showing the Louis XV balustrade and some of the large paintings by Boucher.

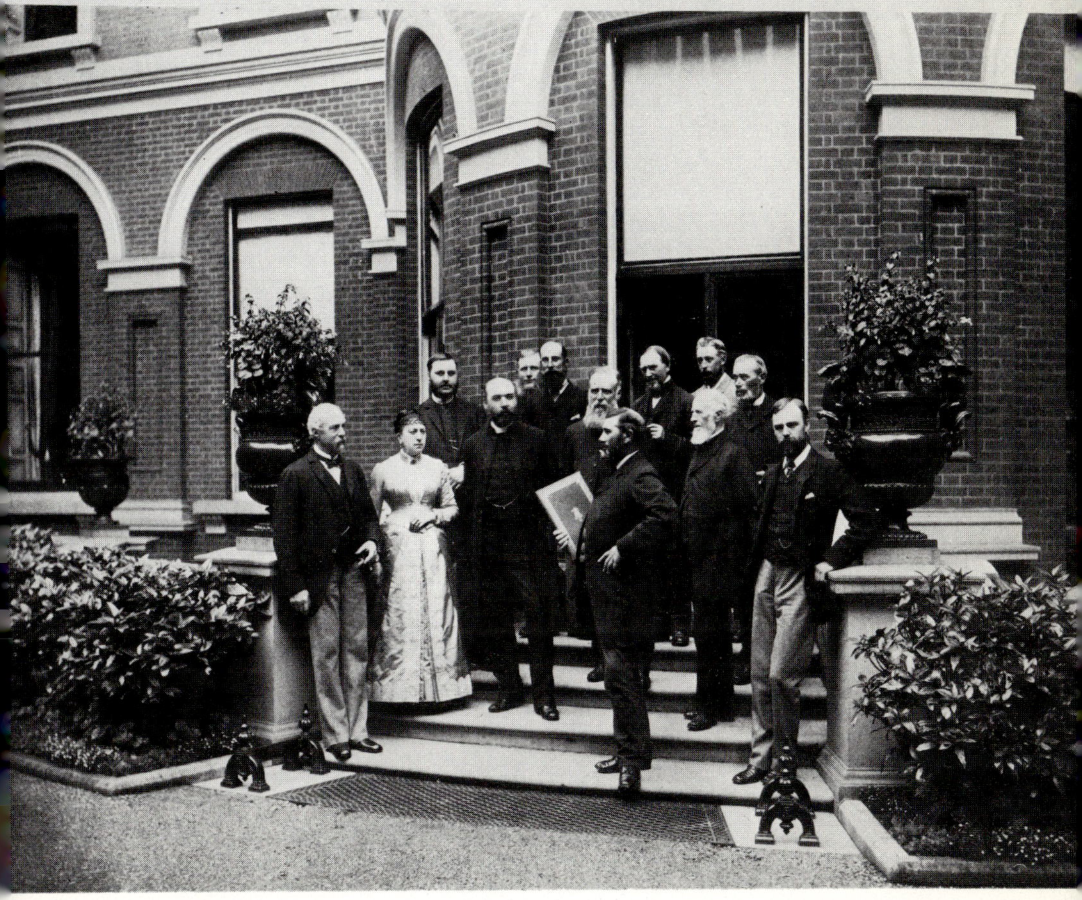

31. Sir Richard and Lady Wallace (left) *in the courtyard of Hertford House with the deputation of Sudbourn tenants who came to present Sir Richard with his portrait by W. R. Symonds in August 1886. Murray Scott stands behind Lady Wallace and the artist is on the extreme right.*

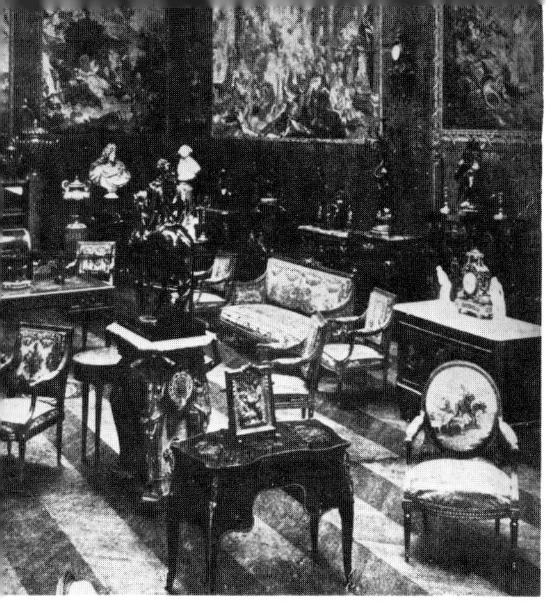

32. *The interior of the rue Laffitte apartment in Murray Scott's time. In the corner is the Houdon bust of Cagliostro (now in Washington); the tapestries are* L'histoire de Psyché, *after designs by Boucher (now in the Philadelphia Museum of Art). In the centre is the bronze equestrian statue of Louis XIV which was stolen during the Second World War.*

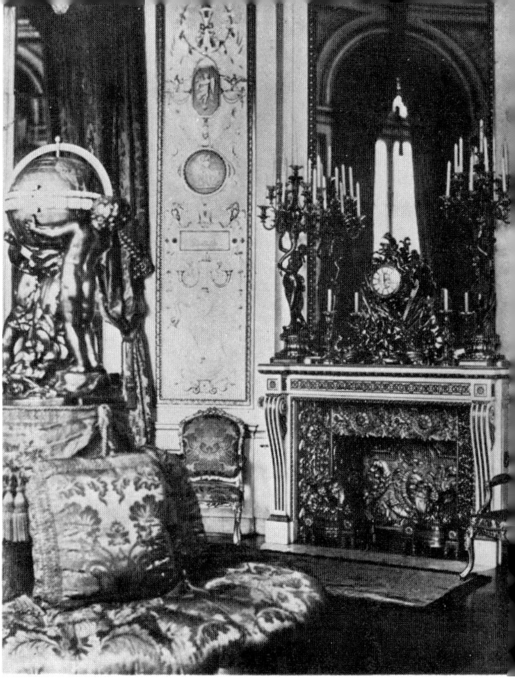

33. *The interior of Bagatelle when Wallace lived there.*

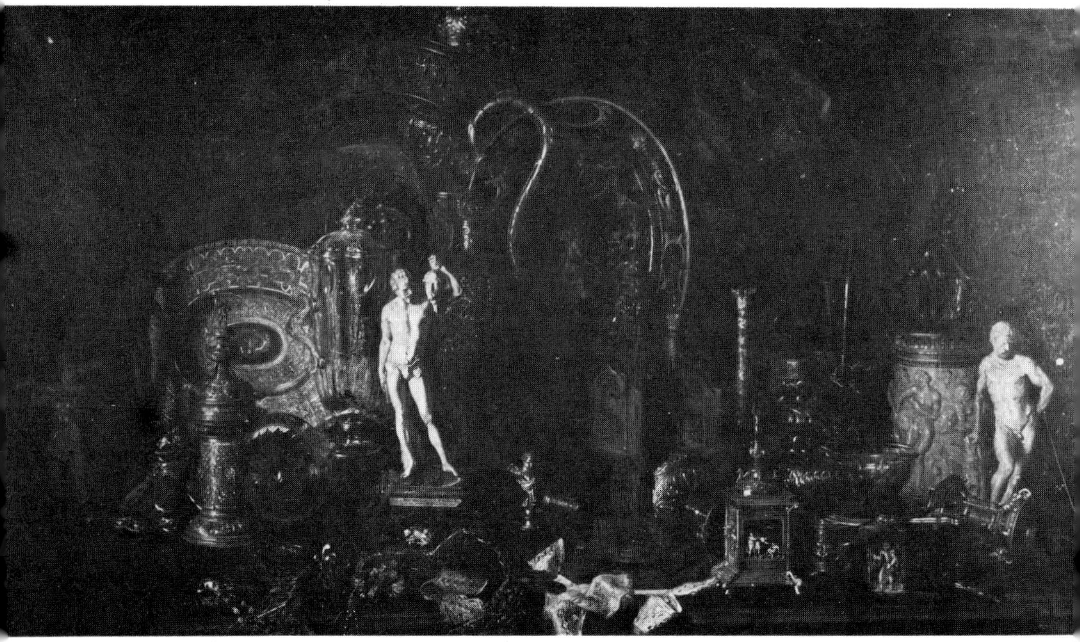

34. *The painting by Desgoffe which Wallace commissioned of objects in the Hertford House collection which he had bought himself. It was hung in the rue Laffitte apartment and is now in a private collection in Nantes.*

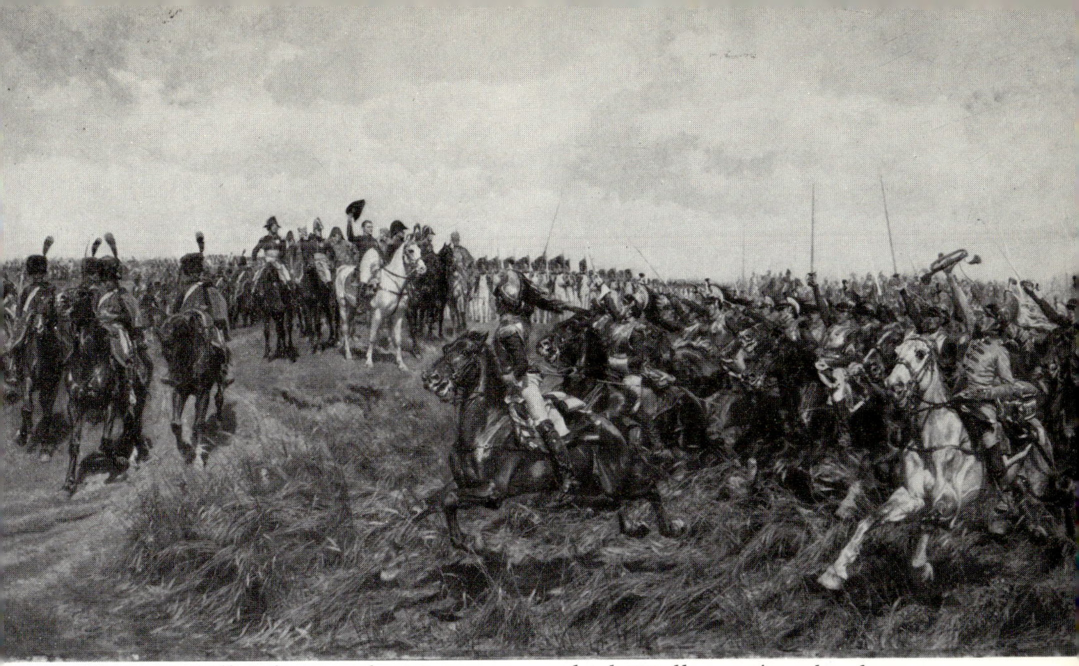

35. Friedland – 1807 *by Meissonier, which Wallace refused to buy. Henry James called it 'the dearest piece of goods I have ever had the honour of contemplating'. It is now in the Metropolitan Museum of Art, New York.*

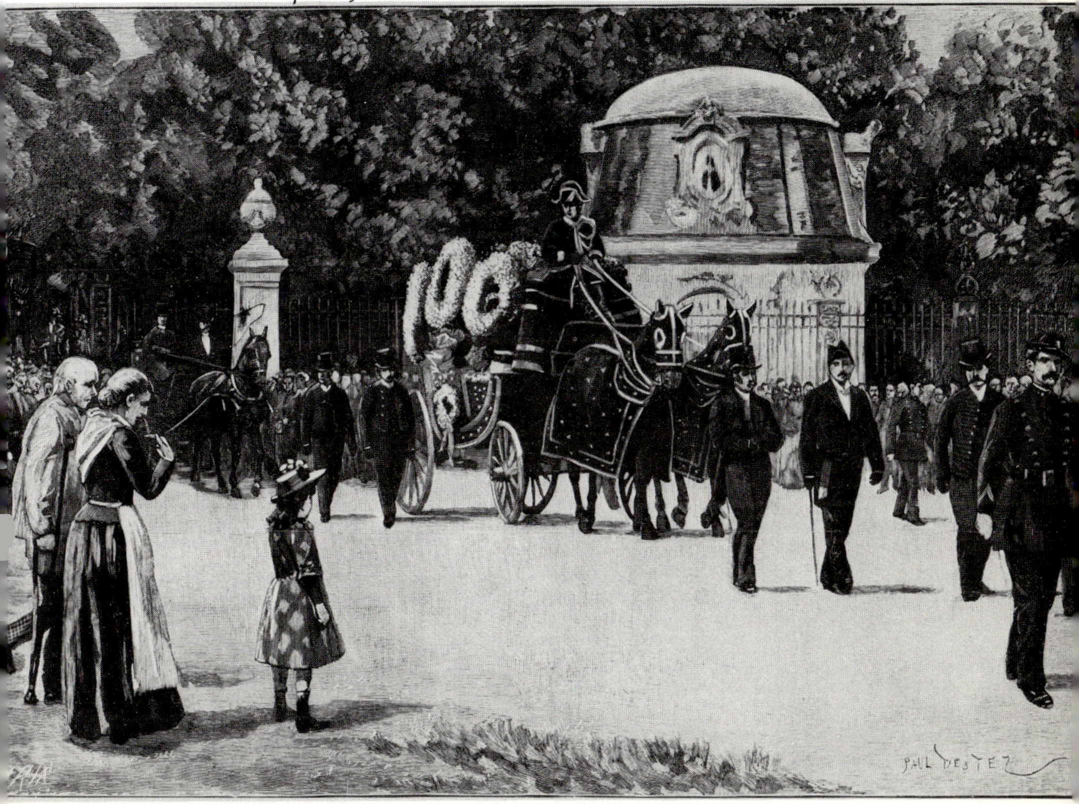

36. Wallace's funeral cortège leaves Bagatelle.

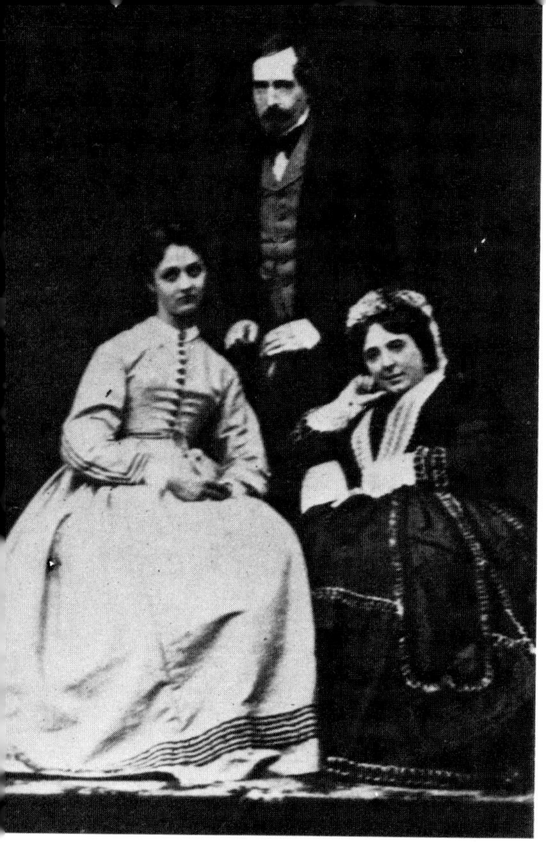

37. *Lord Hertford, Mme Oger and Seymourina, their daughter.*

38. *Bagatelle today.*

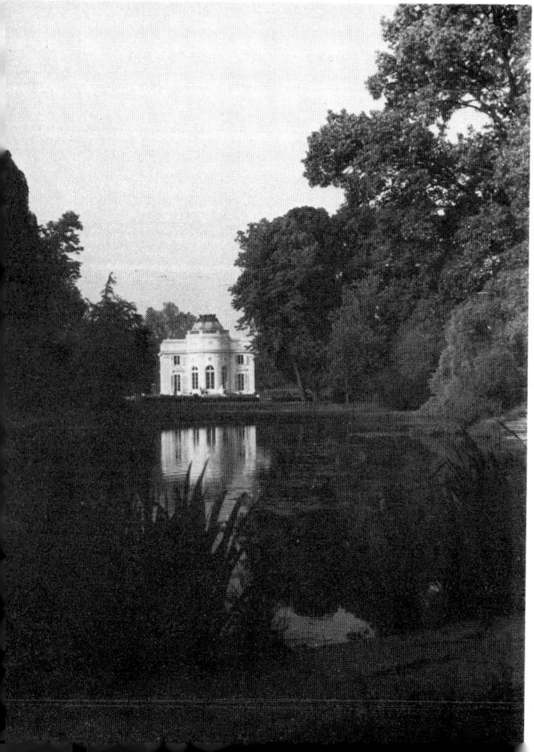

39. *The Wallace fountain at St Germain des Près.*

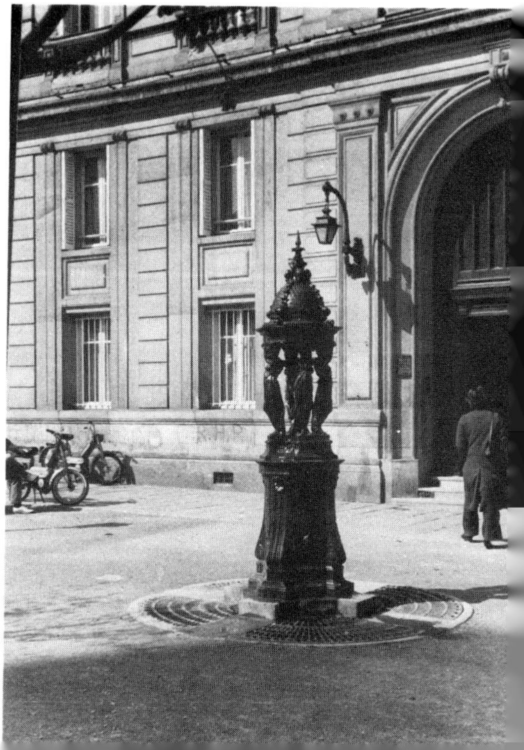

from him, and in the summer of 1876 he took steps to give it a sounder and more permanent existence. He decided to build a hospital, once again in memory of Lord Hertford, to be known as the Hertford–British Hospital. Land was bought at Neuilly, plans were prepared and the next year on 24 August, the seventh anniversary of the death of Lord Hertford, he and Lady Wallace laid the foundation stone. The hospital is there today, and the main frontage has been preserved.

In April 1875 the exhibition at the Bethnal Green Museum had at last closed its doors, and Wallace was looking forward to bringing the whole Collection to Hertford House, newly rebuilt specially to receive it. At last he would be able to live there as he had planned four years before when he had left Paris.

The entrance of the new Hertford House was exactly as it is today, with the new marble Grand Staircase and its Louis XV balustrade, adapted and brought from Paris, leading up from the hall to the first floor. On the right, as one entered, there were four rooms known as state rooms, and Wallace's Turkish-style smoking-room, which was elaborately decorated with tiles. On the left was a breakfast-room and the billiards room, while behind the staircase was the dining-room. There was also a housekeeper's room and the butler's quarters on a mezzanine floor. The kitchen was in the basement.

On the first floor, on the landing at the top of the stairs, was the conservatory. Then came the east drawing-room and two more state rooms which led into the oval drawing-room where Isabella, Lady Hertford, used to receive the Prince Regent. Leading out of the oval drawing-room was another room which was used by Wallace as his study.

On the west side were Lady Wallace's bedroom and boudoir and Wallace's dressing-room and bathroom. High up on the bathroom wall hung a neglected picture in bad condition which had been bought in 1815 by the 3rd marquess, when he was still Earl of Yarmouth. Not until 1900 was it discovered to be the original *Perseus and Andromeda* by Titian and it now hangs in Gallery XVI, the large gallery that Wallace built over the coach-house and stables.

All the remaining rooms on the first floor were given over to galleries to show the Collection.

In the galleries the Collection was arranged in the manner of the time. The pictures were hung crowded on the walls, row upon row above one another, the big pictures fitting in among the smaller ones, so that hardly a square foot of wall-space was left uncovered. The furniture was placed under the pictures, against the wall, in unbroken rows. Again there was little space between each piece of furniture. The centre of the gallery was left empty, except for an occasional writing-table or a pair of large armchairs. The result was an impression of an unbelievably overcrowded and expensive antique shop.

Two entire galleries were needed to display the collections of arms and armour. The European armour was arranged in the west gallery and the oriental armour was put in a gallery between the east drawing-room and the east picture gallery. In these two galleries the effect was less oppressive because the swords, spears, daggers, helmets and gauntlets were hung on the walls in decorative patterns, while the complete suits of armour stood on plinths round the room. This method of displaying armour is still used today in European castles, but it is anathema to the expert on armour because it is impossible to examine closely any individual item. A superb sword of great rarity and value may be one of a trophy of much inferior swords attached high up on the wall.

The great Rubens *Rainbow Landscape* and above it the Salvator Rosa *Apollo and the Sibyl of Cumae* were hung in the place of honour at the east end of the long gallery over the coach-house and stables; but not all the finest treasures were put in the galleries. Some of the most famous works of art were in the private rooms lived in by Sir Richard and Lady Wallace. The major part of the Greuze collection hung in Lady Wallace's boudoir. In her bedroom there were six Bouchers, two Fragonards, one of which was *The Swing*, showing the Baron de St Julien and his mistress, the Lancret painting of Carmago dancing and another Lancret. There were also the Greuze portrait of Sophie Arnould, the actress, and two Paters, in all some of the finest of Lord Hertford's eighteenth-century French paintings.

More eighteenth-century French paintings by Watteau, Boucher, Fragonard and Lancret were to be found in the oval drawing-room, together with a large number of miniatures arranged on the walls between the windows. Cabinets in the room contained Sèvres porcelain and gold snuff-boxes.

Food was the subject of the pictures in the dining-room where the walls were covered with still-life paintings of pheasants and game, pictures of dogs and hunting scenes. There were six paintings by Oudry and two Desportes. There were Sèvres in the billiards room and eleven pictures on the walls. The breakfast-room contained more Sèvres and sixteen Dutch pictures, mainly still lives.

Wallace had chosen for his study mostly watercolours, miniatures and the Limoges enamels he had always loved. In addition, he had kept for himself the great Boucher portrait of Madame de Pompadour with Ines, her favourite spaniel. She had commissioned the picture herself, and it had remained in her possession until her death. The study also contained a bronze statuette of Napoleon, and the portrait of the 3rd marquess by Lawrence.

There were no pictures in the smoking-room, because the walls were covered with elaborate tiles. Instead, there were two famous busts, the marble bust of Louis XIV by Coysevox, and a fine terracotta bust of Charles Le Brun. Wallace could smoke his cigars in good company.

For those who knew the story, if they searched hard among the multitude of pictures on the walls of the east drawing-room they would find, almost hidden, the little *Polichinelle* which Meissonier had painted on the panel of a door in the apartment of Madame Sabatier, who had been Wallace's mistress. Did Lady Wallace know from where that picture came, and why did Wallace hang it in the east drawing-room far away from the other Meissoniers grouped together in the Modern Gallery?

At last Wallace had settled for the first time in a house which was more nearly his own than any other house that he had lived in. It had been almost entirely rebuilt to his wishes and the lease was in his name. He had achieved everything he set out to do. He was the complete Englishman, a Member of Parliament, and as a friend of the Prince of Wales his position in society was firmly established. His life was easy, luxurious even, divided as it was between summers in Paris, shooting at Sudbourn, duties at Westminster and society life in London. He had everything he wanted. Honours continued to be offered him and he always accepted.

He agreed to become one of the Commissioners for the Paris Exposition of 1878 for which he was created K.C.B. It was the Prince of Wales, in a letter in his own handwriting dated 15 October 1878, who had put his name forward to the Prime Minister as being worthy of reward for services rendered. He was a Trustee of the National Gallery and of the National Portrait Gallery.

Every Sunday he and Lady Wallace could be seen walking to church at the now demolished St Thomas's in Orchard Street and each would put a gold sovereign into the collection. He was a model Victorian philanthropist, serious, always gracious and ready to use his wealth to help others. His charm became a legend.

If Wallace enjoyed being a success in London society, the same cannot be said of Lady Wallace. Although she had now lived in England for some years she had never learned to speak English and was clearly out of her element. Dutifully she followed her husband wherever he went, but she could never adapt to the new surroundings and her embarrassing manner and lack of conversation discouraged the few who were brave enough to try to talk to her. She nearly always dressed in black, for French chic had not crossed the Channel with her, and for most of the time she sat alone, a silent, sombre figure while everyone seemed fascinated by her husband.

Lady Wolseley, wife of the field-marshal, met Sir Richard and Lady Wallace at a dinner party and wrote down her impressions after meeting them for the first time:

> Lady Wallace's presence was rather 'springing a mine' on one, but she is most harmless and dowdy, refuses to speak a word of English. Sir Richard Wallace is charming – I made up to him, and he has promised that we shall go alone to see his house in the spring. He is a most attractive man, I think.

This seems to have been the view of everyone on meeting Sir Richard and Lady Wallace for the first time.

The Wolseleys, as Wallace had promised, were invited to Hertford House, where the contents were to 'spring a mine' on the field-marshal. He was profoundly shocked by the nudes 'in every seductive attitude'.

Although Wallace was quietly making additions to the Collection at this time he had no intention of continuing the tireless buying in the manner of Lord Hertford. Having so notably increased the range of the Collection in the early seventies to include medieval and Renaissance objects, he now wished to concentrate on building up the majolica collection. He also bought gold boxes and one or two pictures every year. He made very few additions to the splendid collection of French furniture, but occasionally he would buy a piece, such as the cylinder-top desk by Riesener. This was his only purchase at the great Hamilton Palace sale of 1882, although there were many other fine eighteenth-century French works of art in the sale which Lord Hertford could never have resisted.

One of the pictures he bought was of a landscape near Sudbourn, *Orford on the River Ore*, by the English painter W. C. Stanfield, who started life as a sailor, went on to paint scenery at Drury Lane and eventually became a Royal Academician. Here again he was following Lord Hertford's taste, who had bought two of Stanfield's views of Venice.

His attitude now was much more that of the curator of the Collection than a wealthy collector always in search of new treasures. Unlike Lord Hertford, the Collection was not his whole life and he was happy living in England and enjoyed being a social success.

Chapter Eighteen

RICHARD WALLACE'S DECISION TO LEAVE FRANCE and settle in London had resulted in a life of considerable contentment and undoubted success from every point of view. However, before his happiness could be complete there was one thing which could not be overlooked or forgotten because it concerned his son, Edmond Richard.

Like his mother, the former captain in the French army had not taken to life in England. Although he was now a British subject he had not been able to transform himself into an Englishman. He did not share his father's enthusiasm for English life and society, and as time went by his visits to France became more and more frequent. Wallace, who had hoped that he would find a wife in England, could not understand his attitude and it was a source of great pain and disappointment to him.

In the spring of 1875, hoping, perhaps, that it would influence Edmond, Wallace began to explore the possibility that his son, although illegitimate, might inherit his baronetcy. He was a friend of Disraeli, who was then Prime Minister, and he must have approached him and told him the whole story. Disraeli was sympathetic and instructed the Garter King of Arms to see if there were any precedents which could be invoked in support of such an unusual step. Evidently he succeeded, for on 2 May Disraeli submitted a memorandum to the queen enclosing the precedent which 'Garter has furnished respecting the question concerning Sir Richard Wallace'. He went on to say that the point of view was 'whether the Wallace family with their vast possessions shall become an English or a French family with large estates in Her Majesty's Kingdom left by absentee landlords and their rents consumed in Paris'.

The queen replied promptly. A memorandum dated 3 May

from Sir Thomas Biddulph, Keeper of the Privy Purse, said he could not help thinking that granting the reversion of a dignity to an illegitimate son would open a door to much possible inconvenience. He added that he did not see why, if it was not granted, the Wallace family were bound to become French, instead of English, as all the estates were in England and Ireland. Another memorandum of the same date said that the queen had given the case of Sir Richard Wallace 'the fullest consideration and has come to the conclusion that it would not be advisable to do what it proposed, viz., to create a new Baronetcy with remainder to Mr Edmond Richard Wallace'. It ended by saying 'that it does not follow that this Mr Wallace would settle in France if he were not a Baronet, for many wealthy people are not Baronets and it would not be for the Sovereign to confer such an honour on such an understanding'.

Did Richard Wallace dream of founding a dynasty of Wallace baronets succeeding one another as the owners and occupants of Hertford House and Sudbourn? Perhaps, but whatever his reasons it must have come as a considerable disappointment when Disraeli told him that the queen would not agree to the proposal. At this time his relations with his son were approaching breaking point, although he kept the problem strictly to himself. On the surface life in England and France went on as usual.

Three years later he showed his gratitude to Disraeli, now Lord Beaconsfield, by presenting him with the 3rd marquess's diamond star insignia of the Order of the Garter on the former's return in triumph from the Congress of Berlin. The 3rd marquess had originally intended to leave it to Peel but, as we have seen, changed his mind.

Wallace's last tribute to the memory of Lord Hertford, the Hertford–British Hospital in Paris, was opened in 1879 and that summer the Prince of Wales went to see it. Wallace's friendship with the Prince of Wales had grown closer and on returning to London his Royal Highness paid a visit to Hertford House.

In November he was a guest at one of the lavish shooting parties at Sudbourn. In his diary the Prince of Wales noted that there was covert shooting every morning and that on the last two days they had some snow. He also made an interesting special note that on Wednesday, 19 November, Lady Wallace was at dinner.

It may be that he remembered that night because dinner was not as gay as usual and he had to speak French to his hostess. Equally well, it might have meant that Lady Wallace was not at dinner on the other nights. She was frequently unwell and may often have pleaded illness to absent herself from difficult social occasions.

Edmond Wallace was not at Sudbourn for the prince's visit. But Wallace's secretary, Murray Scott, was present with his two sisters. A big, clumsy bachelor, he seems almost to have been adopted by Wallace. Of course he could speak French, which made him indispensable to Lady Wallace, and although he knew nothing about painting or art he was a permanent member of the Wallace entourage. It is difficult to imagine him at Hertford House, but perhaps, lacking his son's presence, Wallace turned automatically to this man whom he had brought with him from Paris.

Wallace made two unusual additions to the Collection in 1879. Both were relics, one of them Irish, and they represented his personal taste for much earlier works of art than those of the eighteenth century so loved by Lord Hertford. From Spitzer, the dealer from whom he had bought armour, Wallace bought the seventh-century Bell of St Mura, which was long preserved in Ireland at the Abbey of Fahan. It is a bronze cow-bell, without its tongue or striker, decorated with Celtic tracery and semi-precious stones and, according to the legend, it descended from the sky, ringing loudly, on the site of the abbey. Before it touched the earth the tongue was seen to detach itself and return upward to heaven. St Mura was abbot of Fahan, and for centuries it was revered as a relic for its powers of healing.

The second relic was the hunting-horn of Saint Hubert, the patron saint of hunting. The horn, which is painted, gilded and decorated with enamel of the third quarter of the fifteenth century, is believed to have been given by the Bishop of Liège to Charles the Bold, Duke of Burgundy, in return for his help in suppressing an uprising of Liègeois in 1468. Saint Hubert, before his martyrdom in 727, had been Bishop of Liège. Charles the Bold built a chapel for the relic at Chauvirey le Chatel, and with the horn it became the property of the Comte de Scey. He it was who sold the horn to Wallace for 16,000 francs. A year later, when Edmond de Goncourt heard that Wallace had bought the horn of Saint Hubert, he noted it in his journal with the unkind comment that Wallace had not bought it for its value as a work of art but only in order to be able to tell its history to the Prince of Wales.

It may have been about this time that the Prince of Wales sold Wallace the famous Landseer, *The Arab Tent*, which had been exhibited at the Royal Academy in 1866.

Wallace's fame had spread also to the court of Ludwig II, the mad King of Bavaria. In his passion for building castles, the king must have decided that Wallace as a Scotsman was the best person to supply him with illustrations of castles he had never seen but which he imagined were perched on craggy mountains in the Highlands of Scotland. Wallace sent him photographs, drawings and engravings of castles and buildings in the British Isles with which Ludwig was well satisfied, for he is said to have wished to give him a decoration. This did not occur, but as a sign of his gratitude he sent him in 1883, through the German ambassador in London, an engraved portrait of himself which Wallace hung in his study. It is also probable that he may have advised the king on French eighteenth-century decoration and furnishing.

Also in Wallace's study, in the place of honour over his writing-table, was another royal portrait with which he had been presented. It was an oil-painting of Queen Victoria's eldest daughter, the Empress Frederick of Germany, as Crown Princess. She was the favourite sister of the Prince of Wales and she presented the portrait to Wallace. The artist was Heinrich von Angeli, a Hungarian who had a success as a royal portrait painter at the courts of Austria, England and Russia.

Wallace was now completely estranged from his son, who had no thought for the Collection and its future, or for the estates that Wallace would leave him when he died. He had chosen to return to France and had formed a liaison with a woman who was described later by Yriarte as a 'personne de théâtre'. They had children but did not get married, which caused Wallace to exclaim: 'Mon Dieu, est-ce que nous n'aurons jamais fini de bâtards?'

Ill-health was now adding to his troubles. Plagued by gout,

Wallace became the victim of serious bouts of depression during which he brooded on what seemed to him his son's betrayal to such an extent that his general health was affected. In his despondency he lost interest even in the Collection. In the summer of 1884 he did not make his usual visit to Paris, perhaps not wishing to see or be reminded of his son. Instead, he went to Scotland, hoping that a change of air would revive his spirits, but he seems to have derived little benefit from the visit. In August, when Charles Davis wrote to tell him that the Duke of Marlborough was selling some parts of his collections at Blenheim, he could not bring himself to be interested and replied that he was 'too old and too poor' to think of buying anything at the Blenheim sale. 'My miserable galleries are closed,' he added, seeming to admit defeat.

But despite this black mood the famous Wallace charm could still shine from time to time through the clouds of his depression. In 1885 he agreed to sit for his portrait to the Suffolk-born painter W. R. Symonds. Recalling the sittings which took place in his studio at Holland Park Road, Symonds wrote afterwards that Wallace never sat down, always preferring to stand, smoking a cigar, with one hand resting on the back of a chair. 'My impression of Sir Richard was particularly the charm of his personality and his extreme kindness.'

The portrait, which was to be a present to Sir Richard and Lady Wallace from their tenants and friends on the Sudbourn estate, was presented to them at Hertford House by a tenants' deputation and was exhibited at the Royal Academy the same year. Apart from a posthumous marble bust by E. Hannaux it is the only portrait of him in the Collection.

Flashes of the old Wallace were rare and he was seen less and less in society. His world had collapsed. Since the break with his son the future he had planned could never be. What was the point of anything? he asked himself. Just as when he had suddenly decided he could no longer live in France, now he felt he could no longer live in England. In his misery he did exactly what Lord Hertford had done: he went and shut himself up alone at Bagatelle. Lady Wallace remained in London, with John Murray Scott always in attendance to see that she had everything she needed.

In Paris there was someone who could have helped, who could have been closer to him than any friend because she was a relation. She was, in fact, his half-sister, Seymourina, the little girl for whose provision Lord Hertford had added a codicil to his will in 1850 at the time when he also added the codicil leaving everything to Wallace. Now she was married to a M. Paul Poirson and was living in the boulevard Haussmann. She had two children, a daughter born in 1871 and a son born two years later. Wallace was godfather to the daughter, who had been baptised at Bagatelle because the Protestant church at Neuilly had been damaged by shellfire during the war. Moreover, in continuation of the family taste for invented names, she was baptised Richardine. After the baptism, during which Wallace had promised the clergyman that he would pay for the repairs to his church, Seymourina and Wallace had quarrelled and were no longer on speaking terms. The cause of the quarrel is not known, but from an exchange of letters dating from the summer of 1874 it appears that Wallace had offended her.

The first letter, dated 20 August 1874, from Seymourina to Wallace, was written in French and she addressed her half-brother as 'Cher Sir Richard'. She said she was taking up riding again (perhaps after the birth of her son) and asked if she could have a saddle that had been made for her and which she thought was still in the saddle-room at Bagatelle.

Wallace replied saying the saddle was still there and reminded her that a horse he gave her some time ago was still in the stables. She seemed to have forgotten all about it. He said that she also seemed to have forgotten to give him the pleasure of seeing his god-daughter.

Seymourina replied on 22 August refusing Charley, the horse, because she had no stables and thought he would be happier at Bagatelle. Her excuse for not bringing Wallace's god-daughter to see him was that they never knew when he was at Bagatelle until after he had gone. Without giving details she also said that, because of the letter that Wallace had sent her, she could no longer bring Richardine to see him herself, but that the child's father could bring her. She ended by saying that she regretted this state of affairs particularly on the eve of 'un triste anniversaire qui devrait nous réunir'. The sad anniversary which should have united them was in two days' time – the anniversary of the death of Lord Hertford, their father.

There exists a fragment of a letter, which may have been a draft for his reply, in which Wallace suggests that the real reason she does not want Charley is that she thinks he is too old. He also says that she can always find out when he is there and it is impossible to make a woman listen to reason. We do not know whether he ever sent a reply, or whether it was on these lines, but it is unlikely that the breach was healed. No more letters between them have survived. In any case, during this period Wallace seems to have seen very few friends in France, avoiding all connection with the past.

But we do know that Seymourina had become a great beauty, as can be seen in the portrait John Singer Sargent painted of her in 1885, now in the Detroit Institute of Arts. Seymourina came to know Sargent because her husband was the artist's landlord. M. Poirson owned the house in the boulevard Berthier where Sargent had his studio in Paris in the 1880s. Sargent had also painted, the year before, a smaller portrait of her daughter, Richardine, Wallace's god-daughter, who married M. Pierre Girod.

We also know that Wallace was interested enough in Seymourina, despite their quarrel, to ask Capron, his solicitor in London, to find the will of her guardian, who had died in 1874, to see if he had left her any money. This was not Frederick John Cuthbert who had adopted her in 1848 but his brother, Captain James William Cuthbert, who had succeeded as Seymourina's guardian after his brother had died while she was still a child. Capron reported to Wallace, in a letter dated 20 September 1881, that by his will Captain Cuthbert had left everything to his wife but that after her death there were several legacies, 'among others £25,000 to Madame Seymourina Suzanne Poirson....' By a codicil she was also to receive half of his residuary personal estate after the death of his widow.

In 1877 came the terrible blow of Edmond's death in Paris. He had never been reconciled with his father, nor had he lived in the Trianon which Wallace had built for him at Bagatelle. He left four children, some of whose descendants are living in France today. He had never married their mother.

*

In 1888 Wallace went back to London for the opening of the Old Masters Exhibition at the Royal Academy. He had lent several pictures for the exhibition. To record the ceremony H. J. Brooks painted a commemorative group portrait which now hangs in the National Portrait Gallery. The painting shows Wallace standing, silk hat in hand, between Lord Wantage and Lady Jersey, and he looks an ageing and unhappy man.

At this time, no longer having a son to whom he could leave the Collection, Wallace seems to have considered leaving at least part of it to the British nation. He discussed the matter with friends, but the difficulty of getting government support for a special building and the expense of the endowment discouraged him. Pleading ill-health, he dropped the whole idea and returned to France with nothing settled. Back at Bagatelle he became a lonely, melancholy and somewhat eccentric recluse.

There is a story that Lord Warwick and some friends were invited by Wallace to lunch at Bagatelle. On arriving they were told by the butler that Sir Richard was unwell and wished them to excuse him from receiving them. They therefore sat down to lunch without him. During the meal Lord Warwick's attention was attracted by the opening of a small panel in the wall, behind which he saw Wallace's face. For some time he stared at his guest fixedly and without recognition. Then the panel was closed. Lord Warwick said nothing and when lunch was finished he and his friends drove back to Paris without seeing Wallace.

Wallace died suddenly on 20 July 1890, alone in the same room and in the same bed in which Lord Hertford had died. It was a Sunday and the news of his death was first announced in Paris at the morning service at the new English church of St George in the rue des Bassins, to the building of which Wallace had subscribed £8,000.

In London *The Times*, quoting a Reuters telegram from Paris, announced his death on Monday, 21 July, in a short paragraph of only seventeen lines. The next day it devoted a leading article to his death in which it said that it must have come as a surprise to the public at large as only intimate friends were aware of the 'precarious state' of his health. It went on to say that he was not so well known in London as in Paris where he had lived principally since he had given up his seat in Parliament. After telling the story of how he inherited the Collection from Lord Hertford, *The Times* did not hesitate to say that Wallace was Lord Hertford's son.

'When he [Lord Hertford] died, as he could not leave his title or his entailed estates to his son, he left him the house and all it contained, as well as the treasures collected in Paris and a large amount of money.'

The Bethnal Green exhibition and Wallace's collections in London and Paris were mentioned and then *The Times* raised the question of who would inherit them. 'The ungracious question forces itself forward. What will happen to them now? He has left no child.'

Common gossip, according to *The Times*, said he intended to leave everything to the nation: that he had left Hertford House and its contents to England and the rest to France. It added that the 'procrastinating habit' so common in these cases may have prevented him from making a will to 'secure this great object'. If he had, such a public gift has 'hardly been made since Attalus left his all to the Roman people', since the treasures at Hertford House were valued at three million pounds.

The funeral took place on Wednesday, 23 July, in Paris. It was a simple ceremony in accordance with Wallace's wishes. There was no military escort as was the custom at burials of Commanders of the Legion of Honour and no invitations were sent out from Bagatelle.

'The deceased, moreover,' *The Times* reported from Paris the next day, 'had expressed a desire that there should be no display. A third-class hearse and six mourning coaches were accordingly engaged, and only a few intimate friends were admitted to Bagatelle.'

The Préfet of Police and the Mayor of Neuilly who went to Bagatelle were told that there would be no procession on foot leaving Bagatelle and went back to Paris to wait at St Geroge's Church.

Lady Wallace had come from London and 'seemed overcome with grief', according to the *Standard*. The then Lord Hertford, the 6th marquess, had also travelled from London to attend the funeral. The procession of coaches, after crossing the Bois de Boulogne, reached St George's Church near the Arc de Triomphe at 2.30 p.m. After the service a deputation of green-uniformed keepers from the Bois walked behind the hearse to the cemetery of Père Lachaise. There were crowds of Parisians in the streets to watch the funeral procession pass. At the cemetery Monsieur Baudin, on behalf of the Municipality, gave a short address praising not only Wallace's benefactions but also the French patriotism he showed in 1870.

The Prince of Wales had sent a message of condolence to Lady Wallace and on his behalf the Embassy placed a large wreath of red and white roses on the tomb. As he had specifically requested, Wallace was buried in the Hertford family vault, his coffin being placed under the remains of Lord Henry Seymour.

The *Times* correspondent in Paris ended his despatch with more speculation with regard to Wallace's will. 'There is a rumour that Sir Richard Wallace had left two wills, one in English and the other in French, with large bequests to charities.'

The Times was wrong. His son being dead, and any intention he may have had of making a bequest to the British nation having been shelved, Wallace left everything to Lady Wallace, his 'dear wife', under a will made in October 1880 at Sudbourn. One of the witnesses was John Todd, the butler at Sudbourn. Subject to the continuation of pensions and allowances being paid in France and England and the endowment of the Hertford–British Hospital in Paris to be charged to the Irish estates, everything was left unconditionally to her.

There is something infinitely pathetic about Wallace's death. He was the best-known philanthropist of his day, and a social success with everything he wanted. And yet he suddenly gave it all up to go back to Bagatelle to die. Was it an admission of defeat? In a sense it almost certainly was.

Lord Hertford's will had made him rich and famous and he had gone to England to live like a Hertford, with one difference: he had given away much of his wealth and he had always tried to do the right thing. He sat in Parliament for his Irish tenants. He had brought life back to empty Hertford House and Sudbourn. He had lent Lord Hertford's Collection for the public to see. Although he had made himself the complete Englishman, he had not forgotten the English in France, whence he had come. For them he had built and endowed a hospital and given money to help build a church.

All this had brought him recognition and honours, but he had not refused public duties. The year he died he had been appointed High Sheriff of the County of London. He was already Deputy Lieutenant of the counties of Suffolk and Antrim. He was a Trustee of the National Gallery and the National Portrait Gallery, a Governor of the National Gallery of Ireland, and he was a Commander of the Legion of Honour, a K.C.B. and a baronet.

But none of this had made him a Hertford. He had done everything for Lord Hertford's memory, but he would always remain the unrecognised son. Now his own son was dead and his grandchildren were illegitimate. There could be no succession or continuation. It had all, it seemed, been for nothing. So, leaving somebody else to decide the future of the Collection, he had gone back to Bagatelle to die alone in the place where his equally disenchanted father had died.

Chapter Nineteen

IT IS PROBABLY NO EXAGGERATION to say that Lady Wallace was appalled by the responsibility that had suddenly been thrust upon her as a result of the death of her husband. Hitherto she had never been called upon to make any decision and had always remained in the background. Now she was forced into the limelight by his will, in which he left everything to her. She was more than seventy years old; she had never chosen to be in the public eye; and, although as Sir Richard Wallace's wife she had been hostess to the Prince of Wales, she had never sought a position for herself in society. Queen Victoria would never receive her. She had lived very quietly after Wallace left England and was seldom seen outside Hertford House. As the new owner and guardian of this fabulous collection she would have to decide to whom it would be left after her death. It must have been deeply disturbing. The publicity surrounding Wallace's death had aroused enormous public interest and, at the moment when she wished to see nobody, she was inundated with requests from people wanting to visit Hertford House to see the Collection.

In her predicament there was only one person to whom she could turn for help and advice: John Murray Scott, who was still living in Hertford House. During the twenty years he had spent in Wallace's employ he had become much more than a secretary. Wallace and Lady Wallace seem to have adopted him as well as his three brothers and the two sisters who had been invited, as we have seen, to Sudbourn when the Prince of Wales had been the guest of honour. After Wallace's death they all became the intimate friends of Lady Wallace. She was seldom left alone. It was arranged that at least one of the Scott family would dine with her every night at Hertford House. When she took a house at

Brighton where she used to go for a change of air, Murray Scott went there every weekend and other members of the family were frequent visitors.

It was at Brighton, away from Hertford House and the Collection, that on 23 May 1894 she made her will. She probably knew of her husband's intention to leave at least part of the Collection to the British nation and Murray Scott would have told her how he had died before anything could be decided. She had complete confidence in Murray Scott and they must have discussed what she should do. Her chief concern was, without doubt, to carry out her husband's wishes and she therefore decided to bequeath to the British nation everything 'placed on the ground and first floors in the galleries at Hertford House'.

There were certain clearly stated conditions. First, the government should provide a site in a central part of London on which a special museum would be built to house the Collection. It would be kept unmixed with any other objects and be called The Wallace Collection. This condition was her revenge on Lord Hertford for the long years she had been forced to wait before she could marry Richard Wallace. In this way, she hoped, Lord Hertford's name would be forgotten and Wallace only would be remembered as the great collector.

Secondly, she insisted that the famous Louis XV balustrade should be installed in the new museum and that her executors should replace it with a modern balustrade in Hertford House. This was the only object in the Collection that she mentioned in her will and she mistakenly called it a Louis XIV balustrade.

A third condition was that her executors should be empowered to decide what should or should not be included in the Collection and that John Murray Scott should be one of the trustees. The Collection was to remain at Hertford House for not longer than four years at the government's expense and responsibility.

To her only direct descendants, her grandchildren – Marie Richard Georges, Richard Henri, Edmond Georges and Georgette – she left her house on the site of the Bains Chinois at 29 boulevard des Italiens. This house had been intended for their father, Edmond Wallace, had he lived. She left them no money.

On the other hand, she left £16,000 to Seymourina's daughter, Richardine, now Madame Girod. Wallace had left nothing to his god-daughter in his will.

£5,000 was left as an endowment fund for the chaplain at St George's Church. Other charities which received money were the Royal Cambridge Asylum for Soldiers' Widows, £40,000; the National Lifeboat Institution, £10,000; the Artists' General Benevolent Fund, £5,000; L'Assistance Publique, Paris, £10,000; La Société Hospitalité de Nuit, Paris, £10,000. The remainder of her property in England and France, which included the lease of Hertford House, as well as £40,000 was left to John Murray Scott, her residuary legatee.

Having made her will she returned to London and the life of a complete recluse. She never went back to France and remained stoutly British. She had still not learned to speak English so that on the rare occasions when she went out she always took someone with her who could act as an interpreter. After Wallace's death she had given up her first-floor room which contained the Bouchers and the Fragonards, and had moved to a room on the second floor at the back of the house. Here on the balcony which overlooks the courtyard she often used to stand smoking long black cheroots and feeding the pigeons.

Murray Scott remained at Hertford House and also had a room on the second floor next to Lady Wallace. What is one to make of their relationship? She was old enough to be his mother. When Wallace died she was over seventy while Murray Scott was only forty-one. He was a good-tempered giant of a man, rather stupid despite his Marlborough schooling and studies at the Sorbonne, but he seems to have been able to make himself extremely useful. He was six feet four inches tall and weighed twenty-five stones. It is said that he measured five feet round where his waist might have been. He was red-faced and wore mutton-chop whiskers. He knew nothing about art, except what he learned by being with Wallace; but he was to become the master of Hertford House and played an important role in the future of the collections in England and France.

Lady Wallace was nearly eighty when she died on 16 February 1897. She never dreamed, of course, that the Collection would remain at Hertford House and that her plan to have Lord Hertford forgotten would fail. She was buried in Paris at Père Lachaise in the same vault as Lord Hertford and her husband.

The conditions in Lady Wallace's will posed many problems for the government and a committee was appointed under the chairmanship of the Marquess of Lansdowne to decide where, how and at what cost the Collection might be placed on public exhibition. The committee reported that the best solution would be to buy the remainder of the lease of Hertford House from Murray Scott, and the freehold from Lord Portman, so that the Collection could remain where it was. Hertford House would be altered to convert it into a museum. The government adopted this proposal despite a separate report submitted by one of the committee members, Sir Edward Poynter, Director of the National Gallery and President of the Royal Academy. This advocated the building of a new museum next to the National Gallery in Trafalgar Square.

In order to ensure that Lady Wallace's conditions would be observed they were incorporated in a declaration of trust dated 27 July 1899 and a board of trustees was appointed. The first chairman of the board was the Earl of Rosebery. He was shortly afterwards succeeded by Murray Scott who had been nominated as a trustee under the will. It is under this declaration of trust that the Collection is still administered by the trustees today.

The alterations to Hertford House, which were carried out by the Office of Works, were quite considerable. On the ground floor the stables, coach-houses and butler's quarters were converted into galleries; a mezzanine floor on the west side of the building was removed. Sir Richard and Lady Wallace's rooms on the first floor also became galleries. The second floor was converted into offices and workshops. By the summer of 1900 the work was finished and the Collection had been rearranged so as to make use of the new galleries. On 22 June the Prince of Wales formally opened the Wallace Collection as a national museum.

John Murray Scott was the central figure in all these arrangements. As the former secretary of Wallace and the adviser of Lady Wallace, he was listened to as the great authority on the Collection and all matters concerning it. He had also inherited the lease of Hertford House and his agreement to relinquish it had been the first essential step in making the museum there. For all this he was created a baronet in 1899. Unfortunately, his recollections became at times so muddled that he was not always reliable. Nor was he popular with the staff at Hertford House, where he was remembered for being 'close' with money and for refusing a cheap cane chair to a charwoman who had begged him for it. When the house became national property Murray Scott removed everything that was not given to the nation, even the lamp brackets. In his house at 5 Connaught Place there were a number of objects from the Collection which Lady Wallace may or may not have given to him before she died. But among them were Hertford family possessions of great historical and sentimental importance to the Collection and it is extremely unlikely that they would not have been covered by her will; that is to say, they would almost certainly have been on the ground and first floors of Hertford House. One of the paintings that he took to Connaught Place was the Lawrence portrait of the 3rd Marquess of Hertford, the husband of Mie-Mie, which had been bought at the St Dunstan's sale by their son, Lord Hertford. Also at Connaught Place was the miniature of Mie-Mie that Lord Henry Seymour had left in his will to Richard Wallace. Murray Scott took no steps to make sure that they were returned to the Collection and they were sold after his death. (The portrait of the 3rd marquess is now in Washington at the National Gallery.) Except for the Collection, Lady Wallace had left him everything – Sudbourn, the estate in Ulster, the apartment in the rue Laffitte, Bagatelle and all their contents.

Murray Scott's two sisters moved into 5 Connaught Place with him and the family settled down to enjoy his vast fortune. He told his brothers and sisters that Lady Wallace had left this fortune of nearly a million pounds for the whole family and it was only because she did not want to have to put so many Scotts in her will that his name alone had been mentioned. However, somebody else, whose name was not Scott, had her eye on all this money. She was Lady Sackville, at that time the Hon. Mrs Sackville-West, married to her cousin Lionel Sackville-West, who was soon to become the 3rd Lord Sackville. She met Murray Scott in 1899, when she was a member of a party that he had shown round Hertford House. He was fifty-two and she was thirty-six. Lady

Sackville was also a serious collector, not of art but of millionaires and important men. The list by the time of her death was formidable – J. Pierpont Morgan, Rudyard Kipling, Lord Kitchener, W. W. Astor, J. L. Garvin, Sir Edwin Lutyens, Lord Leverhulme, Henry Ford, Gordon Selfridge and even Auguste Rodin. Murray Scott became her most devoted admirer and remained so until his death. He surrendered completely to her domination and could not live without her. Although she bullied him and they frequently quarrelled – Lady Sackville had a violent temper – he always docilely returned to her. He took her to stay in Paris at the rue Laffitte, and every year to Scotland as well. Lady Sackville's daughter, Vita, who always travelled with her mother to Paris and Scotland, christened him Seery and he called her Kidlet. In her diary Vita recalled what it was like to stay in Lord Hertford's apartment in the rue Laffitte where she went with her mother every year after she was eight.

> One could stand at one end of the apartment and look down a long vista of rooms opening one into the other with an unbroken stretch of shining parquet floor, and all the rooms were panelled with cream-white and gilt Louis XV boiserie, or else with faded old green silk. All the furniture was French, with rich ormolu mounts, and there were hanging chandeliers in every room, and sconces on the walls, and, in the big gallery, priceless Boucher tapestries. The big gallery was in a hopeless confusion when we first went there, but Mother soon rearranged that.

Seery, although middle-class, lived in great style in Paris. There was an elderly butler with long white whiskers whose wife did the cooking, about six footmen and a *lingère*. And there were numerous horses and carriages. Murray Scott believed himself to be very methodical and a good organiser, but according to Vita he was the reverse and was always losing his possessions.

Infatuated with Lady Sackville, he showed little concern for the collections in France that he had inherited from Wallace. He must have been a most insensitive man because he left Bagatelle standing empty and Lady Sackville and Vita only went there for picnics during their visits to Paris. Worse, in 1904 he conceived the idea of selling the fifty acres of park to a builder to be cut up and developed as a housing estate. Fortunately his plans reached the ears of the Paris municipal authorities, who decided that Bagatelle must be saved. On 25 March 1904 the Paris Municipal Council voted to expropriate Bagatelle and add it to the Bois de Boulogne. Before they did so Murray Scott insisted first on selling, although he had no need for money, the important French statues that Lord Hertford had collected and placed in the gardens. He also took a number of Louis XVI chimneypieces from Bagatelle to the rue Laffitte. It was an unbelievable and senseless act which destroyed part of the charm of Bagatelle and as a result the City of Paris reduced its offer of seven million francs to 6,500,000 francs. This was accepted by Murray Scott and on 12 January 1905 the Préfet de la Seine signed the deed of sale. Unfortunately, the statues, which included three Houdons and Pigalle's statue of Madame de Pompadour as L'Amitié, were lost. Some found their way to the United States, but it was the beginning of the dispersal of Lord Hertford's collections in France.

All this time Murray Scott had been making gifts of large sums of money to Lord and Lady Sackville to finance the cost of maintaining Knole, the Sackvilles' historic house at Sevenoaks, Kent. He even bought them their railway tickets when they came to visit him. In fact, they shared his riches, although his intimacy with Lady Sackville, it seems certain, never went further than a little hand-patting.

His brothers and sisters watched with alarm. They were powerless as they saw his fortune, which they considered theirs, melting away. They called the Sackvilles 'the locusts' even before they knew that in his will Murray Scott had left the greater part of nearly a million pounds to Lady Sackville. Connaught Place was no longer theirs, for the determined Lady Sackville would decide who should be invited to dinner there and even decreed that only one sister should be present when Murray Scott entertained. She dismissed the cook and used the carriages whenever she wanted. Scott himself was totally unable to stand up to her. Nervous and obsequious, he followed her about carrying her parcels and waiting on her. If she was away he wrote frequent letters to her, in many begging her timidly not to be 'N.G.' (naughty girl). He had told Lady Sackville what she could expect from his will and her only concern after their many quarrels was to make sure that he never revoked it.

His death was sudden. At Hertford House on 17 January 1912

he was seized with a severe heart attack and he died in a chair there almost immediately. In his will he left Lady Sackville £150,000 'in gratitude for all your kindness and affection to me' and the contents of the apartment in the rue Laffitte, estimated to be worth £350,000. Both bequests were to be free of duty.

He left to the National Gallery the copy of a Watteau, a fine Mignard and the four large pictures of battles by Horace Vernet, which Lord Hertford had bought in 1851 at Louis-Philippe's sale. The remainder of his estate, which included his house in London and its contents, was sold in 1913.

In France his will caused deep disappointment, for it had been expected that he would leave to France the collections at the rue Laffitte. Indeed, the French had always blamed him for the fact that Lady Wallace, a Frenchwoman, had left the Collection in England to the British nation.

Naturally, the Scott brothers and sisters were extremely angry and immediately took steps to dispute the will on the grounds that Lady Sackville had alienated their brother's affections from them to secure a disproportionate share of his fortune for herself. Both sides prepared for a great legal battle over what, in fact, was Wallace's money.

It took more than a year before the case came to court. During this time the rue Laffitte apartment, after lawyers had made an inventory, was shut and placed under seals. At the same time the Scott family went ahead with arrangements to sell the contents of Connaught Place. It was a further step in the dispersal of the Collection.

In fact, the whole Collection was doomed. Lady Sackville had no intention of keeping Lord Hertford's treasures in the rue Laffitte, nor did she mean to bring them to Knole, as Murray Scott had hoped. If they became hers she was determined to sell them all. Even before the case came to court she got in touch with the well-known Paris dealer Jacques Seligmann to find out if he would buy everything that was in the apartment. She had already dealt with him a few years before when he had arranged the sale of tapestries from Knole to one of her millionaire friends, J. Pierpont Morgan. She must have had great powers of persuasion because Seligmann agreed, if she won the case, to buy unseen the entire rue Laffitte collection. He was gambling on Lord Hertford's taste and knowledge and on the works of art being of the same high quality as the collection at Hertford House. The price according to the *New York Times* was 1,400,000 dollars. Vita Sackville-West remembers a figure of £270,000.

Both sides waited impatiently for the case to come to court. To Lady Sackville loss meant the ruin of Knole, while to her daughter Vita, if her mother won she would be considered an heiress and she could marry Mr Harold Nicolson after a long engagement.

By a curious coincidence the lawsuit over Murray Scott's will opened in the Probate Court on the same day that the sale of the contents of his house opened at Christie's – 24 June 1913. The sale lasted four days while the hearings in court took eight.

The case had attracted a great deal of publicity in view of the personalities involved and society ladies jammed the public seats when it opened before Sir Samuel Evans, the President of the Probate Division, and a special jury. Sir Edward Carson appeared for the Sackvilles and F. E. Smith for the Scotts.

In his opening speech, which lasted for nine hours, F. E. Smith told the story of Murray Scott's relationship with Lady Sackville who, he said, had spent more than ten years in obtaining 'complete ascendancy and dominion' over him. He revealed that Murray Scott had given Lady Sackville a total of £84,000 in gifts of money at different times while he was alive.

As the case dragged on the crowds outside the law-courts, waiting to see the principals arrive, became bigger every day, while inside there were even ladies sitting on the steps leading to the witness-box. Some had brought picnic lunches with them to avoid losing their places during the lunchtime recess.

Sir Edward Carson rose to cross-examine the first witness on the third day. She was Miss Alicia Florence Scott and he asked her what sort of influence Lady Sackville had had on her brother.

'A mesmeric influence,' replied Miss Scott, adding that she 'had a sort of spell over him'. She denied that anyone thought there had ever been any immoral act.

The Sackville case was a complete denial of all the allegations and Sir Edward Carson took only three and half hours over his opening speech. Even so, it was not until the fifth day that Lady

Sackville went into the witness-box, where she was to remain all the next day as well.

Calm, collected, not at all nervous, an occasional telling gesture with a white-gloved hand, she was an excellent witness. Under the lengthy cross-examination she could not be shaken and there were many sharp exchanges.

'You don't seem to realise, Mr Smith, that Knole is bigger than Hampton Court.'

Vita went into the witness-box after her mother to add her denial to a story that she and her mother had tampered with the drawers in Murray Scott's desk. Then it was Lord Sackville's turn to admit and give a list of the gifts of money from Murray Scott.

The jury retired to consider their verdict on the eighth day of the hearings – it was 8 July. They were out only ten minutes and found for the Sackvilles. Nothing now could stop the dispersal of the collection in Paris. It belonged to M. Seligmann.

Meanwhile, the sale of Murray Scott's possessions at Connaught Place had been over for more than a week. Three hundred and one lots of French decorative objects, furniture, porcelain and tapestry and 153 pictures and drawings, chiefly French and Dutch Schools, had been sold and dispersed at Christie's.

Lot 26 on the opening day was Cosway's miniature, in a gold locket with hair at the back, of Maria Fagiani – Mie-Mie, Lord Hertford's mother. It went for 250 guineas. Happily, it recently came into the hands of a well-known dealer in miniatures through whom it was acquired by the National Art Collections Fund and thus returned to Hertford House.

Four panels of decorative Beauvais tapestry were sold for £18,900 to E. H. Hodgkins, the collector and dealer, since when there has been no trace of their whereabouts.

Among the pictures Lot 1 was a Bonington entitled *Doge's Palace*. This is probably the watercolour called *Ducal Palace, Venice* now in the Manchester City Art Gallery.

Lot 109 was Sir Thomas Lawrence's portrait of the 3rd Marquess of Hertford, which after disappearing for a period is now in the National Gallery in Washington.

Lot 138 was a Watteau described as a *fête champêtre*. It is now in the Boston Museum of Fine Arts and called *La Perspective*. At this sale it fetched £6,510.

The sale included four Bouchers, two Greuzes, two Watteaus and one Nattier.

The dispersal had really begun.

The dispute over Murray Scott's will having been settled in Lady Sackville's favour, Jacques Seligmann was at last authorised to break the seals and enter the apartment at No. 2 rue Laffitte. At last he was going to see what he had bought.

His son Germain Seligman, who was nearly twenty-one at the time, went with his father on his first visit to inspect rue Laffitte and has described what he saw. He knew that more than seven million gold francs had been paid in cash for these works of art, but he had not seen even the few objects that his father already knew about.

To me it was like entering Ali Baba's cave.... Almost every item was of the quality of Hertford House – but in what confusion.

All over the floors, piled up in corners, some carefully covered with slips, others wrapped in papers or, more often, with only a heavy coating of dust to protect them from sight, were some of the greatest sculptures of the eighteenth century and luxurious pieces of furniture made for the royal family. There, rolled in a corner, was the famous set of tapestries after cartoons by Boucher, now in the Philadelphia Museum. Standing on a table was the small marble figure by Lemoyne. Over there, its companion in size and quality, was the first version of the *Cupid Bending his Bow* of Bouchardon. Yonder was the superb Houdon bust of Sophie Arnould, now in the Louvre, as a bequest of Edgar Stern.

All the great cabinet-makers were represented: Riesener, Oeben, Weisweiler, Saunier, and Martin Carlin.... Here, too, were the 'bureau du roi', which my father later gave to the Metropolitan Museum; sets of furniture upholstered in tapestries designed by Casanova and Le Prince; busts by Houdon; drawings and gouaches and paintings by Nattier, Lancret, Boucher, Prud'hon; . . . Among the most impressive of the sculptures were the Coysevox busts of the Grand Dauphin and the Duc d'Orléans, which must certainly have adorned Versailles. They are now part of the Samuel H. Kress Foundation in the National Gallery at Washington.

It is clear that all Lord Hertford's tapestries, most of the sculpture and as much furniture again as in Hertford House comprised this collection in the rue Laffitte. Unfortunately, no complete detailed list of the Collection has survived since the Seligmann records were destroyed in 1940. All that remains is a probate inventory giving no detail, which was made by the lawyers for the executors of Murray Scott's will, dated 16 February 1912. This inventory shows that there was also a library of 3,000 volumes which, as M. Seligmann's firm did not deal in books, was sold to the London bookseller Bumpus. There was sufficient table silver for a regiment, and in the cellar 150 bottles of Mouton Rothschild, 150 bottles of Château Malescot and 600 bottles of Saint Émilion, to mention only a few. There was very little china and linen. There were some very old carriages in the coach-house.

Twelve tapestries hung in the *grande galérie*, another was listed as stored in a cupboard, while four more were on loan to the Musée des Arts Décoratifs. Thirteen pages in the list were devoted to paintings, watercolours and drawings.

The first private collector to see the Collection while it was still at the rue Laffitte was Henry C. Frick. Germain Seligman recalls that he came straight from playing golf wearing plus-fours. Frick, undisturbed by the confusion, made his selection and the deal for an outright purchase was concluded on the spot.

Shortly after Frick's visit the entire Collection was moved to a new gallery at the Hôtel de Sagan, which was the headquarters of Messrs Seligmann in Paris. Its exhibition drew buyers from all over Europe and North and South America. But it was June 1914 and when war was declared the Hôtel de Sagan was closed and the sale of fine art was halted for four years. This delayed the dispersal of Lord Hertford's Collection. After the war many of the finest objects, after being in the possession of the great private collectors, found their way to museums in Europe and America. In the next chapter we shall discuss the search for these missing works of art and the whereabouts of those that it has been possible to trace.

In May 1919 Lady Sackville quarrelled with her husband and left Knole. The last act in the tragic dispersal of the Collection took place in Brighton as recently as the 21 June 1953, when Lady Sackville's possessions were sold after her death. In the sale were the last of the objects that Murray Scott had given her and which had not been previously sold.

Among them was the red elephant-cloth embroidered with gold thread that Lord Hertford had sent to the Musée Rétrospectif with his oriental armour in 1865. It was described as: 'The rich cloth of gold trappings for an Elephant, in 4 parts, worked in various raised floral motifs and finished with tasselled fringe. (These wrappings were worn by the private elephant belonging to Lord Hertford at Bagatelle.)'

Lord Hertford never kept an elephant at Bagatelle.

Chapter Twenty

PERHAPS THE GREATEST LOSS caused by the dispersal of the Collection was the breaking up of Lord Hertford's unique collection of French eighteenth-century sculpture. At the time of Lady Wallace's death it was certainly the largest collection in private hands and one of the most remarkable ever assembled, a further proof of Lord Hertford's knowledge and expert eye. He must have acquired most of it before 1865 because he lent some of the earliest and finest smaller pieces to the Musée Rétrospectif that year and they can be identified in the photographs that have survived of his exhibits. He placed the larger pieces in the gardens at Bagatelle and later Richard Wallace brought some of the more important statues to London and placed them in the new courtyard at Hertford House. Photographs exist of these too.

The breaking up of the Collection started when Murray Scott sold those statues which he did not take from Bagatelle to the rue Laffitte. This was just before Bagatelle was bought by the City of Paris in 1904. Next there was the sale of Murray Scott's possessions at Connaught Place after his death, which included statuary that had been at Hertford House. Finally, all that was in the apartment at rue Laffitte, which included five outstanding works by Houdon and others by Coysevox, Bouchardon, Lemoyne and Clodion, was sold by Lady Sackville to M. Jacques Seligmann, the Paris dealer.

Today the majority of these statues have found their way to the United States, but one at least has remained in England. In 1964 the Victoria and Albert Museum bought a marble group of *Ganymede and the Eagle*, signed Guillaume Coustou Fils, which probably dates from around 1760. It can be seen in photographs of the courtyard at Hertford House taken after Sir Richard Wallace's death, and later it was in the collection of Sir

Victor Leon before its purchase by the Victoria and Albert Museum.

As recently as 1977 two more eighteenth-century French statues which may have belonged to Lord Hertford have been identified on the lower terrace at Cliveden. One by Cayot and the other by Poirier, they represented the nymphs of Diana and were made for the park at Marly; they are said to have been at Bagatelle. They were bought by the first Lord Astor, probably from Duveen who acquired them when Murray Scott sold the statuary at Bagatelle.

Two marble busts from the rue Laffitte are today in the National Gallery of Art in Washington. When Lord Hertford owned them they were both attributed to Coysevox and believed to be of Louis XIV and the Grand Dauphin. The first bust is still attributed to Coysevox but is called *The Grand Dauphin, son of Louis XIV*, and the second bust is believed to be the work of an unknown early eighteenth-century French sculptor and is thought to be of the eldest son of the Grand Dauphin, Louis, Duc de Bourgogne, who was the father of Louis XV.

The National Gallery in Washington has another of Lord Hertford's early eighteenth-century statues which can be seen in photographs of the Musée Rétrospectif. It is the Bouchardon statue of Cupid making a bow out of the club of Hercules. Its companion piece at the Musée Rétrospectif, the *Baigneuse* by Lemoyne, passed from M. Seligmann into the collection of the Baron Edmond de Rothschild, to whose descendants it now belongs.

But it was Lord Hertford's unique collection of the works of Jean Antoine Houdon (1741–1828) which was to suffer the most severely from the dispersal of the works at Bagatelle and rue Laffitte. He possessed at least seven works by Houdon in marble and bronze. The two splendid marble busts of Madame Victoire de France and Madame de Serilly are at Hertford House still, but five other works, which were in France, were sold either by Murray Scott or Seligmann. Of these only one has remained in France, the four others are in the United States. The list is as follows:

Paris, Louvre: Marble bust of Sophie Arnould as Iphigénie in the part she created in the opera by Gluck.

Washington, National Gallery: Marble bust of Cagliostro.

New York, Metropolitan Museum: Marble figure, *La Baigneuse assise*; bronze figure, *La Frileuse*.

San Marino, California, Henry E. Huntington Library and Art Gallery: Bronze figure of Diana.

At Bagatelle there was also an important work by Jean Baptiste Pigalle (1714–85). This was a marble life-size figure of Madame de Pompadour, clad as 'L'Amitié'. It was sold by Murray Scott in 1904 and passed into the collection of the Baron Edouard de Rothschild, whose son presented it to the Louvre in 1977.

Lord Hertford also possessed some terracotta statuettes by Claude Michel, called Clodion (1738–1814). Two have been traced. One, a figure of Flore, appeared in the sale of Murray Scott's sister Mary in London in 1924 and was bought by a private collector. Another was at the rue Laffitte and was mentioned in the inventory. It is described as *Satyresse tenant deux enfants* and is now at Baltimore in the Walters Art Gallery.

Some pieces of sculpture have disappeared leaving no trace. One was the equestrian statue of Louis XIV, a large bronze reduction of the statue by Girardon which stood in the place Vendôme until it was destroyed during the Revolution. The original bronze was stolen from M. Seligman's house in Paris during the Second World War, but there is a version of it at Windsor Castle.

This list, of course, does not include the many small eighteenth-century bronze statuettes and groups which can be seen standing on the furniture in the photographs of the rue Laffitte apartment. Nor does it include another important marble bust by Houdon of an elderly man, said to resemble Benjamin Franklin, which may have belonged to Lord Hertford and which may also have been the bust which Wallace lent to an exhibition in Paris just before his death. This also has disappeared and its whereabouts are unknown today.

Tapestries

When it comes to wall tapestries the dispersal of Lord Hertford's Collection has been almost complete and many, despite their size, have totally disappeared. He is thought to have possessed thirty-two tapestries, most of them of the very finest quality, but after his death they were sold and some have disappeared.

One reason for the loss of what was once a very important part of Lord Hertford's Collection of eighteenth-century French art was that there was no room to hang tapestries at Hertford House because all the wall space was taken up by the eight hundred pictures. This may explain why in April 1876 Wallace sold at Christie's twelve important French eighteenth-century tapestries described in the catalogue as 'three splendid sets of Beauvais and Gobelins tapestries'. They were, in fact, all from famous series and in three sets of four panels:

Four Gobelins panels with subjects from Don Quixote on a red ground.

Four Gobelins panels with the royal cipher in the corners and with similar subjects on a yellow ground.

Four Gobelins tapestries with subjects from the history of Jason in brilliant colours from the designs of de Troy.

All these are now in the United States. The four Don Quixote panels on a red ground were formerly in the J. Pierpoint Morgan collection, but are now in the Philadelphia Museum of Art, bequeathed by Mrs Widener Dixon; and those on a yellow ground were in the possession of the late Mr Clarence Mackey and then his daughter, Mrs Robert Z. Hawkins. The last four are now in Hartford, Connecticut, after having been in the possession of the Guinness family.

The Philadelphia Museum of Art has five more tapestries which belonged to Lord Hertford. They are the set of five Louis XV Beauvais panels representing *L'Histoire de Psyche* after designs by Boucher, bequeathed by Mrs A. Hamilton Rice, who bought them direct from Seligmann.

One more tapestry is in New York at the Metropolitan Museum of Art. It is *Le Repos*, one of a Louis XV Beauvais series called *Jeux rustiqués* from designs by Le Prince, the gift of Mrs Oliver Gould Jennings.

Four more decorative Beauvais panels, which Murray Scott had at his house in Connaught Place, have not been traced. At the sale at Christie's after his death, they were bought for 18,900 guineas by E. H. Hodgkins, but there has been no trace of them since.

Ten more tapestries – four Beauvais, five Gobelins and one Brussels – were in the probate inventory at rue Laffitte, but they also have disappeared without trace.

In London the only tapestry to be seen in the Wallace Collection at Hertford House today is confined to the upholstery of chairs and sofas, including, it must be admitted, valuable Beauvais series after designs by Francesco Casanova.

But if we are to complete the list of missing tapestries we must include four early sixteenth-century Flemish tapestries which Sir Richard Wallace bought in 1872 and exhibited at the fifth Musée Rétrospectif in 1876. These also probably descended to Sir John Murray Scott from Lady Wallace. These 'Gothic' tapestries were very large, but despite this they too, surprisingly, have disappeared.

Furniture

The sale of the contents of the apartment in the rue Laffitte meant that an even larger collection of high-quality French furniture than can be seen in London at the Wallace Collection was broken up and dispersed. Much of it has disappeared because it is more difficult to trace furniture than paintings or sculpture, both of which are recorded in sales catalogues in much more detail. Here again photographs of the Musée Rétrospectif exhibition and the interior of the rue Laffitte have provided valuable clues.

The rue Laffitte collection seems to have been particularly rich in furniture with Boulle marquetry. There were two immense wardrobes, a large chest of drawers by the now famous B.V.R.B., and three medium-size cupboards in the Boulle technique.

The first collector to visit the rue Laffitte after Seligmann had been authorised to enter the apartment was, as we have seen, Mr Henry Frick, who chose only Louis XVI pieces which can be seen today in New York at the Frick Collection. The list is as follows:

A Riesener table.
A pair of console tables.
A pair of lacquer *étagères*.

A pair of gilt-bronze candelabra.
A gilt-bronze clock.

Also in New York at the Metropolitan Museum is a late Louis XVI roll-top desk by Guillaumne Beneman which was presented in 1919 by Seligmann himself in memory of J. Pierpont Morgan and of the United States' help to France during the war of 1914–18.

In Ohio the Cleveland Museum of Art has a bed made by Georges Jacob which is believed to have belonged to Marie Antoinette. This bed still has its original Philippe de Lasalle embroidered satin upholstery and covers. Three other items at this museum came from the rue Laffitte – a pair of Clodion gilt-bronze candelabra and a Louis XV desk, and a fine pair of gilt-bronze fire-dogs.

At Kansas City the William Rockhill Nelson Gallery of Art has a pair of monumental French seventeenth-century red porphyry urns.

Many other pieces have been acquired by private collectors in America, such as Mr George Rasmussen of Chicago and Mr and Mrs Charles Wrightsman of New York.

Not everything, however, went to America. The Jacob furniture, which was in the *grand salon* at the rue Laffitte, remained in Paris. It consisted of two large sofas, a smaller sofa, ten chairs and a firescreen, all in carved and gilded wood and upholstered in Beauvais tapestry. Together with a pair of Beauvais tapestry screens it is now in the Musée Nissim de Camondo, Paris.

Pictures

The greater part of Lord Hertford's and Sir Richard Wallace's collections of pictures is still to be seen at the Wallace Collection in London. The eight hundred pictures at Hertford House comprise nearly all the finest paintings that were in London at the time of Lady Wallace's death.

When tracing pictures that were formerly in the collections in London and Paris and which have passed into other hands it should be remembered that both Lord Hertford and Sir Richard Wallace during their lifetimes sold pictures in their possession. For example, the famous Greuze *Les Oeufs cassés* now in New

York at the Metropolitan Museum was in the Collection until Wallace sold it in 1885 to Lord Dudley after it had been exhibited at Bethnal Green. Then Wallace, as mentioned above, made a gift in 1871 to the National Gallery of the famous Terborch *The Peace of Munster*. Although a small picture, it is possible to identify all the seventy-seven persons shown taking part in the ceremony of swearing the oath of the ratification of the Treaty of Munster in 1648. There is also in the National Gallery a Veronese, *The Vision of St Helena*, which had belonged to the 3rd Marquess of Hertford and was sold in 1855 by Countess Zichy as part of the contents of his villa, St Dunstan's, in Regent's Park.

Some important pictures which were not in the collections were in the possession of Sir John Murray Scott at his house in Connaught Place. He had inherited them from Lady Wallace and in his will he left to the National Gallery in London the four battle pictures by Horace Vernet, a fine Mignard, and a painting after Watteau. The rest of his pictures were sold after his death including, as we have seen, the portrait of the 3rd Marquess of Hertford by Lawrence, which Lord Hertford, his son, had bought at the same sale at St Dunstan's when the Veronese, mentioned above, was sold. This portrait is now in the National Gallery in Washington.

In the National Portrait Gallery in London is a Bonington watercolour, believed to be a self-portrait, which was given by Lord Hertford to Richard Wallace in 1864. Written on the back in Wallace's handwriting is:

> Portrait en charge de Bonington fait par luimême. 51 Francs
> Vente Villot 25 Janvier 1864
> Given to me by the Marquess of Hertford 26 January 1864
>
> R. WALLACE

Wallace seems to have made a mistake. He probably meant 'Portrait a charge' which means a caricature – 'en charge' has no meaning.

At the rue Laffitte there were a number of important Bouchers. Lord Hertford had a passion for Boucher and his collection of Bouchers was, and still is, despite the sale of those at the rue Laffitte, the largest ever assembled by one man. The whereabouts of five that were in the rue Laffitte is known – four are in America:

New York Metropolitan Museum: *The Birth and Triumph of Venus.*
Frick Collection: *Le Dessin* and *Portrait de jeune femme.*
Washington, National Gallery: *Diane et Endymion.*

The fifth Boucher, *Cupid and the Graces*, passed into the Gulbenkian Collection and is now in Lisbon.

Lord Hertford had others, five of which, it is known, were sold to private collectors.

Other paintings in America are:

San Francisco, M. H. de Young Museum: A set of four half-moon-shaped over-doors by Lancret.

Detroit, Museum of Art: *Mme. Henriette de France en Vestale* by Nattier.

Boston, Museum of Fine Art: *La Perspective* by Watteau, sold in London at the Murray Scott sale.

Finally, when pondering over the whereabouts of these missing works of art, it must be remembered that some of them may have been destroyed by fire. Not only did Wallace lose part of the Collection, valued at £120,000, in 1874 in the fire at the Pantechnicon warehouse, but what was described as 'part of the Wallace Collection valued at £75,000' was damaged in a fire at Dixon's Depository, Harrow Road, London, in 1902. These must have been objects in the possession of Murray Scott and could have been pieces for which he had no room at Connaught Place, including perhaps the four missing 'Gothic' tapestries.

Postscript

TODAY NO TRACE REMAINS of Lord Hertford's long residence in Paris. Soon after Seligmann had bought his Collection his house at the corner of the rue Laffitte was sold and pulled down to make way for a block of offices.

More recently, the two English churches that Lord Hertford and Wallace knew have also been pulled down to make room for modern buildings. The old church opposite the British Embassy in the rue d'Arguesseau, where Wallace went in as Richard Jackson and came out calling himself Richard Wallace, and where the funeral service for Lord Hertford was held, has gone. Services are now held in a new church in the basement of the block of offices that has been built on the site of the old church. The new church is no longer known as the Embassy church but is called St Michael's.

The same thing has happened to St George's in the rue Auguste-Vacquerie, the church that Wallace and Lady Wallace supported at the end of their lives. Known at one time as the Victoria Church, because it was built in the year of Queen Victoria's Jubilee, it had only been consecrated a year when Wallace died. He had given money towards its building and his funeral was held there. After his death Lady Wallace continued to be interested in the church and she left an endowment for the chaplain in her will. There were three windows in the church dedicated to the memory of Sir Richard and Lady Wallace, given in February 1898 by 'their affectionate and devoted friend' John Murray Scott. The new St George's has just started its basement life under another modern block of flats which has been built above it.

Only the fountains have survived as a memorial to Richard Wallace's connection with Paris. In addition to the original fifty fountains which he gave in September 1872, another thirty were cast by the city authorities. Today sixty-four are still 'en service' in the streets of Paris and are looked after by the municipality. Known as 'les Wallaces', they have been the cause of a French word being made out of his name.

In the Bois de Boulogne Bagatelle still survives, little changed since Wallace went back there to die. No one has lived there since. Murray Scott never lived there and it has remained uninhabited since he sold it to the City of Paris. The park and gardens, which cover fifty acres, are open to the public. The rose-garden is famous and in the spring Parisians flock in hundreds to admire the masses of daffodils and tulips growing wild under the trees which give the park a very English atmosphere. In the middle, the little château stands empty, its shutters closed, and it is not open to the public. Recently central heating was installed and the ground-floor rooms were restored and redecorated, but funds ran out before the upstairs rooms could be tackled. There is no furniture.

Occasionally the City of Paris gives receptions in these newly restored rooms and the shutters are pulled back from the windows of Lord Hertford's white and gold panelled drawing-room. Then the large circular room under the dome, painted in *trompe l'oeil*, comes to life again for a brief period. Upstairs the rooms are sadly neglected. The wallpaper is peeling from the walls of the bedroom where both Lord Hertford and Richard Wallace died; adjoining it is a small sitting-room and dressing-room. There is only one other bedroom on the first floor.

The garden has remained largely the same as it was in Lord Hertford's time. Even the head gardener's cottage, which used to stand in the middle of the kitchen garden, is there, but today it is surrounded by herbaceous plants instead of vegetables. Lord Hertford was responsible for the orangery, the labyrinth and the lakes with their water-lilies and swans. However, few of the hundreds of Parisians who enjoy walking in this garden realise they owe their pleasure to an Englishman.

Descendants of the beautiful Madame Poirson, who as the little girl Seymourina Cuthbert played in the gardens at Bagatelle, still live in France. As could have been expected with Lord Hertford, her parentage was surrounded with mystery. Her birth was registered two days later at the *mairie* of the Third Arrondissement by the midwife, who gave the mother's name as Clémence

Amélie Barjonnet, and her age as nineteen. Two witnesses, who were described as workmen, were there to support this statement and they also signed the declaration of birth.

Seven months later, on 29 December 1846, the child was baptised Suzanne Seymourina at the Evangelical Church of the Redemption, when Lord Hertford and Madame Oger stood as the godparents. Lord Hertford described himself as 'Richard Seymour Hertford, militaire', and Madame Oger used her original name – Louise Suzanne Bréart. The name of the father was given as Jean Vincent, 'propriétaire, natif de Lille (Dept. du Nord) demeurant à Paris (domicile non déclaré)'. As we have seen, two years later Seymourina acquired yet another father, when she was adopted by Mr Cuthbert.

What remains of Lord Hertford's collections are still in his house in Manchester Square. Since they were opened to the public in June 1900 by King Edward VII, then still Prince of Wales, they have twice had to be packed up and moved for reasons of safety. In the 1914–18 war the main treasures were first stored in the basement, but when the air-raids began in 1917 the entire Collection was taken to the new Post Office Tube station at the Paddington district Post Office. In September 1939 the Collection was sent outside London for the duration of the Second World War. In 1940 a high-explosive bomb fell in the forecourt of Hertford House, and incendiary bombs fell on the roof. But, although shaken, Hertford House survived.

Recently air-conditioning has been installed which will save the furniture and other objects from being damaged by the London climate. It is intended to maintain the atmosphere of a private house rather than a museum and to this end the rooms where Sir Richard and Lady Wallace lived are to be recarpeted. Only the galleries which he built on to the house will have parquet floors. Of the forty clocks in Hertford House thirty-three are still working.

In making her great gift to the British nation Lady Wallace, so to speak, stopped the clocks. The Collection remains unchanged and nothing can be added to it. If one regrets the many fine works of art which once were part of it and are no longer there it is still, nevertheless, the finest collection of French eighteenth-century art in the world.

Bibliography

Aldington, Richard, *Wellington* (London, 1946)
Alsop, Susan Mary, *Lady Sackville* (London, 1978)
Alton-Shée, Edmond d', *Mes Mémoires, 1826–48* (Paris, 1869)
André-Maurois, Madame S., *Miss Howard – La femme qui fit un empereur* (Paris, 1956)
Aspinall, A. (ed.), *Correspondence of George, Prince of Wales, 1806–9* (London, 1969)
——, *The Letters of King George IV, 1812–30* (London, 1938)
Aulard, F. V. A., *Paris sous le Consultat* (Paris, 1903)
Barbey d'Aurevilly, Jules A., *Du dandysme et du George Brummell* (Paris, 1926)
Belleroche, Maud Sacquard de, *Cinq personnages en quête d'empereur* (Paris, 1962)
Berry, Miss Mary, *Extracts from the Journals and Correspondence, 1783–1852*, edited by Lady Theresa Lewis (London, 1866)
Bertaut, Jules, *Le Boulevard* (Paris, 1957)
Billy, André, *La Présidente et ses amis* (Paris)
Blanc, A. A. P. Charles, *Le Trésor de la curiosité, tiré des catalogues de ventes* (Paris, 1858)
Blayney, A. T. B., *Narrative of a Forced Journey through Spain and France as a Prisoner of War in the Years 1810 to 1814* (London, 1814)
Blessington, Marguerite Gardiner, *The Idler in France* (London, 1841)
Blount, Edward, *Memoirs, 1815–1902* (London, 1902)
Brightfield, Myron F., *John Wilson Croker* (London, 1951)
Broglie, Raoul de, *Chantilly* (Paris, 1964)
Brooke, John, *King George III* (London, 1972)
Bullen, Roger, *Palmerston, Guizot and the Collapse of the Entente Cordiale* (London, 1974)
Castelot, André, *Napoleon III* (Paris, 1973–4)
Clark, Kenneth, *Another Part of the Wood* (London, 1974)
Coleridge, E. H., *The Life of Thomas Coutts, Banker* (London, 1920)

Croker, John Wilson, *The Croker Papers*, edited by Louis J. Jennings (London, 1885)
Dansette, Adrien, *Histoire du Second Empire*, Vol. I, *Louis Napoleon à la conquête de pouvoir* (Paris, 1961)
Debuchy, Victor, *Les Ballons du Siège de Paris* (Paris, 1973)
Du Camp, Maxime, *Souvenirs d'un demi-siècle* (Paris, 1949)
Duchesne, Henri Gaston, *Le Château de Bagatelle, 1715–1908* (Paris, 1909)
Evans, Thomas William, *Mémoires* (translation) (Paris, 1910)
Falk, Bernard, *Old Q.'s Daughter* (London, 1951)
Fleury, Général Comte, *Souvenirs* (Paris, 1897–8)
Fleury, M. and Sonolet, L., *La Société du Second Empire* (Paris, 1912–13)
Fonvielle, Wilfred de, *Le Siège de Paris vu à vol d'oiseau* (Paris)
Gladwyn, Cynthia, *The Paris Embassy* (London, 1976)
Goncourt, Edmond de and Jules de, *Journal* (Paris, 1888)
Gower, Lord Ronald C. Sutherland-Leveson-, *My Reminiscences* (London, 1883)
Gramont, Elizabeth de, *Le Comte d'Orsay et Lady Blessington* (Paris)
Gronow, R. H., *The Reminiscences and Recollections of Captain Gronow* (London, 1892)
Guest, Ivor, *Napoleon III in England* (London, 1952)
Gwynn, S. L. and Tuckwell, G. M., *The Life of Sir Charles W. Dilke* (London, 1917)
Henrey, Robert (ed.), *Letters from Paris, 1870–5* (London, 1942)
Hibbert, Christopher, *George IV* (London, 1972)
Horne, Alistair, *The Fall of Paris* (London, 1965)
Ilchester, Earl of, *Chronicles of Holland House, 1820–1900* (London, 1937)
Jekyll, Joseph, *Correspondence with Lady Gertrude Sloane Stanley, 1818–38* (London, 1894)
Joffet, Robert, *Bagatelle, histoire-guide* (Paris, 1961)
Jollivet, Gaston, *Souvenirs de la vie de plaisir sous le Second Empire* (Paris, 1927)
Keppel, Sonia, *The Sovereign Lady* (London, 1974)
Kurtz, Harold, *The Empress Eugénie* (London, 1964)
Lewis, Michael, *Napoleon and his British Captives* (London, 1962)
Loliée, Fréderic, *Les Femmes du Second Empire* (Paris, 1927)
——, *La Fête impériale* (Paris, 1926)
Malmesbury, J. H. H., *Memoirs of an ex-minister* (London, 1885)
Mérimée, Prosper, *Correspondence générale: établie et annotée par Maurice Parturier* (Toulouse, 1946–61)

Moneypenny, W. F. and Buckle, G. E., *Life of Benjamin Disraeli* (London, 1929)
Newton, T. W. L., *Lord Lyons* (London, 1913)
Nicolson, Nigel, *Portrait of a Marriage* (London, 1973)
Nouvelle histoire de la France contemporaine, Editions du Seuil (Paris, 1972–)
Porché, François, *Baudelaire et La Présidente* (Paris, 1959)
Quennell, P. and Powell, D. (eds.), *The Private Letters of Princess Lieven to Prince Metternich, 1820–6* (London, 1937)
Raikes, Thomas, *Journal* (London, 1856)
Reitlinger, Gerald, *The Economics of Taste* (London, 1951)
Renoir, Jean, *Renoir* (Paris, 1926)
Rheims, Maurice, *La Vie étrange des objets* (Paris)
Richardson, Joanna, *The Courtesans* (London, 1967)
Robinson, Lionel G., *Letters of Dorothea, Princess Lieven, during her Residence in London, 1812–34* (London, 1903)
Rochegude, Félix de, *Guide pratique à travers le vieux Paris* (Paris, 1903)
Rumbold, Horace, *Recollections of a Diplomatist* (London, 1902)
Sackville-West, Victoria, *Pepita* (London, 1937)
Sarcey, Francisque, *Le Siège de Paris: impressions et souvenirs* (Paris, 1871)
Seligman, Germain, *Merchants of Art, 1880–1960* (New York, 1961)
Stern, Jean, *Lord Seymour dit Milord l'Arsouille* (Paris–Genève, 1954)
Sweeney, John L. (ed.), *The Painter's Eye* (Essays of Henry James) (London, 1956)
Valvet, Roger, *Paris et sa Poste* (Paris, 1957)
Washburne, E. B., *Recollections of a Minister to France, 1869–77* (London, 1877)
——, *The Correspondence of E. B. Washburne* (Washington, 1878)
Whitehurst, Felix M., *My Private Diary during the Siege of Paris* (London, 1875)

Source Notes

The main unpublished sources are, of course, to be found in the archives at the Wallace Collection. In addition to letters, bills, catalogues of sales, etc., use has also been made of the extracts from the Harrowby MSS., and letters and extracts from the diary of the 5th Marquess of Hertford and his wife.

Other unpublished sources have been:

Royal Archives, Windsor.

Egerton MSS., the British Library.

Reports, minutes and correspondence of the Science and Art Department, the Victoria and Albert Museum.

Henry Cole diaries and correspondence, Victoria and Albert Museum.

Van book, 1872, Bethnal Green Museum.

Two published works should be mentioned because they are the main source of biographical material about the Seymour-Conway family and have been used in several chapters. They are, in English, *Old Q.'s Daughter* by Bernard Falk and, in French, *Lord Seymour dit Milord l'Arsouille* by Jean Stern. Details of the sources for each chapter will be found in the Bibliography when they are not given in full below.

With regard to objects in the Collection, their history and date of purchase, great use has been made of the excellent detailed catalogues of the Collection.

Finally, I was able to examine the nearly nine hundred letters from the 3rd Marquess of Hertford to John Wilson Croker, which suddenly came on to the market in July 1978, after the text of this book had been completed. They contained nothing which made it necessary to change anything that I had already written.

Chapter One

Early Seymours, founders of the Collection: Falk and *General Guide to the Collection*. Regent arriving in Manchester Square: Gronow. Lord Yarmouth's marriage: Falk. Hertford seats in Parliament: Aldington.

Police reports on Lord Yarmouth in Paris: Aulard. Life in Verdun: Blayney. Lord Yarmouth's letters from Verdun: Egerton MSS. Lord Yarmouth brought to Paris when Mie-Mie pregnant: Jules Bertaut article, *Figaro Litteraire*, 29 December 1951. Lord Yarmouth's negotiations with Talleyrand: Egerton MSS.

Chapter Two

Minny Seymour and the Hertfords' relations with the Prince of Wales: Hibbert. Prince's letters to Lady Hertford: Egerton MSS., Aspinall, *Correspondence of George, Prince of Wales*. Lord Yarmouth's letters from Verdun: Egerton MSS. Receptions at Hertford House: Miss Berry. Lady Holland's chef: Keppel. Lord Yarmouth's letters about his son's education: Egerton MSS. Stephen Demainbray: Brooke. Richard swindled at cards: Falk, Egerton MSS. Richard's letters to Mie-Mie: Egerton MSS. Lord Yarmouth's friendship with Croker: *Croker Papers*. Princess Lieven on Lord and Lady Hertford: Robinson, Quennell. Lord Hertford's request for a dukedom: Aspinall, *Letters of King George IV*.

Chapter Three

Mie-Mie's character: Falk. Richard Jackson is brought to Paris: Falk. Lady Blessington on 3rd marquess: Blessington. 3rd marquess and the Strachan family: Falk, *Croker Papers*. Demidoff family: Belleroche. Café de Paris *habitués*: Bertaut.

Chapter Four

Lord Henry Seymour: Stern. Lord Yarmouth buys Bagatelle: Raikes. Lord Yarmouth's affairs with women: Falk.

Chapter Five

Lord Henry Seymour's racing: Stern. Death of 3rd marquess, his will and subsequent lawsuit: *Croker Papers*, Brightfield. Letters to Mrs Dawson-Damer: Wallace Collection archives. Disraeli on will of 3rd marquess: Moneypenny and Buckle.

Chapter Six

Richard Jackson becomes Richard Wallace: Falk. Letters to Mrs Dawson-Damer: Wallace Collection archives. Irish visit: Falk. Lord Hertford and family flee to England: Malmesbury. Lord Henry Seymour returns to France: Stern.

Chapter Seven

Lord Hertford's letters to Mawson: Wallace Collection archives. Meetings with Louis Napoleon at Miss Howard's house: Fleury, André-Maurois. Lady Blessington and Louis Napoleon: Gramont. Life in Boulogne: Stern. Lord Hertford changes his will: Falk and Wallace Collection archives. Lord Hertford orders copies of furniture: *Furniture Catalogue*, Wallace Collection.

Chapter Eight

Queen Victoria's visit to Paris: Castelot. Lord Henry Seymour and Mrs Minchin: Stern. Death of Mie-Mie, Lord Hertford's grief: Wallace Collection archives. Manchester Art Treasures Exhibition: Wallace Collection archives. Lord Henry Seymour's will: Wallace Collection archives.

Chapter Nine

Wallace and Madame Sabatier: Billy, Porché, Richardson. Meissonier: Reitlinger, catalogue *Le Musée de Luxembourg en 1874*, exhibition Grand Palais, 1974. Lord Hertford at Compiègne: Mérimée, Vol. II, Kurtz. Napoleon III's taste in pictures: Du Camp.

Chapter Ten

Lord Hertford's exhibit at Musée Rétrospectif: F. J. B. Watson, *Apollo*, special number June 1965. Lord Hertford's letters to Mawson: Wallace Collection archives. The Salon des Refusés: Castelot. Millet: catalogue Millet exhibition, Grand Palais, 1975.

Chapter Eleven

Lord Hertford's meanness and indifference: Goncourt, Yriarte, *La Revue de Paris*, September 1902. Castiglione on Lord Hertford and women: Loliée. The dandy in Lord Hertford's character: Barbey d'Aurevilly. French eighteenth-century painting: Rosenberg catalogue, Louis XV exhibition, Hôtel de la Monnaie, 1974. Night-life on the boulevard and Lord Hertford looking into the windows of the Maison Dorée: Jollivet. Private collections in Paris: Vol. I *Paris-Guide*, 1867; Wilhelm, *L'Oeil*, June 1956.

Chapter Twelve

Outbreak of Franco-Prussian war: Castelot, Kurtz. Blount's drive to Bagatelle: Blount. 5th marquess at Bagatelle and funeral of 4th marquess: diary of 5th marquess, Wallace Collection archives. Letters of Dudley Ryder: Harrowby MSS. Whitehurst on Lord Hertford's bequest to Wallace: Whitehurst.

Chapter Thirteen

Paris during the Siege: Horne, Whitehurst. Balloons: Fonvielle, Valvet. Le Marin de Wallace: Debuchy. Wallace gets married: Blount. British Embassy during Siege: Gladwyn.

Chapter Fourteen

Irish lawsuit: *Belfast Morning News*, August 1871. Acquires lease of Hertford House: diary 5th marquess, Wallace Collection archives. Alterations to Hertford House: Wallace Collection archives.

Chapter Fifteen

Bethnal Green Museum: *History of Victoria and Albert Museum*, H.M. Stationery Office. Wallace tells Cunliffe-Owen he wishes to show the Paris collection at Bethnal Green: Henry Cole correspondence, Victoria and Albert Museum. The offer is accepted: Minutes, Resorts and Correspondence, Science and Art Department, Victoria and Albert Museum. Van book 1872: Bethnal Green Museum. Opening ceremony, Bethnal Green Museum: Cole diaries, Victoria and Albert Museum. Henry James goes to Bethnal Green: Sweeney. Purchase of Sudbourne: diary of 5th marquess, Clark.

Chapter Sixteen

Wallace elected M.P. for Lisburn: *Lisburn Herald*, 21 February 1869. Wallace at Westminster, his accent and appearance: Gwynn and Tuckwell. T. P. O'Connor: Falk. Pantechnicon fire: *The Times*, February–March 1874. Impressionist Exhibition 1874: Hélène Adhémar, catalogue *Centenaire de l'Impressionisme*, Grand Palais, 1974. Shooting at Sudbourn, F. J. B. Watson, *Apollo*, June 1965.

Chapter Seventeen

Letters of Meissonier: Wallace Collection archives. Henry James on *Friedland – 1807*: Sweeney. Its purchase in America: catalogue, French Paintings, Metropolitan Museum of Art. The Collection in Hertford House from photographs: Wallace Collection archives. Prince of Wales recommends Wallace for an honour: Royal Archives, Windsor. Lady Wolseley on Lady Wallace quoted by Falk.

Chapter Eighteen

Disraeli's memorandum to Queen Victoria: Royal Archives, Windsor. Wallace gives Disraeli 3rd marquess's Garter Star, Moneypenny and Buckle. Prince of Wales at Sudbourn: P.O.W.'s engagement books, Royal Archives, Windsor. Wallace and Ludwig of Bavaria:

letter from German Ambassador, 25 May 1883, Wallace Collection archives, see also *The Times* obituary notice, 17 June 1886. Letter to Charles Davis: Wallace Collection archives. Symonds on painting Wallace's portrait: Wallace Collection archives. Seymourina's correspondence with Wallace: Wallace Collection archives. Lord Warwick's experience at lunch at Bagatelle quoted by Falk. Wallace's will: Wallace Collection archives.

Chapter Nineteen

Lady Wallace and the Scott family: *Daily Telegraph*, June 1913, statements made in court during lawsuit over Murray Scott's will. Lady Wallace's will: Wallace Collection archives. Murray Scott's meanness: statements by staff at Hertford House, Wallace Collection archives. Murray Scott sale: Christie's catalogue, Wallace Collection archives. Lady Sackville: V. Sackville-West, N. Nicolson. Murray Scott's plan to sell Bagatelle to builders: Joffet. Murray Scott's will: Wallace Collection archives. Lawsuit over will: reports of court proceedings, *Daily Telegraph*, June 1913. Seligmann buys rue Laffitte collection: Seligman. Lady Sackville's sale: Wallace Collection archives.

The quotation on page 184 appears by kind permission of Nigel Nicolson.

Chapter Twenty

The lost collection: Robert Cecil, *Burlington Magazine*, June 1950, April 1956, and (letter) March 1958, *Apollo*, June 1965; Seligman, A.F. Morris, *The Connoisseur*, August 1910, April 1911; Gustave Babin, *L'Illustration*, 20 and 27 June 1914.

Index

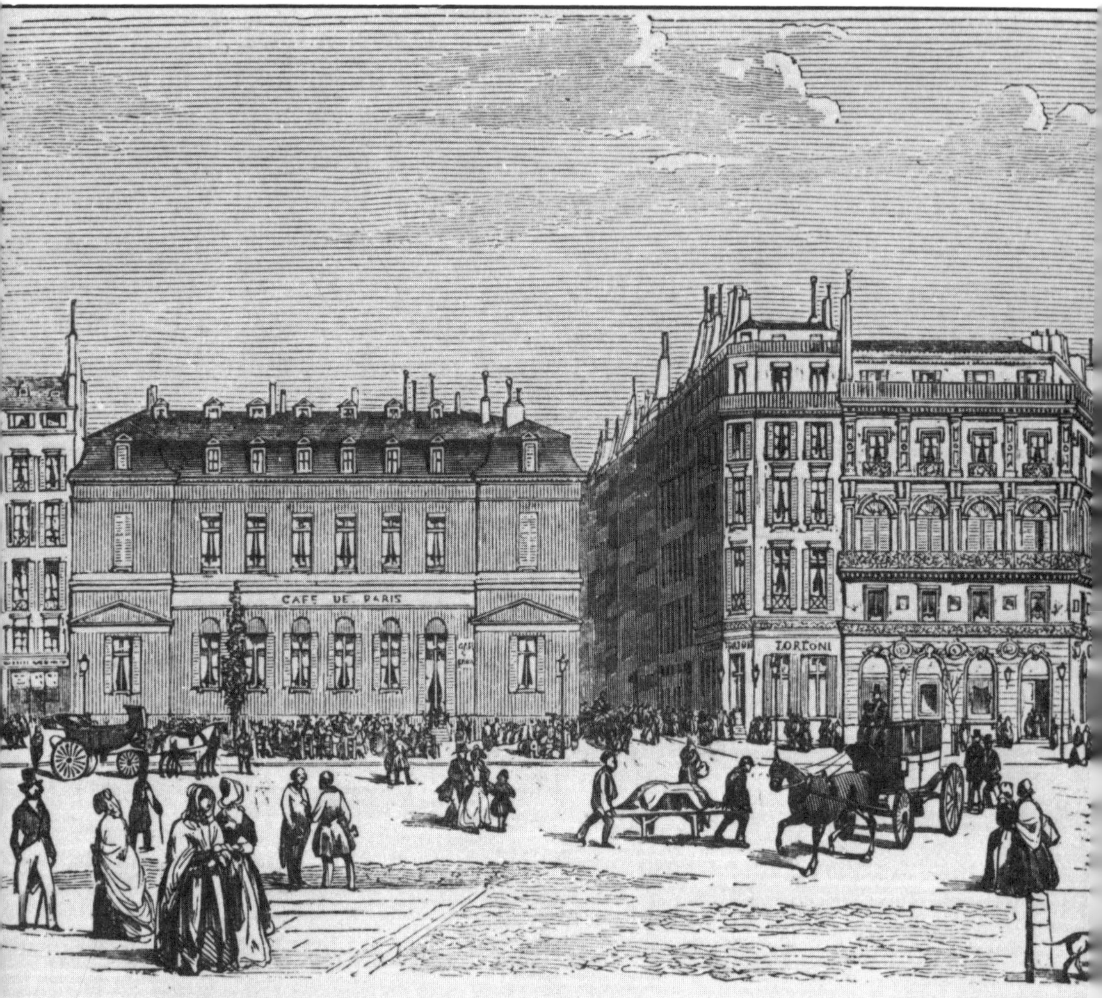

Café de Paris. Rue Taitbout. Tortoni. Maison-Dorée.